AL-FAWA'ID
A COLLECTION OF WISE SAYINGS

Ibn Al-Qayyim Al-Guzyah

International Publishing House

All rights reserved. No part of this publication may be reproduced, stored in a retrieval system, or transmitted in any form or by any means including electronic, mechanical, photocopying, recording, or otherwise without written permission from the publisher.
For more information, please contact:

Table of Contents

TABLE OF CONTENTS V
TRANSLITERATION SYSTEM XII
TRANSLATOR'S NOTES XIV
IMPORTANT RULES: CONDITIONS ONE MUST MEET IN ORDER TO BENEFIT FROM THE QUR'ÂN 1
CHAPTER: THE BEGINNING OF CREATION, RESURRECTION AND THE PRINCIPLES OF MONOTHEISM MENTIONED IN CHAPTER QÂF 5
THE STATUS OF THE PEOPLE OF BADR 24
A PRECIOUS GEM OF WISDOM: 28
THE INTERPRETATION OF THE QUR'ÂNIC VERSE, ... 28
A PRECIOUS GEM: AL-FÂTIHAH AND THE WISDOM IT CONTAINS 30
A PRECIOUS GEM: TWO WAYS TO KNOW ALLAH 33
A PRECIOUS GEM: PROPHETIC HADITHS ELIMINATING GRIEF AND DISTRESS 36
A PRECIOUS GEM: 47
THE THRONE AND THE HEART 47
A PRECIOUS GEM: 49
THE CONTENT OF THE QUR'ÂN 49
A PRECIOUS GEM: NO PLACE FOR TWO CONTRADICTIONS 51
INTERPRETATION OF CHAPTER AT-TAKÂTHUR 53
NOTE: PERFECT WISDOM 54
CHAPTER ON THE RIGHTS OF ALLAH 57
A PRECIOUS GEM: TWO KINDS OF JEALOUSY 58
CHAPTER: MORE WISDOM 61
CHAPTER: SALMÂN AL-FÂRISY 63
A PRECIOUS GEM: LESSONS 68
A PRECIOUS GEM: THIS LIFE OF DECEPTION 71

CHAPTER: A WONDROUS REALITY 72

A PRECIOUS GEM: SOURCES OF UNLAWFULNESS 73

A PRECIOUS GEM: BENEFITS 73

AN IMPORTANT RULE: THERE IS NO POWER OR STRENGTH EXCEPT WITH ALLAH 80

A PRECIOUS GEM: KNOWLEDGE IS FOLLOWED BY LOVE 82

A RULE: TWO RESTRAINTS THAT RESCUE 83

A PRECIOUS GEM: GOOD CHARACTER IS A PART OF PIETY 85

A PRECIOUS GEM: EXAMPLES AND LESSONS 85

AN IMPORTANT RULE: EFFECT OF "THERE IS NO GOD BUT ALLAH" AT THE TIME OF DEATH 87

A PRECIOUS GEM: FEAR ALLAH, FOLLOW HIS ORDERS, AND AVOID WHAT HE HAS FORBIDDEN 92

A PRECIOUS GEM: SIN AND DEBT 92

A PRECIOUS GEM: FIGHTING IN THE CAUSE OF ALLAH 92

CHAPTER: ENMITY BETWEEN THE MIND AND IMAGINATION 93

A PRECIOUS GEM: THE MESSENGER'S VICTORY 95

CHAPTER: THE VANITY OF FALSE HOPES 98

CHAPTER: WHY WAS ADAM CONSIDERED THE LAST OF CREATURES? 100

CHAPTER: VARIOUS PRECIOUS GEMS 104

CHAPTER: THE MANIFESTATION OF THE LORD 109

CHAPTER: THE MERITS OF ABU BAKR 111

WARNING: GREAT PEARLS OF WISDOM 115

WARNING: LESSONS AND WARNINGS 116

CHAPTER 120

A PRECIOUS GEM: FORMS OF REJECTING THE QUR'ÂN AND UNCERTAINTY ABOUT IT 126

A RULE: THE PERFECTION OF ONESELF 127

A PRECIOUS GEM: THE REWARD OF BEING BUSY IN THE SERVICE OF ALLAH 129

A PRECIOUS GEM: ELEMENTS OF KNOWLEDGE 130

AN IMPORTANT RULE: THE APPARENT AND HIDDEN ASPECTS OF FAITH 132

A PRECIOUS GEM: TRUST IN ALLAH 132

A GREAT AND IMPORTANT RULE: "O YOU WHO BELIEVE! ANSWER ALLAH (BY OBEYING HIM) AND (HIS) MESSENGER" 136

A PRECIOUS GEM: JIHAD IS ORDAINED FOR YOU 143

A PRECIOUS GEM: ASCETICISM DURING THIS WORLDLY LIFE 147

IMPORTANT RULE: THE BASIS OF GOODNESS 155

PRECIOUS GEMS 158

A PRECIOUS AND VALUABLE GEM: THE (RELIGIOUS) SCHOLAR WHOSE DEEDS ARE INCONSISTENT WITH HIS KNOWLEDGE 160

A PRECIOUS GEM: 165

THE IGNORANT WORSHIPPER AND THE IMMORAL (RELIGIOUS) SCHOLAR 165

A GREAT AND PRECIOUS GEM: 168

THE BEST ACQUIREMENT FOR THE SOUL 168

CHAPTER: FAITH AND THOSE WHO DISAGREE WITH IT 172

A VALUABLE AND PRECIOUS GEM: THE ORIGIN OF HAPPINESS 174

A VALUABLE AND IMPORTANT RULE: THE PEOPLE OF GUIDANCE AND THE PEOPLE OF MISGUIDANCE 175

CHAPTER: TEN USELESS MATTERS 179

CHAPTER: THE RIGHT TO SUBMIT TO ALLAH 180

CHAPTER: THE SWEETNESS OF TRUSTING IN ALLAH 182

ADVICE: HOW TO SET YOUR STATE ARIGHT 186

CHAPTER: THE SIGN OF GOOD WILL 187

CHAPTER: ASCETICISM IN THIS WORLDLY LIFE 187

CHAPTER: KINDS OF ASCETICISM (ABSTINENCE) 188

CHAPTER: REMEMBERING ALLAH AND BEING GRATEFUL TO HIM .. 206

CHAPTER: GUIDANCE LEADS TO MORE GUIDANCE AND ABERRATION LEADS TO MORE ABERRATION 210

CHAPTER 216

CHAPTER: GUIDANCE IS THE PARTNER OF MERCY AND ABERRATION IS THE PARTNER OF MISERY 220

CHAPTER: BESTOWING AND PREVENTING 227

CHAPTER: THE EVIL OF FALSEHOOD 228

CHAPTER: "AND IT MAY BE THAT YOU DISLIKE A THING WHICH IS GOOD FOR YOU" 230

CHAPTER: THE CONDITIONS OF BEING SATISFIED WITH KNOWLEDGE 233

CHAPTER: THE DANGER OF SUBMITTING TO ONE'S DESIRES 235

CHAPTER: THE LIMITS OF ONE'S CHARACTERISTICS 236

CHAPTER: PIETY WITHIN THE HEART 239

CHAPTER: THE ORIGIN OF PRAISED AND DISPRAISED MORALS 242

CHAPTER: THE REQUIREMENTS OF ACHIEVING GREAT TARGETS .. 243

CHAPTER: THE WISDOM OF IBN MAS'ÛD 243

CHAPTER: SINCERITY AND LOVE THAT ARE PRAISED CANNOT COEXIST 250

CHAPTER: PLEASURE DEPENDS UPON DETERMINATION 252

CHAPTER: THE PIETY OF 'UMAR BIN 'ABDUL 'AZÎZ 256

CHAPTER: THE BENEFITS OF DESERTING EVIL HABITS 258

CHAPTER: HINDRANCES 259

CHAPTER: ATTACHMENTS 259

CHAPTER: THE STATUS OF THE MESSENGER (PEACE BE UPON HIM) 259

CHAPTER: SIGNS OF HAPPINESS AND MISFORTUNE 260

CHAPTER: DEEDS ARE AN ESTABLISHMENT WHOSE FOUNDATION IS FAITH 262

CHAPTER: THE BASES OF INFIDELITY 265
A MOST PRECIOUS GEM 267
CHARACTERISTICS OF THOSE WHO DO NOT KNOW ALLAH 267
CHAPTER: THE TREE OF SINCERITY 276
CHAPTER: DEGREES OF HAPPINESS 277
CHAPTER: THE BODY AND SOUL 281
CHAPTER: THREE PRECIOUS GEMS 283
CHAPTER: KNOWING ALLAH 283
CHAPTER: LICIT AND ILLICIT GAINS 285
CHAPTER: CONSOLATION OF THE BELIEVERS 286
CHAPTER: UNAWARENESS CAUSES HARDSHIP 286
CHAPTER: THE JOURNEY TO ALLAH, EXALTED BE HE, AND ITS OBSTACLES 287
CHAPTER: KINDS OF GRACE 288
A GREAT PRINCIPLE: THE BEGINNING OF KNOWLEDGE AND ACTION 289
CHAPTER: THE HEART IS NEVER VOID OF THOUGHTS 291
CHAPTER: HE WHO DOES NOT KNOW HIMSELF, DOES NOT KNOW HIS CREATOR 297
A PRECIOUS GEM: LEVELS OF KNOWING ALLAH 299
A PRECIOUS GEM: ALLAH WILL NOT CHANGE THE CONDITION OF A PEOPLE UNTIL THEY CHANGE THEMSELVES 300
CHAPTER: THE BEAUTY OF ALLAH, THE EXALTED 301
CHAPTER: ALLAH IS FULL OF GRACE AND HE LOVES GRACE 304
CHAPTER: KINDS OF BEAUTY 307
CHAPTER: SINCERITY OF DETERMINATION AND DEEDS 309
A PRECIOUS GEM: THE WILL OF THE SERVANT 310
CHAPTER: GLORIFYING ALLAH 311
A PRECIOUS GEM: LIFE IS A JOURNEY 315

A PRECIOUS GEM: OBSERVING 316

A PRECIOUS GEM: THE SATANIC WAYS OF TEMPTING 316

A PRECIOUS GEM: THE WAY TO SUCCESS 317

A PRECIOUS GEM: THE BEST KINDS OF REMEMBRANCE 317

CHAPTER: THE MOST USEFUL AND THE MOST HARMFUL OF PEOPLE 318

A PRECIOUS GEM: FORBIDDEN PLEASURE 318

A PRECIOUS GEM: THERE IS RIGHT AND WRONG IN EVERYTHING .. 319

CHAPTER: THE PEOPLE OF PARADISE AND THOSE OF HELLFIRE .. 320

CHAPTER: SOME QUALITIES OF MONOTHEISM 321

A PRECIOUS GEM: ONLY THE HEART THAT IS FOUNDED ON MONOTHEISM WILL COMPREHEND THE PRECIOUS QUALITIES OF ALLAH 322

A PRECIOUS GEM: AL-INÂBAH AND AL-I'TIKÂF 322

A PRECIOUS GEM: SIGHING WHILE LISTENING TO THE QUR'ÂN 325

A USEFUL RULE: KINDS OF THOUGHTS 326

AN IMPORTANT RULE: MAKING A REQUEST AND PATIENCE THEREAFTER 328

AN IMPORTANT RULE: THE SERVANT EXISTS BETWEEN THE HANDS OF ALLAH 329

AN IMPORTANT RULE: THE PLEASURE OF THE HEREAFTER IS MORE LASTING 330

A PRECIOUS GEM: AND AYYÛB (JOB) WHEN HE CRIED TO HIS LORD! 330

A PRECIOUS GEM: YOU ARE MY PROTECTOR IN THIS LIFE AND IN THE HEREAFTER 331

AN IMPORTANT RULE: AND THERE IS NOT A THING BUT THE STORES THEREOF ARE WITH US 332

A PRECIOUS GEM: LOVING ALLAH 334

A VALUABLE RULE: ALL BLESSINGS ARE FROM ALLAH 335

CHAPTER: THE CAUSES OF FAILURE 337

CHAPTER: THE INTERPRETATION OF THE BEGINNING OF CHAPTER AL-'ANKABÛT 341

SAYYID AL-ISTIGHFÂR 352

Transliteration System

1. The Arabic Alphabet

No.	Letter	By	Example	
1.	أ	A	Asad	أسد
2.	ب	B	Badr	بدر
3.	ت	T	Tabûk	تبوك
4.	ث	Th	Al-Haytham	الهيثم
5.	ج	J	Jâbir	جابر
6.	ح	H	Al-Hiwâlah	الحوالة
7.	خ	Kh	Khadîjah	خديجة
8.	د	D	Dinâr	دينار
9.	ذ	Dh	Dhul-Qa'dah	ذو القعدة
10.	ر	R	Ar-Ribâ	الربا
11.	ز	Z	Zaynab	زينب
12.	س	S	Sûrah	سورة
13.	ش	Sh	Ash-Shâfi'y	الشافعي
14.	ص	S	Al-Ansâr	الأنصار
15.	ض	D	Diyâ'	ضياء
16.	ط	T	At-Tawâf	الطواف
17.	ظ	Zh	Azh-Zhihâr	الظهار
18.	ع	'A, 'I, 'U	'Aly, Al-'Ilm, 'Umar	علي، العلم، عمر
19.	غ	Gh	Al-Mughîrah	المغيرة
20.	ف	F	Al-Fâtihah	الفاتحة
21.	ق	Q	Banû Qaynuqâ'	بنو قينقاع
22.	ك	K	Umm Kulthûm	أم كلثوم

23.	ل	L	Abû Lahab		أبو لهب
24.	م	M	Umaymah		أميمة
25.	ن	N	An-Nasî'ah		النسيئة
26.	هـ	H	Hind		هند
27.	و	W	Al-Wâqi'ah		الواقعة
28.	ي	Y	Yathrib		يثرب

2. Vowels & Diacritical Marks

No.	Letter	By	Example	
1.	الفتحة	A	Fahd	فهد
2.	المد بالألف	Â	Al-Isnâd	الإسناد
3.	الضمة	U	Al-Jumu'ah	الجمعة
4.	المد بالواو	Û	Al-H̱udûd	الحدود
5.	الكسرة	I	Ash-Shirk	الشرك
6.	المد بالياء	Î	Ibn Sirîn	ابن سيرين
7.	الألف المفتوحة	A	Al-A̱hzâb	الأحزاب
8.	الألف المضمومة	U	Usâmah	أسامة
9.	الألف المكسورة	I	Al-I̱hsâr	الإحصار
10.	العين الساكنة	'	Sa'd, As-Sa'y	سعد، السعي

Translator's Notes

All praise and thanks are due to Allah. We praise Him and seek His help, guidance and forgiveness. We seek refuge with Allah from the consequences of our evil conduct and the sins we have committed. Whosoever Allah guides, no one can mislead and whosoever He sends astray, no one can guide.

I bear witness that there is no god but Allah Alone, who has no partner and I bear witness that Muhammad is His servant and Messenger. Allah sent him (peace be upon him) as a witness, a bearer of good news and a warner, and as one who invites to Allah by His leave, and as a lamp spreading light.

This book, *Al-Fawâid: A Collection of Wise Sayings* is one of the well-known compilations of Imam Shams Ad-Dîn Ibn Qayyim Al-Jawziyyah, who is well known by the name Ibn Al-Qayyim (may Allah have mercy upon him). This blessed book is not like others that simply contain sections, chapters and themes, but it consists of the elevated thoughts that Allah, Exalted be He, bestows upon some of His servants as He wills. So whenever any of these scattered pearls of wisdom occurred to the Imam, he would immediately record them. I am sure that he did not sit down and write this book in one or two weeks, but surely it was developed over a long period of time. Whenever something came to his mind, he would record it, and whenever he learnt a lesson or anything crucial in his life, he would illuminate the lines of his page with the ink of his pen.

I remember the first time I read this book, which was twenty years ago in 1980. It was beyond my ability at that time to fully comprehend the meaning that Ibn Al-Qayyim (may Allah have mercy upon him) was trying to impart in the book. However, in the course of time, Allah, the Almighty bestowed His favors upon me, and I began to understand the light and guidance that these words contain.

The book is not concerned with juristic subjects nor does it deal with any of the instrumental sciences that anyone can understand and memorize, but rather, it consists of the landmarks of guidance, and light, and the firebrands of piety that Ibn Al-Qayyim pondered in the fields of piety, asceticism and vivid exhortation toward the truth.

He focuses on the role and duty of the hearts, and makes them clear to us to the extent that we are moved and motivated to learn and practice them. He explains to us the diseases of the heart so that we may know how to avoid and overcome them. He ponders on the depths of the nature of the human self and moves inside its hidden sphere, from one part to the other, which might be difficult for many people to understand. This book has reached the peak of understanding regarding this particular point. Ibn Al-Qayyim is renowned in the field of ascetics and one of the most knowledgeable people of Allah.

So, dear reader, here is the book. Take it as one of your close friends, and when you find life's difficulties facing you, read it and ponder the meaning that is applicable to you. Surely, you will find your way out, for you will be living in the world of insight, where there is permanent comfort, the yearning to be close to the Lord of the worlds and the strong desire to enter the Gardens of Delight.

We ask Allah, the Exalted, to bestow upon our hearts that which He bestows upon His righteous servants, and reward Imam Ibn Al-Qayyim and the Muslims with the best reward, and gather us with him at the place of His mercy along with the Prophets,, the truthful, the martyrs and the righteous. How excellent these companions are!

The translations of the Glorious Qur´ân were quoted from The Noble Qur´ân, by Dr. Muhammad Taqî-ud-Dîn Al-Hilâly and Dr. Muhammad Muhsin Khân; King Fahd Complex for the Printing of the Holy Qur´ân, Madinah, K.S.A.

Although the hadith were translated without their full chains of transmission, attribution has been made to their original recording in the different hadith compilations, which include Sahîh Al-Bukhary, Sahîh Muslim, Sunan Abu Dâwûd, etc.

The translation process of this book took a great effort from all members of the team.

We would like to express our thanks to everyone who took part or contributed to the reproduction of this translation, particularly the translators, the revisers and the editor. May Allah reward them all for their work and make it helpful for those who seek guidance to the True Path.

Finally, we pray that this translation will provide useful information and advice to all its readers, regardless of their background, and that they may all benefit from it. We also hope that all our efforts on this book will be counted among our good deeds with Allah, the Almighty. Amen.

In the Name of Allah

Imam and sheikh Abu 'Abdullâh is known as Ibn Qaiyim Al-Jawziyyah (may Allah be merciful to him). He revived the Sunnah and restrained innovation. He said what follows:

Important Rules: Conditions One must Meet in Order to Benefit from the Qur'ân

If you want to benefit from the Qur'ân, you must concentrate and devote your heart solely when reciting and listening to it. You must pay attention, and try to comprehend the fact that what you are reading is the word of Allah. As you read, you must know that Allah is addressing you in and through this Qur'ân. Indeed, it is the words of Allah to you through the tongue of His Messenger. Allah says,

﴿ إِنَّ فِي ذَٰلِكَ لَذِكْرَىٰ لِمَن كَانَ لَهُۥ قَلْبٌ أَوْ أَلْقَى ٱلسَّمْعَ وَهُوَ شَهِيدٌ ۝ ﴾

which means, "Verily, therein is indeed a reminder for him who has a heart or gives ear while he is heedful." (Qâf, 50:37)

Obtaining the perfect effect depends upon the stimulus, the place of the receiver, the condition for the effect to occur, and the absence of any obstacle that may obstruct the effect. The above verse explains all that in the most precise, and clear words. When Allah says which means, "Verily, therein is indeed a reminder" it is a sign for what had passed from the beginning of the chapter until this verse. His saying, "for him who has a heart" refers to the place of the receiver and it means the living heart, which comprehends what Allah says. For example when Allah says,

﴿ ...إِنْ هُوَ إِلَّا ذِكْرٌ وَقُرْءَانٌ مُّبِينٌ ۝ لِّيُنذِرَ مَن كَانَ حَيًّا... ﴾

which means, "This is only a Reminder and a plain Qur'ân. That he or it (Muhammad or the Qur'ân) may give warning to him who is living (a healthy minded believer)." (Yâsîn, 36:69-70)

"Who is living." means the one who has a living heart. And when Allah says which means, "Or gives ear" means the person listens to what is being said to him. And this is the condition in order to be truly affected by the words.

And His saying, "While he is heedful..." means to be aware; that his heart is conscious and not distracted by any worldly matter.

Ibn Qutaibah[1] said, "He is listening to the Book of Allah while his heart is present and understands; not being inattentive or unaware. If the heart is inattentive; lacking understanding concerning what is being said, as well as failing to see or meditate on it, then there is an obstruction. If however, the Qur'ân produced an effect on the receiver, which is the living heart, and the condition of listening was fulfilled, and the heart is not engaged with something other than the meaning of the speech, the desired effect will occur, which is obtaining benefit from the Qur'ân and remembrance."

The Living Heart

Some people may say, "If the effect will take place by the combination of these matters, what is the purpose of the article 'or' in 'Or gives ear' while it is the article 'and,' which joins two matters and not 'or,' which indicates only one. To this, it can be said, "This is a good question and the answer is as follows:

---

[1] Ibn Qutaibah is 'Abdullâh bin Muslim bin Qutaibah Ad-Dainûry. He is one of the chiefs of literature and has produced many works. He was born in Baghdad in 213 A.H. He settled down in Kûfah, and was appointed as the judge of Ad-Dainûr and attributed to it. He (may Allah be merciful to him) passed away in Baghdad 276 A.H. From among his works are *Al-Ma'ârif*, *Adab Al-Kâtib*, *Al-Ma'âly*, and *Ta'wîl Mukhtalif Al-Qur'ân*. See *Al-Bidâyah wa An-Nihâyah*, vol.11, p.61.

"The speech includes the article 'or' because it considers the case of the one being addressed and called. Many people have a naturally living heart and so whenever he thinks and meditates, his heart and mind will lead him to the truth of the Qur'ân, and his heart will believe in what the Qur'ân has said. And here the passing of the Qur'ân over his heart will only increase his natural light. This is the description of those, about whom Allah says,

﴿ وَيَرَى ٱلَّذِينَ أُوتُواْ ٱلْعِلْمَ ٱلَّذِىٓ أُنزِلَ إِلَيْكَ مِن رَّبِّكَ هُوَ ٱلْحَقَّ... ﴾

which means, "And those who have been given knowledge see that what is revealed to you (O Muhammad) from your Lord is the truth." (Saba', 34:6)

And He, the Almighty says about them,

﴿ ٱللَّهُ نُورُ ٱلسَّمَٰوَٰتِ وَٱلْأَرْضِ مَثَلُ نُورِهِۦ كَمِشْكَوٰةٍ فِيهَا مِصْبَاحٌ ٱلْمِصْبَاحُ فِى زُجَاجَةٍ ٱلزُّجَاجَةُ كَأَنَّهَا كَوْكَبٌ دُرِّىٌّ يُوقَدُ مِن شَجَرَةٍ مُّبَٰرَكَةٍ زَيْتُونَةٍ لَّا شَرْقِيَّةٍ وَلَا غَرْبِيَّةٍ يَكَادُ زَيْتُهَا يُضِىٓءُ وَلَوْ لَمْ تَمْسَسْهُ نَارٌ نُّورٌ عَلَىٰ نُورٍ يَهْدِى ٱللَّهُ لِنُورِهِۦ مَن يَشَآءُ وَيَضْرِبُ ٱللَّهُ ٱلْأَمْثَٰلَ لِلنَّاسِ وَٱللَّهُ بِكُلِّ شَىْءٍ عَلِيمٌ ﴾

which means, "Allah is the Light of the heavens and the earth. The parable of His Light is as (if there were) a niche and within it a lamp, the lamp is in glass, the glass as it were a brilliant star, lit from a blessed tree, an olive, neither of the east (i.e. neither it gets sun-rays only in the morning) nor of the west (i.e. nor it gets sun-rays only in the afternoon, but it is exposed to the sun all day long), whose oil would almost glow forth (of itself), though no fire touched it. Light upon Light! Allah guides to His Light whom He wills." (An-Nûr, 24:35)

This is the natural light of the pious heart that recognizes the light and beauty of the Divine light contained in the truth of the Qu'rân, and this is the state of the owner of a living heart that is aware.

Ibn Al-Qaiyim said, "We have mentioned some of the lessons contained in this verse in the Book *Ijtimâ' Al-Juyûsh Al-Islâmiyah 'alâ Ghazw Al-Mu'atilah wa Al-Jahmiyah.* The owner of the heart combines his own heart and the meanings of the Qur'ân. He finds that it is as if it was written in his heart and he reads and comprehends it with his heart. Many people do not possess a perfectly prepared and aware heart, namely a completely living heart. Such a heart needs a witness to distinguish between right and wrong. The life of his heart; his light, and his natural brightness do not reach the level of the owner of a living and aware heart. The way to lead him to this guidance is to dedicate his hearing to the words of the Qu'ran and his heart to think, meditate, and comprehend its meaning. He will then know that it is the truth.

One: The state of he who sees with his own eyes what is he is being called to and told about.

Two: The state of he who knows the truthfulness and piety of he who is informing him and says, "His truthfulness is enough for me." Such is the level of Faith while the first is the level of Ihsân. The first reaches 'Assured Knowledge' and his heart is promoted to the rank of the 'Assured eye' while the other has definite belief, which rescued him from disbelief and enabled him to enter into Islam.

The Assured eye is of two kinds: one in this worldly life and the other in the hereafter. The one, which is found in this life is attributed to the heart, like an eye witness. Whatever the Messenger told us about unseen matters, will be seen in the hereafter with our own eyes and in this life such things will be 'seen' by insight.

Chapter: The Beginning of Creation, Resurrection and the Principles of Monotheism Mentioned in Chapter Qâf

This chapter mentions many principles of faith that are sufficient for us, and that serve us instead of the speech and opinions of people, and their reasoning. It contains information about the beginning of creation, resurrection, monotheism, prophethood, belief in Angels, division of people into miserable conditions and happy ones. It also includes the attributes of Allah, and talks about Allah in a way that depicts Him as being free from all defects and faults. Allah also mentions the two resurrections and the two worlds: the bigger world is the Hereafter and the smaller world is this worldly life. He mentions the creation of mankind, death, and resurrection, and his state both in death and on the Day of Resurrection. Allah Knows all that the servant does, even what he conceals within himself. Allah appoints guardian Angels that record every word that is uttered. , He will come on the Day of Resurrection accompanied by an angel to drive him and an angel to bear witness. When the angel drives him along he will say what Allah says,

$$\text{﴿ وَقَالَ قَرِينُهُ هَٰذَا مَا لَدَيَّ عَتِيدٌ ﴾}$$

which means, "Here is (this Record) ready with me." (Qâf, 50:23)

which means, "O Allah! Here is what You ordered me to bring. Then it will be said when he is brought to Allah, what Allah says,

$$\text{﴿ أَلْقِيَا فِي جَهَنَّمَ كُلَّ كَفَّارٍ عَنِيدٍ ﴾}$$

which means, "Both of you throw (Order from Allah to the two angels) into Hell, every stubborn disbeliever (in the Oneness of Allah, in His Messengers, etc.)." (Qâf, 50:24)

This is what is usually done when a criminal is brought into the presence of the King. It would be said, "This is so and so. I have brought him." And the King would say, "Take him to jail! Punish him with what he deserves!"

The Resurrection is for the Body itself

This chapter clearly shows that Allah, the Exalted returns the same body that had obeyed or disobeyed Him in life, in order to reward or punish it just like He rewards the soul itself, which believes in Him and punishes the one, which disbelieves in Him. That does not mean that Allah, the Exalted creates another soul, which will be rewarded or punished, as some people say. Such people do not understand the nature of the Resurrection, which the Messengers informed mankind about. They claim that Allah, the Exalted will create another body that is different in all aspects and that Allah will reward or punish it. They also say that the soul is simply a part of the body, so Allah will create another soul other than this one and a body other than this body. This belief is contrary to what the Messengers taught, and what the Qur'ân, Sunnah, and other Books of Allah, the Exalted say. This is in fact denial of the Resurrection and adopting the belief of the disbelievers. Such people find it difficult to comprehend that Allah, the Exalted will recreate the very same body and soul that had known life. They cannot imagine how the body will become bones and dust and Allah will create it again in its original form. Allah quotes them as saying,

﴿ أَءِذَا مِتْنَا وَكُنَّا تُرَابًا وَعِظَامًا أَءِنَّا لَمَبْعُوثُونَ ﴾

which means, "When we are dead and have become dust and bones, shall we (then) verily be resurrected? (As-Saffât, 37:16)

And such people also say,

$$\{ ...\ذَٰلِكَ رَجْعٌ بَعِيدٌ ۝ \}$$

which means, " That is a far return." (Qâf, 50:3)

If what they assert is true and another body other than the one that had known in life is rewarded or punished, this will neither be Resurrection nor returning back, indeed, it would be a new creation altogether. And the following verse would be rendered meaningless. May Allah forbid! Allah says,

$$\{ قَدْ عَلِمْنَا مَا تَنقُصُ ٱلْأَرْضُ مِنْهُمْ... ۝ \}$$

which means, "We know that which the earth takes of them (their dead bodies)." (Qâf, 50:4)

Allah answered the question that He, the Exalted will separate these pieces which had mixed with the earth and turned it into elements which are difficult to be separated. So Allah, the Exalted told mankind that He knows what the earth is taking from their flesh, bones, and hair and just as He knows these pieces He is capable of separating, and gathering them after being separated, and creating them again. He, the Exalted decides the time of Resurrection by His perfect knowledge, power, and wisdom.

Those who doubt the resurrection are of three kinds:

The Suspicion of Those Who Deny the Resurrection

One: The body and the earth is mixed in such a way that prevents any separation or the possibility of separation.

Two: The resurrection is not related to power.

Three: If a generation died and another one is created to take its place, it is not wisdom to destroy them all and then resurrect them again.

The Proof of Resurrection

One: Stating the perfection of Allah's knowledge, as He said while answering those who said,

﴿ ...مَن يُحْىِ ٱلْعِظَٰمَ وَهِىَ رَمِيمٌ ۝ قُلْ يُحْيِيهَا ٱلَّذِىٓ أَنشَأَهَآ أَوَّلَ مَرَّةٍ ۖ وَهُوَ بِكُلِّ خَلْقٍ عَلِيمٌ ۝ ﴾

which means, "Who will give life to these bones when they have rotted away and became dust?" Say: (O Muhammad) "He will give life to them Who created them for the first time! And He is the All-Knower of every creation!" (Yâsîn, 36:78-79)

And He, the Exalted says,

﴿ ...وَإِنَّ ٱلسَّاعَةَ لَءَاتِيَةٌ ۖ فَٱصْفَحِ ٱلصَّفْحَ ٱلْجَمِيلَ ۝ إِنَّ رَبَّكَ هُوَ ٱلْخَلَّٰقُ ٱلْعَلِيمُ ۝ ﴾

which means, "And the Hour is surely coming, so overlook (O Muhammad), their faults with gracious forgiveness. [This was before the ordainment of *Jihâd holy fighting in Allah's Cause*]. Verily, your Lord is the All-Knowing Creator." (Al-Hijr, 15:85-86)

And He, the Exalted says,

﴿ قَدْ عَلِمْنَا مَا تَنقُصُ ٱلْأَرْضُ مِنْهُمْ... ۝ ﴾

which means, "We know that which the earth takes of them (their dead bodies)." (Qâf, 50:4)

Two: Stating the perfection of Allah's power. Allah says,

﴿ أَوَلَيْسَ ٱلَّذِى خَلَقَ ٱلسَّمَٰوَٰتِ وَٱلْأَرْضَ بِقَٰدِرٍ عَلَىٰٓ أَن يَخْلُقَ مِثْلَهُم... ۝ ﴾

which means, "Is not He, Who created the heavens and the earth Able to create the like of them? (Yâsîn, 36:81)

And He, the Exalted says,

$$\left\{ \text{بَلَىٰ قَٰدِرِينَ عَلَىٰٓ أَن نُّسَوِّيَ بَنَانَهُۥ} \right\}$$

which means, "Yes, We are Able to put together in perfect order the tips of his fingers." (Al-Qiyâmah, 75:4)

And He, the Exalted says,

$$\left\{ \text{ذَٰلِكَ بِأَنَّ ٱللَّهَ هُوَ ٱلۡحَقُّ وَأَنَّهُۥ يُحۡيِ ٱلۡمَوۡتَىٰ وَأَنَّهُۥ عَلَىٰ كُلِّ شَيۡءٍ قَدِيرٌ} \right\}$$

which means, "That is because Allah, He is the Truth, and it is He Who gives life to the dead, and it is He Who is Able to do all things." (Al-Hajj, 22:6)

Allah, the Exalted combines these two matters when He says,

$$\left\{ \text{أَوَلَيۡسَ ٱلَّذِى خَلَقَ ٱلسَّمَٰوَٰتِ وَٱلۡأَرۡضَ بِقَٰدِرٍ عَلَىٰٓ أَن يَخۡلُقَ مِثۡلَهُم ۚ بَلَىٰ وَهُوَ ٱلۡخَلَّٰقُ ٱلۡعَلِيمُ} \right\}$$

which means, " Is not He, Who created the heavens and the earth Able to create the like of them? Yes, indeed! He is the All-Knowing Supreme Creator." (Yâsîn, 36:81)

Three: The perfection of His wisdom. Allah says,

$$\left\{ \text{وَمَا خَلَقۡنَا ٱلسَّمَٰوَٰتِ وَٱلۡأَرۡضَ وَمَا بَيۡنَهُمَا لَٰعِبِينَ} \right\}$$

which means, "And We created not the heavens and the earth, and all that is between them, for mere play." (Ad-Dukhân, 44:38)

And He, the Exalted says,

$$\left\{ \text{وَمَا خَلَقۡنَا ٱلسَّمَآءَ وَٱلۡأَرۡضَ وَمَا بَيۡنَهُمَا بَٰطِلاً ...} \right\}$$

which means, "And We created not the heavens and the earth and all that is between them without purpose!" (Sâd, 38:27)

And He, the Exalted says,

$$\text{أَيَحْسَبُ ٱلْإِنسَٰنُ أَن يُتْرَكَ سُدًى}$$

which means, "Does man think that he will be left *Suda* [neglected without being punished or rewarded for the obligatory duties enjoined by his Lord (Allah) on him]?" (Al-Qiyâmah, 75:36)

And He, the Exalted says,

$$\text{أَفَحَسِبْتُمْ أَنَّمَا خَلَقْنَٰكُمْ عَبَثًا وَأَنَّكُمْ إِلَيْنَا لَا تُرْجَعُونَ ۞ فَتَعَٰلَى ٱللَّهُ ٱلْمَلِكُ ٱلْحَقُّ لَآ إِلَٰهَ إِلَّا هُوَ رَبُّ ٱلْعَرْشِ ٱلْكَرِيمِ}$$

which means, "Did you think that We had created you in play (without any purpose), and that you would not be brought back to Us?" So Exalted be Allah, the True King." (Al-Mu'minûn, 23:115-116)

And He, the Exalted says,

$$\text{أَمْ حَسِبَ ٱلَّذِينَ ٱجْتَرَحُوا ٱلسَّيِّئَاتِ أَن نَّجْعَلَهُمْ كَٱلَّذِينَ ءَامَنُوا وَعَمِلُوا ٱلصَّٰلِحَٰتِ سَوَآءً مَّحْيَاهُمْ وَمَمَاتُهُمْ سَآءَ مَا يَحْكُمُونَ}$$

which means, "Or do those who earn evil deeds think that We shall hold them equal with those who believe (in the Oneness of Allah Islamic Monotheism) and do righteous good deeds, in their present life and after their death? Worst is the judgment that they make." (Al-Jâthiyah, 45:21)

The resurrection is a reality. It is known by the mind that Allah is perfect His names, and attributes obligate this matter and Allah is in no need of those who deny this truth, and His perfection is free from any defects or faults.

Allah, the Exalted told mankind that whoever disbelieves, is confused but that they did not gain anything from this confusion. Allah says,

$$﴿ ...فَهُمْ فِي أَمْرٍ مَّرِيجٍ ﴾$$

which means, "so they are in a confused state (cannot differentiate between right and wrong)." (Qâf, 50:5)

Then in this chapter, Allah invited them to consider the heavens: the way they have been built, their height, straightness, and beauty, and then to look at the earth and how He spread it out, prepared it for its purposes, fixed it with mountains, and provided all the means of life. He produces every good kind of plant with their different shapes, colors, amounts, benefits, and qualities. This indeed provides an insight and a reminder for every servant who turns to Allah, (that is to say, who believes in Allah, obeys His commands, and always begs for His forgiveness). If he ponders on this, he will perceive the meaning, which the Messengers told us about concerning Monotheism and the Resurrection. Whoever looks at the heavens and the earth will firstly meditate and secondly remember, and this will provide deeper insight to the servant who always turns to Allah with his body, heart and soul.

Allah then invited them to think about the source of their subsistence; food, clothing, ships, and gardens. The source is water, which Allah sends down from the sky and blessed it until He produces therewith gardens and grain, different kinds of fruit: black, white, red, yellow, sweet, and sour. Allah shows the difference in their use and kinds, and He also shows the grain and its use, qualities, shapes, and amounts. He then mentions the palm trees as they contain a lesson and meaning, which will not be left a secret for the one who meditates. Allah, the Almighty says,

$$\left\{ ...\text{فَأَحْيَا بِهِ ٱلْأَرْضَ بَعْدَ مَوْتِهَا} ... \right\}$$

which means, "And makes the earth alive therewith after its death." (Al-Baqarah, 2:164)

Then He, the Almighty says,

$$\left\{ ...\text{كَذَٰلِكَ ٱلْخُرُوجُ} \right\}$$

which means, "Thus will be the resurrection (of the dead)." (Qâf, 50:11)

It means that just as plants, fruit, and grain are brought out from the earth, you will be resurrected from the earth after having been mixed with it.

We have mentioned this analogy and examples of other analogies mentioned in the Qur'ân in the Book entitled *Al-Ma'âlim*, and we explained some of their lessons.

Then Allah determines prophethood using the best of determinations, the most concise words, and far removed from all suspicion and doubt. He informed mankind that He sent Messengers to the people of Nûh (Noah, peace be upon him), 'Âd, Thamûd, the people of Lût (Lot, peace be upon him), and the people of Fir'awn (pharaoh), but they disbelieved in them. So He destroyed them with different kinds of destruction and He proved the truth of what the Messengers had promised them. This is proof of their prophethood and the prophethood of he who informed us about them. This is the prophet who had neither learnt from a teacher nor read from a book. He informed us about it in detail exactly like the people of the Book. Nothing refutes this except the question of those liars who deny the final resurrection. Whoever asks this question is a liar and such is the one who denies what has been proven and what has been passed down through the generations by the prophets and those who follow in their footsteps. Denying such a matter is like denying the existence of famous kings, scientists, and remote countries.

The Meaning of Lethargy:

Allah, the Exalted again mentions the Resurrection. Allah says,

$$﴿ أَفَعَيِينَا بِٱلْخَلْقِ ٱلْأَوَّلِ ... ﴾$$

which means, "Were We then tired with the first creation?" (Qâf, 50:15)

And He, the Almighty says,

$$﴿ ...وَلَمْ يَعْىَ بِخَلْقِهِنَّ... ﴾$$

which means, "And was not wearied by their creation." (Al-Ahqâf, 46:33)

And He, the Almighty says,

$$﴿ ...وَمَا مَسَّنَا مِن لُّغُوبٍ ﴾$$

which means, "And nothing of fatigue touched Us." (Qâf, 50:38)

Then He, the Almighty said,

$$﴿ ...فِي لَبْسٍ مِّنْ خَلْقٍ جَدِيدٍ ﴾$$

which means, "They are in confused doubt about a new creation (i.e. Resurrection)?" (Qâf, 50:15)

Their point of confusion is that Allah, the Almighty will recreate mankind as a new creation on the Day of Resurrection. Allah drew the attention of such people to His greatest proofs of power, to the evidence of His Divinity. and proof of the

Resurrection, as it is among the greatest proofs of Monotheism.

There is no greater evidence than the formation of this human being with its organs, abilities, and properties, and the flesh, bones, veins, nerves, ligaments, openings, systems, desires, and insight that it contains. All that is simply a drop in the ocean. The idea of the creation of man is enough to make any person ponder, and if he does, he will remember what the Messengers told us about Allah: His names and attributes. Allah, the Exalted then told mankind that His Knowledge encompasses humanity and that He, the Exalted knows what each individual whispers to himself. He informed us that He is close to man through His knowledge and is close to man like a vein that is inside his body. Moreover, He is even closer to him than this vein; He has more power over him and more knowledge of him.

Our sheikh said, "The meaning of "We" here is the Angels. As Allah says,

$$\text{﴿ فَإِذَا قَرَأْنَاهُ فَاتَّبِعْ قُرْآنَهُ ﴾}$$

which means, "And when We have recited it to you [O Muhammad through Jibrîl (Gabriel)], then follow you its (the Qur'ân's) recital." (Al-Qiyâmah, 75:18)

So Gabriel recited it to him. Our sheikh said, "The evidence is what Allah says,

$$\text{﴿ إِذْ يَتَلَقَّى ٱلْمُتَلَقِّيَانِ ... ﴾}$$

which means, "That the two receivers (recording angels) receive (each human being after he or she has attained the age of puberty)." (Qâf, 50: 17)

Writing the Deeds of Man and the Two Resurrections

Allah, the Exalted informed us about the two angels that are on the right and left of each human being and they write his words and deeds. He paid attention to the process of reckoning and writing words more than He did with writing deeds, which are less in amount as actions are the aims of words and their ultimate ends Then He mentioned the minor resurrection which is the stupor of death and that it came with the truth which is meeting with Allah, the Exalted and the soul will be brought to judgment and will have its reward or punishment which will be advanced to it before the major Day of Resurrection. Then He mentioned the major Resurrection as He, the Almighty says,

﴿ وَنُفِخَ فِى ٱلصُّورِ ۚ ذَٰلِكَ يَوْمُ ٱلْوَعِيدِ ﴾

which means, "And the Trumpet will be blown, that will be the Day whereof warning (had been given) (i.e. the Day of Resurrection)." (Qâf, 50:20)

After that He, the Exalted told us about the states of all creatures on this Day and that each of them will come to Allah, the Exalted accompanied by an angel that will drive him and an angel that will bear witness against him. This is besides the witness of his limbs, and the earth, which will testify concerning what he has and the rights he has taken from others. This includes the rights of Allah, the Exalted, the rights of the messenger (peace be upon him) and the rights of the believers. Allah, the Exalted will take the testimony of the Guardians, the Prophets, the places on which bad deeds were committed, and the skin and body parts that were used in committing sins. He, the Exalted will not judge them only according to His knowledge even though He is the most Just. That is why He told His Prophet (peace be upon him) that He judges between people according to what He heard from their confession as well as evident testimony and not according to

His knowledge alone. How can any ruler judge according to his knowledge without neither sign nor confession? Then He, the Exalted mentioned the heedless state of mankind concerning this matter while they should not be apathetic at all. Allah, the Almighty says,

﴿ ...فِى غَفْلَةٍ مِّنْ هَـذَا... ﴾

which means, "Indeed you were heedless of this." (Qâf, 50:22)

In another verse, He, the Almighty says,

﴿ ...وَإِنَّهُمْ لَفِى شَكٍّ مِّنْهُ مُرِيبٍ ﴾

which means, "And indeed they are in grave doubt concerning it (this Qur'ân)." (Hûd, 11:110)

The Companion and his Dispute

Then Allah informed us that every human being has a companion who is constantly with him and that companion is an angel. This angel writes down his words and deeds, whether they are good or bad. When the angel brings him to Allah, he will say, "This is the one that You had appointed me to accompany in life. I brought him to You." This is the saying of Mujâhid.[2]

Ibn Qutaibah said, "The meaning is that this is what I have written and counted from his words and deeds. They are all recorded here. The verse includes both meanings. That is to say, this person is the one whom I have been accompanying

---

[2] He is Mujâhid bin Jabr, Abu Al-Hajâj from Mecca. He is from the followers and is a scholar of recitation and exposition. He learned exegesis from Ibn 'Abbâs, a famous scholar of this nation. He passed away in 104 A.H. See *Tahdhîb At-Tahdhîb*, vol.1, p.42, *Al-Jarh wat-Ta'dîl*, vol.8, p.1469, *Mîzân Al-I'tidâl*, vol.3, p.439, *Lisân Al-Mîzân*, vol.7, p.349, and *Siyar A'lâm An-Nubalâ'*, vol.4, p.449.

and these are his deeds, which I have counted. Then Allah, the Almighty will say,

$$\text{﴿ أَلْقِيَا فِى جَهَنَّمَ ... ﴾}$$

which means, "(And it will be said), "Both of you throw (Order from Allah to the two angels) into Hell." (Qâf, 50:24)

The order may be referring to the two angels or to the angel that accompanied him during life, and it is the same. The way this speech is written is quite famous among the Arabs. Allah then mentioned six characteristics of the person who would be thrown into Hellfire:

One: He is a disbeliever in Allah, His rights, His religion, Monotheism, His Names, His attributes, His Messengers, and His Angels. He disbelieved in His Books and the Resurrection.

Two: He rejects the truth due to his stubbornness and denial.

Three: He hinders good and that includes both the good that would be done to him if he performed good deeds and the good done to other people. There is no good in him neither for himself nor for his people and this is the state of most creatures.

Four: Besides hindering good to people, he transgresses against man with his hand and his tongue. He is unjust and an oppressor.

Five: He is doubtful, in fact he is suspicious.

Six: Although being a polytheist, who sets up another god with Allah, he worships, loves and hates for His sake, swears by Him, gives oaths to Him, and takes friends and enemies for His sake. The disbeliever might even quarrel with his companions from the devils and Satan would accuse him of wronging himself and that he is the one who pushed himself to transgress. His companion would say that it never had the power to mislead him but he was himself in error and far astray so he chose his condition for himself. Allah says that Satan would say to the people of Hellfire,

﴿ ...وَمَا كَانَ لِيَ عَلَيْكُم مِّن سُلْطَانٍ إِلَّا أَن دَعَوْتُكُمْ فَاسْتَجَبْتُمْ لِي... ﴾

which means, "I had no authority over you except that I called you, so you responded to me." (Ibrâhîm, 14:22)

So his companion here is Satan and they are disputing in the presence of Allah.

Another group said, "His companion here is the Angel. He will claim that the angel exaggerated in his writing, was unjust, and that he did not commit all these sins, and that the angel was quick and did not give him a chance to repent before he wrote. The Angel would say that he did not add anything in his writing more than what was really done and that he was not quick to write. Allah says that Angel would say,

﴿ ...وَلَٰكِن كَانَ فِي ضَلَالٍ بَعِيدٍ ﴾

which means, "But he was himself in error far astray." (Qâf, 50:27)

Allah, the Almighty would say,

﴿ قَالَ لَا تَخْتَصِمُوا لَدَيَّ... ﴾

which means, "Dispute not in front of Me." (Qâf, 50:28)

Allah informed us about the quarrels between the disbelievers and Satan in His presence in chapter of As-Sâfât and Al-A'râf, the disputes of people in His presence in chapter Az-Zumar, and the disputes of people of Hellfire in chapter Ash-Shu'arâ' and Sâd.

After that Allah, the Exalted told us that the Punishment He decrees cannot be changed. This is mentioned in the following verse,

$$\text{﴿ ...لَأَمْلَأَنَّ جَهَنَّمَ مِنَ ٱلْجِنَّةِ وَٱلنَّاسِ أَجْمَعِينَ ﴾}$$

which means, "Surely, I shall fill Hell with jinns and men all together." (Hûd, 11:119)

Also His promise to the people of faith to enter Paradise and this will never be changed or reneged. Ibn 'Abbâs said, "He wants to say that My promise will never be changed either concerning people who obey Me or those who disobey." Mujâhid said, "As if He says, "I have executed what I had decreed." And these are the most correct explanations of this verse."

There is another opinion that the meaning is: sayings would never be changed just because of some lies and false reports, as often occurs in the presence of kings and rulers. So the saying here is that of those who dispute with each other. This is the opinion of Al-Farrâ'[3] and Ibn Qutaibah.

As Al-Farrâ' said, "The meaning is that no one will tell lies in the presence of Allah as He knows the unseen." And Ibn Qutaibah said, "It means that sayings will never be distorted, increased, or decreased in Allah's presence. As he said, "The sayings in My presence and not My sayings." This is, "Lies will never be told in My presence." So from this one point the following two verses bear the same meaning. Allah says,

---

[3] Al-Farrâ' is Yahyâ bin Ziyâd bin 'Abdullâh bin Mansûr, Abu Zakariyyâ from Kûfah. He is a scholar of grammar and linguistics. They used to say to him, "The emir of believers in grammar." He passed away in 207 A.H. See *Tahdhîb At-Tahdhîb*, vol.121, p.212, *Al-Ansâb*, vol.10, p.155, and *Târîkh Baghdâd*, vol.14, p.149.

$$\{ ... وَمَا أَنَا بِظَلَّامٍ لِلْعَبِيدِ \}$$

which means, "And I am not unjust (to the least) to My slaves." (Qâf, 50:29)

And He, the Exalted says,

$$\{ مَا يُبَدَّلُ الْقَوْلُ لَدَيَّ ... \}$$

which means, "The Sentence that comes from Me cannot be changed." (Qâf, 50:29)

That is to say, whatever I said and promised will be done and it will always be just. From the other point, Allah described Himself with two things:

One: sayings would never be changed in Allah's presence as He has perfect knowledge.

Two: He will never be unjust toward His servants as He is perfectly just.

Then He told us about the large space in Hellfire and that whenever people would be thrown inside it, Allah says that it would say,

$$\{ ... هَلْ مِن مَّزِيدٍ \}$$

which means, "Are there anymore (to come)?" (Qâf, 50:30)

He is wrong who says that this verse indicates the negative, that is to say: that there would be no more to come. Many authentic hadiths refutes this interpretation.

Attributes of the People of Paradise

Allah told us that Paradise will be brought near the pious people and that its people have four characteristics:

One: They are oft-returning to Allah in sincere repentance. These believers always return to Allah after committing sins and start to obey and remember Allah. 'Ubaid bin 'Umair said, "The repentant is the one who remembers his sins and asks forgiveness for them." Mujâhid said, "He is the one who asks forgiveness when he remembers his sins while he is alone. And Sa'îd bin Al-Musaiyab[4] said, "He is the one who commits sin, repents, commits again, and repents again."

Two: They preserve their covenant with Allah. Ibn 'Abbâs said, "Whatever Allah orders him to do, he does it. Qatâdah[5] said, "It is he who preserves the rights and blessings granted to him by Allah." The Soul has two special abilities: the power to ask and the power to preserve. The repentant person uses his power of asking to ask forgiveness from Allah, to return to Him, seek His pleasure and obey Him. The power of preserving is found in keeping himself away from sins and all that is forbidden. The repentant person comes nearer to Allah by obeying Him.

Three: Allah, Exalted says,

$$﴿ مَنْ خَشِيَ الرَّحْمَٰنَ بِالْغَيْبِ ... ﴾$$

---

[4] He is Sa'îd bin Al-Musaiyab bin Hazan bin Abu Wahab Al-Makhzûmy Al-Qurashy. His surname was Abu Muhammad. He was the head of the followers and one of the seven top jurists in Medina. He used to be called the narrator of 'Umar because he was the best among people to memorize laws under the leadership of 'Umar bin Al-Khattâb. He (may Allah be merciful to him) passed away in 94 A.H. See *Tahdhîb At-Tahdhîb*, vol.4, p.84, *Târîkh Al-Bukhâry Al-Kabîr*, vol.3, p.510, *Al-Jarh wat-Ta'dîl*, vol.4, p.262, and *Siyar A'lâm An-Nubalâ'*, vol.4, p.217.

[5] He is Qatâdah bin Du'âmah bin 'Azîz, Abu Al-Khattâb As-Sudûsy from Basra. He was an exegete and a memorizer. He was blind and passed away in 118 A.H. See *Tahdhîb At-Tahdhîb*, vol.8, p.351, *Târîkh Al-Bukhâry Al-Kabîr*, vol.7, p.185, *Al-Jarh wat-Ta'dîl*, vol.7, p.756, *Mîzân Al-I'tidâl*, vol.3, p.385, and *Lisân Al-Mîzân*, vol.7, p.341.

which means, "Who feared the Most Beneficent (Allah) in the *Ghaib* (unseen): (i.e. in this worldly life before seeing and meeting Him)." (Qâf, 50:33)

This verse declares the Existence, Divinity, and Power of Allah and His knowledge of every detail of His servants' conditions, His Books, Messengers, orders and prohibitions, His promise, threat, and standing before Him on the Day of Resurrection.

Four: Allah, the Almighty says,

$$ ﴿ ...وَجَاءَ بِقَلْبٍ مُّنِيبٍ ۝ ﴾ $$

which means, "And brought a heart turned in repentance (to Him - and absolutely free from each and every kind of polytheism)." (Qâf, 50:33)

Ibn 'Abbâs said, "He is far from sins and rushes to obey Allah. The reality of repentance is to devote the heart to obedience, love, and striving to be near to Allah." Allah then mentioned the reward of the one, who has these attributes. Allah says,

$$ ﴿ ادْخُلُوهَا بِسَلَامٍ ۖ ذَٰلِكَ يَوْمُ الْخُلُودِ ۝ لَهُم مَّا يَشَاءُونَ فِيهَا وَلَدَيْنَا مَزِيدٌ ۝ ﴾ $$

which means, "Enter you therein in peace and security; this is a Day of eternal life! There they will have all that they desire, and We have more (for them, i.e. a glance at the Almighty, All-Majestic)." (Qâf, 50:34-35)

Then He frightened them with the destruction that had happened to those who were before them. Such were stronger in power but that did not prevent their destruction. And when the time of destruction came, they ran seeking refuge in the land! Could they find any place of refuge to save themselves from destruction? Qatâdah said, "The enemies of Allah got into a fix and found that the order of Allah would catch up with them." Az-Zajjâj said, "They ran seeking refuge but did not find any other way except death." They searched for any other refuge other than death but they did not find any."

Allah, the Exalted informed us about that as He says,

﴿ ...لَذِكْرَىٰ لِمَن كَانَ لَهُۥ قَلْبٌ أَوْ أَلْقَى ٱلسَّمْعَ وَهُوَ شَهِيدٌ ﴾

which means, "A reminder for him who has a heart or gives ear while he is heedful." (Qâf, 50:37)

He then told us that He created the heavens and the earth and all between them in six Days and that nothing of fatigue touched Him. He accused His enemies from among the Jews of lying when they said that Allah rested on the seventh day. Then He ordered His Prophet to follow His example and be patient toward what his enemies are saying about him, as Allah was patient toward what the Jews had said about Him. And there is no one more capable of being patient than Him. He ordered him to do something that will help him to be patient, and that is to glorify the Praises of His Lord, before the rising of the sun and before its setting (i.e. the *Fajr*, *Zhuhr*, and *'Asr* prayers), as well as during a part of the night also, glorify His praises (i.e. *Maghrib* and *'Ishâ'* prayers). Likewise there are more prayers other than the *Fard* prayers: (As-Sunnah, Nawâfil optional and additional prayers). It was said that after the *Isha* prayer is Al-Witr prayer (Odd prayer) and said it means the two rak'ahs after Maghrib (Sunset Prayer). The first is the opinion of Ibn 'Abbâs and the other is of 'Umar, 'Aly, Abu Hurairah, and Al-Hasan bin 'Aly. And there is a third opinion from Ibn 'Abbâs that it means glorifying Allah verbally after every obligatory prayer.

Then Allah ends the chapter by mentioning the Resurrection and the call of the caller that indicates the souls returning to their bodies for Resurrection. This call will be from a near place that will be heard by all. Allah says,

$$\{ \text{يَوْمَ يَسْمَعُونَ الصَّيْحَةَ بِالْحَقِّ} ... \}$$

which means, "The Day when they will hear *As-Saihah* (shout, etc.) in truth." (Qâf, 50:42)

It will be the sign of Resurrection and standing in front of Allah. On the Day when the earth shall be cleft from off them, as with plants. They will come out hastening forth. That will be a gathering, quite easy for Allah.

Then Allah, the Exalted said that He knows all the things that His enemies say about Him, and He will punish them for their words. He mentions His power and knowledge and that He will punish them.

He told His Messenger that he is not a tyrant over them and was not sent to force them to believe. He ordered him to warn by the Qur'ân, he who fears Allah's Threat. The righteous will benefit from being warned but those who do not believe in the Resurrection and neither fear His threat nor hope for His reward, will not benefit from being warned.

The Status of the People of Badr

The Prophet (peace be upon him) said to 'Umar (may Allah be pleased with him), "'Who knows, perhaps Allah has looked at the warriors of Badr and said (to them), 'Do whatever you like, for I have forgiven you.'"[6] Many people have misinterpreted this hadith, for the obvious meaning is that everything has been allowed for them and that they can do whatever they want. But this, in fact is not the case. According to a group of people,

---

[6] Recorded by Al-Bukhâry, in *Kitâb Al-Jihad was-Siyar*, section: the spy, no. (3007). And Muslim, in the book of *Fadâil As-Sahâbah*, section: among the excellence of the people of Badr (may Allah be pleased with them)... no. (2494).

among whom is Ibn Al-Jawzy, [7] "By this statement it does not mean that their future sins are included, but what is meant is the past sins. That is to say, "I have forgiven every bad thing you did before." He (Ibn Al-Jawzy) said, "and there are two things that prove that:

If it was supposed to mean future sins, the answer would have been: I will forgive you.

The second thing is that it would have been a sort of freedom to commit sins, and there is no reason for that.

The true meaning of this response is: I have forgiven your previous sins because of this battle. But it is a weak argument in two ways:

Firstly, because the statement, "Do whatever you like, for I have forgiven you," includes future sins and not the past only. And the statement, "I have forgiven you," does not necessarily mean, "I will forgive you" in order to include future sins, for the statement "I have forgiven" is a confirmation that there will be forgiveness in the future, just like the following statements in the Qur'ân which means: "The event (the Hour or the punishment of the disbelievers and polytheists or the Islamic laws or commandments) ordained by Allah will come to pass), and that which means (and your Lord comes) and so on.

Secondly: the hadith itself replies to him, for the cause of it is the story of Hatib and his spying on the Prophet (peace be upon him), and that is a sin that was committed after the battle of

---

[7] Ibn Al-Jawzy: His full name is, 'Abdur-Rahman bin 'Aly bin Muhammad Al-Jawzy, Al-Qurashiy, Al-Bagdâdiy, Abu Al-Faraj, the scholar of history and hadith of his time. He was born 508 A. H. and died (may Allah have mercy upon him) 598 A. H. adopted from *Al-Bidâyah wan-Nihâyah* (vol, 13\ p, 35).

Badr [8] and not before it, therefore, the second opinion is definitely coorect.

Allah knows best, but we think that this is a statement about people that Allah knew would not leave their religion, and that they would die in the state of Islam. He also knew that they might commit some sins like other people do, but He would not leave them to persist in them, but would make it easy for them to turn to Him with sincere repentance, seek His Forgiveness and do righteous deeds that wipe out the trace of their sins. And this would be specified for them only and not for others.

This is because their truthfulness has been provenand so they have been forgiven. It can also be that they were granted forgiveness because of these reasons, and it does not mean that they should stop performing religious duties, because of having been forgiven, and if that had happened without fulfilling orders, they would not have needed to pray or Fast or perform Pilgrimage or pay Zakât or do Jihad.

Just because someone is certain to be forgiven, it does not mean that repentence should be delayed. This point is mentioned in another hadith. Abu Hurairah (may Allah be pleased with him) narrated that, 'I heard the Prophet (peace be upon him) saying, "If somebody commits a sin and then says, 'O my Lord! I have sinned, please forgive me!' And his Lord says, 'My slave knows that he has a Lord who forgives sins and punishes for it, I therefore have forgiven My slave (his sins).' Then he remains without committing any sin for a while and then again commits another sin and says, 'O my Lord, I have committed another sin, please forgive me,' and Allah says, 'My slave knows that he has a Lord who forgives sins and punishes for it, I therefore have forgiven My slave (his sin).

---

[8] The statement "Committed after the Battle of Badr:" it occurred six years after it.

Then he remains without Committing any sin for a while and then commits another sin (for the third time) and says, 'O my Lord, I have committed another sin, please forgive me,' and Allah says, 'My slave knows that he has a Lord Who forgives sins and punishes for it, therefore I have forgiven My slave (his sin), he can do whatever he likes." [9]

This does not mean that the person is allowed to do forbidden things, but it means that as long as the person repents, whenever he commits sins, Allah will forgive him.

And the reason this servant has been distinguished with this is because it is known that he does not insist on a sin, and that whenever he commits a sin he repents. It is just as certain for this servant as it is for the people of Badr, as well as anyone the Messenger of Allah (peace be upon him) gave the good news of entering Paradise or told him that his sins had been forgiven. It was not understood from him or any of the Companions that the person is free to commit sins and neglect religious duties. In fact these people were even busier in exerting more effort and feared more after they received the good news than before. This applies more to the ten people who were given the good news of entering Paradise. Abu Bakr, for instance was known to be even more cautious and he feared Allah a great deal. Likewise, 'Umar believed that this good news is limited by its conditions, and so remained constant in piety until his death. Obviously, 'Umar continued to avoid anything that was forbidden. None of them understood that they were given absolute permission to do whatever they wanted.

---

[9] Recorded by Al-Bukhâry, from the book of At-*Tawhîd*, section of the following Qur'anic verse,..." يريدون أن يبدلوا " which means, (They want to change.....). No. (7507), and Muslim, from the book of At-Tawbah, section of acceptance of repentance even if the sins have been repeated. No. (2758). Both of them have been narrated by Abu Hurairah, and they are traceable hadiths.

A Precious Gem of Wisdom: The Interpretation of the Qur'ânic Verse,

Allah, the Almighty says,

﴿ هُوَ ٱلَّذِى جَعَلَ لَكُمُ ٱلْأَرْضَ ذَلُولًا فَٱمْشُوا۟ فِى مَنَاكِبِهَا وَكُلُوا۟ مِن رِّزْقِهِۦ ۖ وَإِلَيْهِ ٱلنُّشُورُ ۝ ﴾

which means: "He it is, Who has made the earth subservient to you (i.e. easy for you to walk, to live and to do agriculture on it, etc.), so walk in the path thereof and eat of His provision, and to Him will be the Resurrection." (Al-Mulk, 67:15)

Allah, Exalted be He, told us that He made the earth subservient for mankind to tread, dig, cultivate and build on. He did not make it difficult for people who need to do all these things in life. Allah, the Almighty also said that He made the earth like a bed, a resting place, a wide expanse, a fixed abode and a receptacle. And He also said that He has spread it, brought forth water from it, and pasture. He has fixed mountains on it, placed therein broad highways and roads. He caused rivers and springs of water to flow, and bestowed blessings upon it and predestinated its substance.

Among its blessings is that every kind of animal and their sustenance come from the earth Also when a seed is put into the earth, it brings it forth multiplied for the benefit of mankind. The earth also carries dirt on itself and brings forth from within itself the best of things and everything that benefits man. It hides all foul things and brings forth all that is sweet. Among its blessings, is that it covers the waste of people and brings forth food and drink for them. Therefore, it is the most perfect thing for bearing harm, and the most perfect thing for bringing about benefit. Nothing that comes out of the earth is better than the earth itself. What is meant here is that Allah, the Almighty made the earth for us like a docile camel that allows itself to be ridden by anyone. The Arabic word "*Manâkibhâ*" means its paths, and is the best expression to convey the meaning of subservience concerning roads and pathways. The walker treads on its paths, which is its highest point. That is why the word "*Manâkib*" has been explained as the shoulders of a human being. They said, "That means that walking on its plains is easier." Another group said, "The word "*Manâkib*" means, sides and areas, as well as the sides of man. What is meant is that "*Manâkib*" means, the raised parts of the earth, and the surface that the animal walks on is the highest part of the earth, for the outside of the ball is its surface, and walking takes place on its surface. That is why it is a good expression to use the word, "*Dhalûl*" which means, subservient.

Then He ordained that mankind should eat from His Provision, which He provided. He subjugated it for them, leveled it and made ways and roads in it which people walk on. He also provided their provision in it. And He mentioned the preparation of residence for benefit and moving around it; back and forth, and eating from that which is provided for the resident. Then He warned mankind by saying the following verse, "*Ilaihi An-Nushûr*" to mean that we are not destined to stay in this abode forever, but we have simply entered it as a passer by. Therefore, we should not take it as a real homeland and a permanent abode, as the only reason for us entering it is to provide ourselves with provision for the Hereafter. The verse indicates Allah's Lordship and Oneness, His Power, Wisdom, Mercy, the remembrance of His Favors and His Kindness. It also contains a warning not to rely on this present life and take it as one's permanent homeland and abode, but rather, we should speed up and move toward His Paradise. Therefore, this verse speaks about His Knowledge, His Oneness, the remembrance of His Favors, the desire to return to Him, the preparation to meet Him, the coming to Him, the knowledge that Allah, the Almighty will roll up this world as if it had not existed and then He will resurrect its people after He had caused them to die, and indeed to Him will be the Resurrection.

A Precious Gem: Al-Fâtihah and the Wisdom it Contains

Man's endeavors in life arise from two main capacities: (i) a theoretical capacity of awareness, and (ii) a practical capacity of willingness to act. Therefore his complete happiness depends on both. The perfection of the theoretical capacity of awareness comes about by knowing his Creator, and His Beautiful Names and Attributes. It also lies in knowing the road that leads to Him and its obstacles, and by knowing his own self and its flaws. By means of these things, he will attain perfection of the theoretical capacity of awareness. The most knowledgeable people are those who know them best.

The perfection of the practical capacity of willingness to act, does not occur unless the rights of Allah, the Almighty are observed by the servant. The rights of Allah are fulfilled by performing one's obligations with sincerity, honesty, advice, kindness, and acknowledging His favor upon him.

Therefore, the servant of Allah feels shy to stand before Him with the small amount of service he did for Allah, because he knows that it is far below what He deserves. He also knows that there is no way to perfect these two capacities unless Allah helps Him. So he desires to be guided to the Straight Way, to which He guides His sincere servants and helps them avoid the things that would let them stray from that Way, either by an imperfection in his capacity of awareness, or by an imperfection in his practical capacity. Going astray incurs the wrath of Allah, the Almighty.

Therefore, man's perfection and happiness cannot be complete without these things. Sûrat Al-Fâtihah has mentioned them and has arranged them perfectly.

Allah, the Almighty says,

﴿ ٱلْحَمْدُ لِلَّهِ رَبِّ ٱلْعَٰلَمِينَ ۝ ٱلرَّحْمَٰنِ ٱلرَّحِيمِ ۝ مَٰلِكِ يَوْمِ ٱلدِّينِ ۝ ﴾

which means, "All praise and thanks are due to Allah, the Lord of the Âlamîn (mankind, jinn and all that exits). The Most Gracious, the Most Merciful. The Only Owner (and Only Ruling Judge) of the Day of Recompense (i.e. the Day of Resurrection)." (Al-Fâtihah, 1:1-4)

These Qur'ânic verses contain the first principle, and that is to have knowledge of the Lord, Exalted be He, and to have knowledge of His Beautiful Names, Attributes and Deeds. The Names that are mentioned in this Sûrat are the bases of the Beautiful Names of Allah, the Almighty, namely Ar-Rabb and Ar-Rahman.

The Name 'Allah' belongs to the Divine Attributes, and the Name 'Ar-Rabb' belongs to His attributes of Lordship and the Name 'Ar-Rahman' belongs to the qualities of Benevolence and Generosity.

His statement,

﴿ إِيَّاكَ نَعْبُدُ وَإِيَّاكَ نَسْتَعِينُ ۝ ﴾

which means, "You (Alone) we worship, and You (Alone) we ask for help (for each and everything). (Al-Fâtihah, 1:5)

This Qur'ânic verse contains the knowledge of the road that leads to Him, which is only found by worshipping Him Alone with that which He loves and prefers, and by asking His Help to worship Him properly.

And His statement,

$$\text{﴿ ٱهْدِنَا ٱلصِّرَٰطَ ٱلْمُسْتَقِيمَ ۝ ﴾}$$

which means, "Guide us to the Straight Way" (Al-Fâtihah, 1:6)

This Qur'ânic verse declares that the servant has no way to achieve happiness except by keeping on the Straight Way, and that there is no way to this straight path without the guidance of Allah. And just as he cannot worship Him, except with His Help, he cannot stand firm on the road except with His guidance.

The following Qur'ânic statement,

$$\text{﴿ ...غَيْرِ ٱلْمَغْضُوبِ عَلَيْهِمْ وَلَا ٱلضَّآلِّينَ ۝ ﴾}$$

which means, "Not (the way) of those who earned Your Anger (such as the Jews), nor of those who went astray (such as the Christians). (Al-Fâtihah, 1:7)

This Qur'ânic verse declares that there are two ways to deviate from the Straight Way, and that one way is corruption of knowledge and belief, and the other is that concerned with the corruption of one's intentions and actions.

Therefore, the beginning of the Sûrat speaks about mercy, the middle speaks about guidance and the end speaks about favor and blessings. The servant receives blessings according to his level of guidance, and the guidance he receives is according to the amount of mercy he receives from Allah. So the whole issue returns to His Blessings and Mercy, which are the characteristics of Lordship.

Therefore, He is Merciful and the Benefactor, and that is one of the characteristics of Divinity. He is the true God, even if the ungrateful choose to deny it and even if the polytheists treat others like they should only treat Him. So, whoever complies with the meaning of Al-Fâtihah in terms of knowledge, action, and a way of life, the person will have then successfully perfected himself, and his submission will have become the same as those whose degree has been raised above the common worshippers. And it is Allah whose aid is to be implored.

A Precious Gem: Two Ways to Know Allah

Allah, the Exalted invites His servants to know Him in two ways:

The first one is: by observing His creation and pondering.

The second one is: by reflecting on His Qur'ânic Verses. The first one is His signs in the universe, and the second one is the comprehension of His Verses of the Qu'ran.

The first one is illustrated in the following Qur'ânic verse,

﴿ إِنَّ فِى خَلْقِ ٱلسَّمَٰوَٰتِ وَٱلْأَرْضِ وَٱخْتِلَٰفِ ٱلَّيْلِ وَٱلنَّهَارِ وَٱلْفُلْكِ ٱلَّتِى تَجْرِى فِى ٱلْبَحْرِ بِمَا يَنفَعُ ٱلنَّاسَ وَمَآ أَنزَلَ ٱللَّهُ مِنَ ٱلسَّمَآءِ مِن مَّآءٍ فَأَحْيَا بِهِ ٱلْأَرْضَ بَعْدَ مَوْتِهَا وَبَثَّ فِيهَا مِن كُلِّ دَآبَّةٍ وَتَصْرِيفِ ٱلرِّيَٰحِ وَٱلسَّحَابِ ٱلْمُسَخَّرِ بَيْنَ ٱلسَّمَآءِ وَٱلْأَرْضِ لَءَايَٰتٍ لِّقَوْمٍ يَعْقِلُونَ ﴾

which means, "Verily! In the creation of the heavens and the earth, and in the alternation of night and day, and the ships which sail through the sea with that which is of use to mankind, and the water (rain) which Allah sends down from the sky and makes the earth alive therewith after its death, and the moving (living) creatures of all kinds that He has scattered therein, and in the veering of winds and clouds which are held between the sky and the earth, are indeed Ayât (proofs, evidences, signs, etc.) for people of understanding." (Al-Baqarah, 2:164)

And the following Qur'ânic verse,

﴿ إِنَّ فِي خَلْقِ ٱلسَّمَٰوَٰتِ وَٱلْأَرْضِ وَٱخْتِلَٰفِ ٱلَّيْلِ وَٱلنَّهَارِ لَآيَٰتٍ لِّأُو۟لِى ٱلْأَلْبَٰبِ ﴾

which means, "Verily! In the creation of the heavens and the earth, and in the alternation of night and day, there are indeed signs for men of understanding." (Âl-'Imrân, 3:190)

There are many other verses having the same meaning.

The second is illustrated by the Qur'ânic verse, which goes as follows:

﴿ وَإِذَا جَآءَهُمْ أَمْرٌ مِّنَ ٱلْأَمْنِ أَوِ ٱلْخَوْفِ أَذَاعُوا۟ بِهِۦ ۖ وَلَوْ رَدُّوهُ إِلَى ٱلرَّسُولِ وَإِلَىٰٓ أُو۟لِى ٱلْأَمْرِ مِنْهُمْ لَعَلِمَهُ ٱلَّذِينَ يَسْتَنۢبِطُونَهُۥ مِنْهُمْ ۗ وَلَوْلَا فَضْلُ ٱللَّهِ عَلَيْكُمْ وَرَحْمَتُهُۥ لَٱتَّبَعْتُمُ ٱلشَّيْطَٰنَ إِلَّا قَلِيلًا ۝ ﴾

which means, "Do they not then consider the Qur'ân carefully?" (An-Nisâ', 4:83).

﴿ أَفَلَمْ يَدَّبَّرُوا۟ ٱلْقَوْلَ ... ۝ ﴾

which means, "Have they not pondered over the Word (of Allah, i.e. what is sent down to the Prophet)." (Al-Mu'mimûn, 23:68)

﴿ كِتَٰبٌ أَنزَلْنَٰهُ إِلَيْكَ مُبَٰرَكٌ لِّيَدَّبَّرُوٓا۟ ءَايَٰتِهِۦ وَلِيَتَذَكَّرَ أُو۟لُوا۟ ٱلْأَلْبَٰبِ ۝ ﴾

which means, "(This is) a Book (the Qur'ân) which We have sent down to you, full of blessings that they may ponder over its Verses, and that men of understanding may remember." (Sâd, 38:29)

There are many other Qur'ânic verses that have the same meaning.

Creation indicates actions, and actions indicate attributes, for the creation indicates the existence of a creator, and that requires His existence, ability, will and knowledge. It is impossible that a voluntary action proceeds from something that is nonexistent, helpless, lifeless, ignorant and having no will.

Moreover, the various characteristics in the creation prove the existence of the Creator's will, and that His action is repetitive. The elements of creation concerning interests, and praiseworthy purposes, indicate His wisdom. Those parts of creation, which are beneficial, and good, indicate His Mercy. In the same way, the fact that He Seizes, takes retribution and metes out punishment, indicates His Anger. The honor He bestows on His creatures, their closeness and care, indicate His Love. The fact that He banishes and abandons, indicates His Hatred and Abhorrence.

Every element of nature begins in a weak and incomplete state, then develops and grows to its complete and final state and this fact points to the reality of the Hereafter. The conditions of plants and animals, and the flow of water indicate the reality of the Hereafter. Man continually witnesses the effects of mercy and blessings upon creation and these indicate the fulfillment of prophecies. The creation of Allah is perfect to the extent that if any of its elements are removed there would be some kind of inadequacy, and this indicates that the Giver of perfection is truly deserving of praise and thanksmore than anyone or anything else.

Therefore, His creation really shows His Attributes and the truthfulness of that which His Prophets reported about Him. The creation is then evidence that confirms the verses of Qu'ran to be true and draws our attention to the signs in creation.

Allah, the Almighty said,

﴿ سَنُرِيهِمْ ءَايَٰتِنَا فِى ٱلْءَافَاقِ وَفِىٓ أَنفُسِهِمْ حَتَّىٰ يَتَبَيَّنَ لَهُمْ أَنَّهُ ٱلْحَقُّ... ﴾

which means, "We will show them Our Signs in the universe, and in their ownselves, until it becomes manifest to them that this (the Qur'ân) is the truth." (Fussilat, 41:53)

This simply means that the Qur'ân is the truth. And He said that He will show them (the disbelievers) some of His signs that can be seen, and will make clear to them the truthfulness of His Verses (the Qur'ân).

He then said that His witness is sufficient for the truthfulness of the evidence and proof that He provided concerning the authenticity of His Prophet. Therefore, His Verses are true evidence, and He is a true witness for His Prophet through His verses. So He is the Witness and the witnessed for, and He is the Evidence and the Indicated to. He is the Evidence by Himself about Himself, as some of the most knowledgeable people of Allah said, "How can I ask for the Evidence of whom is an Evidence for me over all things? If you ask for any evidence of Him, you will find that His Existence is more evident than that." That is why the Messengers (peace be upon them) said, "What! Can there be a doubt about Allah?" (Ibrâhîm, 14:10) Therefore, He is more Known than all that is known and more evident than all evidence. Realistically, everything in the universe is proven to be a created object by the fact that there must be a creator, which is Allah, the Almighty; yet, and by way of deductive reasoning, He Himself is recognized through the existence of such creatures as well as through His actions and laws, which organize the course of all creatures in the universe.

A Precious Gem: Prophetic Hadiths Eliminating Grief and Distress

It is recorded in Musnad Ahmad and Sahîh Abu Hâtim on the authority of 'Abdullâh bin Mas'ûd that the Messenger of Allah (peace be upon him) said, "Whoever was afflicted with grief and distress and says, **'Allâhumma inny 'abduk, wa ibn 'abdik,**

wa ibn amatik, nâsiyaty biyadik, mâdin fiyya hukmuk, 'Adlun fiyya qadâ'uk, as'aluka bikul ism huwa lak, sammaita bihi nafsak, aw anzaltahu fy kitâbik, aw 'allamtahu ahadan min khalqik, aw ista'tharta bihi fy 'ilmil-ghaibi 'indik, an taj'ala al-qur'âna rabî'a qalby, wa nûra sadry, wa jalâ' huzny, wa dhahâba hammy (O Allah! I am Your Servant, the son of Your Servant, the son of Your Maid servant. You have control over me. Your Judgment is executed on me. Your Decree on me is just. I ask You by each Name of Yours by which You have called Yourself, revealed in Your Book, taught to any of Your servants, or kept as a secret in the knowledge of the unseen with You, to make the Qur'ân the spring (delight) of my heart, the light of my chest, the eliminator of my sorrow, and the remover of my worries),' Allah, the Exalted and Ever-Majestic, will remove his grief and will change his sorrow into happiness." It was said, "O Messenger of Allah! (Do) we have to learn these words?" He said, "Yes, whoever hears them should learn them."

This great prophetic tradition implies certain matters of knowledge, monotheism and submission, for example the supplicant starts by saying, "I am Your servant, the son of Your servant, and the son of Your maid servant." This includes the forefathers of the supplicant until we reach Adam and Eve. In other words, the supplication indicates submission and full compliance to Allah, besides the confession of being His servant along with his forefathers.

It asserts the fact that the servant has no one but his Lord, His blessings and His graces. Whenever his Lord ignores him, surely he is a looser, with no refuge or support.

This confession means, I am in dire need of You, and I have no supporter or refuge other than You and it infers that the supplicant is submissive, obedient, and forbearing. He acts according to his submission to Allah, not according to his feelings of self-sufficiency. To provide help and comfort is the role of kings and masters, not servants. However, the actions of servants are based on submission, in order to reach the level of those obedient servants described by Allah, the Exalted. Allah says,

$$\text{﴿ إِنَّ عِبَادِي لَيْسَ لَكَ عَلَيْهِمْ سُلْطَانٌ ... ﴾}$$

which means, "Certainly, you shall have no authority over My slaves." (Al-Hijr, 15:42)

And He, the Almighty says,

$$\text{﴿ وَعِبَادُ الرَّحْمَٰنِ الَّذِينَ يَمْشُونَ عَلَى الْأَرْضِ هَوْنًا ... ﴾}$$

which means, "And the slaves of the Most Beneficent (Allah) are those who walk on the earth in humility and sedateness." (Al-Furqân, 25:63)

Other kinds of servants are those slaves of submission and lordship. Ascribing them to Allah resembles ascribing houses to His Kingdom, or ascribing the Sacred Mosque to Him, or like ascribing the Camel to Him, or His Paradise, and finally ascribing the submission of His Messenger to Him in the following Qur'ânic verse,

$$\text{﴿ وَإِن كُنتُمْ فِي رَيْبٍ مِّمَّا نَزَّلْنَا عَلَىٰ عَبْدِنَا ... ﴾}$$

which means, "And if you (Arab pagans, Jews, and Christians) are in doubt concerning that which We have sent down (i.e. the Qur'ân) to Our slave (Muhammad)..." (Al-Baqarah, 2:23)

And He, the Almighty says,

$$\text{﴿ سُبْحَانَ الَّذِي أَسْرَىٰ بِعَبْدِهِ ... ﴾}$$

which means, "Glorified (and Exalted) be He (Allah) [above all that (evil) they associate with Him] Who took His slave (Muhammad SAW) for a journey by night." (Al-Isrâ', 17:1)

And He, the Almighty says,

$$\text{﴿ وَأَنَّهُ لَمَّا قَامَ عَبْدُ اللَّهِ يَدْعُوهُ ... ﴾}$$

which means, "(It has been revealed to me that) When the slave of Allah (Muhammad SAW) stood up invoking (his Lord Allah) in prayer to Him..." (Al-Jinn, 72:19)

Submission

The correct meaning of, "I am Your servant" indicates full submission, compliance, and repentance to Allah, as well as being obedient to one's Lord and avoiding His prohibitions, depending on Him, seeking His help and support, seeking refuge in Him from evil, and finally being related to Him with feelings of love, fear and hope. It also indicates, "I am Your servant in all cases, whether young or grown up, living or dead, obedient or disobedient, in a good condition or otherwise (i.e. being afflicted in the soul, heart, tongue or bodily organs)."

Moreover, it means, "I am all Yours, both my money and myself," for the servant and all that which he possesses belong to his master.

It also means, "You are the one who bestowed all those blessings upon me, so those blessings are really Yours."

It also includes, "I can't act freely in that which You granted me, either my money or myself, except by Your orders, as no servant can behave freely except with his master's permission. I can neither hurt nor benefit myself, and I possess no power (of causing) death, nor (of giving) life, nor of raising the dead. So, if he really believes in all that which was previously mentioned, then he has confessed his full submission to Allah.

The sentence, "My forelock is in Your hands," means, "I cannot act freely as far as my soul is concerned," for how can he act freely when his soul is possessed by his Lord, his forelock is in His hands, his heart is between two of His fingers, and moreover, his death, life, happiness, misery, good-condition, and affliction are in the charge of his Lord, the Exalted? By no means is the servant in the charge of himself. The master owns him, and he is weaker than any worthless slave whose forelock is in the grasp of a powerful and mighty ruler. It is so much more than that.

Whenever the servant of Allah confesses the fact that his forelock and the forelock of all other servants are in the grasp of Allah (i.e. under His control), he will neither fear nor aspire to any worldly sovereign nor will he overestimate them, because he knows quite well that they are but subdued servants, whose destiny is controlled by Allah. Whoever confesses this fact, surely will stand in need of Allah and whenever he witnesses the reality of other people, he will neither overestimate them nor exaggerate in seeking their support. In this way, his belief, trust and submission will be turned to Allah alone. This is the reason behind Hûd's speech to his people when he said in the Qur'ânic verse,

﴿ إِنِّى تَوَكَّلْتُ عَلَى ٱللَّهِ رَبِّى وَرَبِّكُم ۚ مَّا مِن دَآبَّةٍ إِلَّا هُوَ ءَاخِذٌۢ بِنَاصِيَتِهَآ ۚ إِنَّ رَبِّى عَلَىٰ صِرَٰطٍ مُّسْتَقِيمٍ ۝ ﴾

which means, "I put my trust in Allah, my Lord and your Lord! There is not a moving (living) creature but He has grasp of its forelock. Verily, my Lord is on the Straight Path (the truth)." (Hûd, 11:56)

The sentence, "Your Judgment is executed on me. Your Decree on me is just," implies two themes, the first of which is the execution of His judgment on His servant.

The second theme implies praising Him and that His Decree is just, in addition to the fact that Allah, the Exalted, is the Dominion, and that to Him belong all praise and thanks, and that is the meaning of Hûd's words, "There is not a moving (living) creature but He has grasp of its forelock," and also his words, "Verily, my Lord is on the Straight Path (the truth)." In other words, despite the fact that Allah is the Dominion, the Almighty and the Controller of the destiny of His servants as their forelocks are in His grasp, yet He is on the straight path. He is the Just One, Who oversees His servants' affairs justly. He is on the straight path in His words, His actions, His judgment, His destiny, His commandments, His prohibitions, His rewards and His punishment. His verses are truthful, His Judgment is correct, and His commandments are beneficial. He prohibited all that which is evil and mischievous. His reward descends upon those who deserve His mercy and grace. His punishment descends upon those who deserve torment by means of His Justice and wisdom.

Judgment and Decree

There is a distinction between judgment and decree, because judgments are executed and decrees are just.

The judgment of Allah, the Exalted, implies His legitimate judgment and His preordained judgment upon the whole universe. Both judgments are executed on human beings, who are subjected to them, either willingly or unwillingly. However, there is only one distinction between the two, the preordained universal judgment is compulsory, whereas the religious judgment is optional.

On the other hand, decree means completion and perfection whenever it is executed. The expression "Your decree is just" means "Your decree which you completed, and perfected is the rightful one.

The word "judgment" refers to every commandment prescribed by Allah, the Exalted. The judgment of Allah is ordained. Religious judgments will surely be executed, and universal ones will be executed if it is ordained by Allah. Verily, Allah executes that which He ordains, and anyone else can decide whichever judgment he wants but he may still lack the ability to execute it. Allah alone has the power of judgment and implementation. The expression, "Your decree is just" comprises all the decrees ordained by Allah upon His servant: illness or health, luxury or poverty, pleasure or pain, life or death, punishment or reward etc.

Allah, the Exalted, says,

﴿ وَمَآ أَصَٰبَكُم مِّن مُّصِيبَةٍ فَبِمَا كَسَبَتْ أَيْدِيكُمْ وَيَعْفُواْ عَن كَثِيرٍ ۝ ﴾

which means, "And whatever of misfortune befalls you, it is because of what your hands have earned. And He pardons much." (Ash-Shûrâ, 42:30)

And He, the Almighty also says,

﴿ ...وَإِن تُصِبْهُمْ سَيِّئَةٌ بِمَا قَدَّمَتْ أَيْدِيهِمْ فَإِنَّ ٱلْإِنسَٰنَ كَفُورٌ ۝ ﴾

which means, "but when some ill befalls them because of the deeds which their hands have sent forth, then verily, man (becomes) ingrate!" (Ash-Shûrâ, 42:48)

Every decree ordained upon the servant of Allah is just.

The Perception of Destiny and Decree in Other Sects

It was argued, "If sin is preordained by Allah's decree and destiny, then, where is justice?" Justice here is concealed.

It was replied, "That's a good question, and for that reason a sect once claimed that only justice is preordained but injustice is inconceivable." They answered, "Injustice is the disposal in other's property, and Allah is the Owner of all things. Accordingly, His disposal of affairs is just, concerning His creation.

Another sect claimed, "Justice means to abstain from punishing for that which is preordained and predestined, so as long as He approved of the punishment, then sin is neither preordained nor predetermined. Thus, punishment for one's sin is just, and it is the consequence of one's words and deeds in this worldly life."

It was difficult for this sect to combine justice and destiny. They claimed that whoever believes in destiny, should never believe in justice, and likewise whoever believes in justice should never believe in destiny. It was hard for them, as well, to combine monotheism with the validity of the Attributes of Allah. They claimed that it is impossible to validate monotheism except by disbelieving in the Attributes of Allah. In brief, their monotheism turned out to be suspension, and their justice turned out to disbelief in Justice.

On the other hand, the Sunnis believe in both (i.e. justice & destiny). Their definition of Injustice is putting a matter in other than its place, like punishing the obedient and innocent person. Verily, Allah is too Exalted for this, which is His characteristic as explained in the Glorious Qur'ân. The fact that Allah, the Exalted, sends astray whom He wills, and preordained sin and transgression on whomever He wills, is simply justice, because He places mischief and aberration in its right place. It is worth mentioning that one of the Names of Allah is 'the Just,' whose judgments are correct, proper and rightful.

Moreover, Allah clarified all paths, by sending His Messengers, and revealing His Divine Books. He facilitates the ways of guidance and obedience by means of hearing, insight and the use of the mind, which is justice.

Furthermore, Allah guides him who wants to be guided which is a great blessing. On the other hand, He sends astray those who are unworthy as well as those who are unwilling to receive the blessings of Allah, so He deprived them of His blessing but not His justice. Such people are divided into two kinds.

The first kind is him whom Allah leaves to stray due to his misguidance as he turned away from Allah, preferring His enemy and neglecting to remember and thank Him. As a result, he deserves to be abandoned by Allah.

The second kind is those whom Allah is initially unwilling to support, because He knows that they underestimate the guidance of Allah. Such people are not thankful to Allah and do not praise Him, and this is the reason behind their being deprived of His blessings.

Allah, the Exalted, says,

﴿ وَكَذَٰلِكَ فَتَنَّا بَعْضَهُم بِبَعْضٍ لِّيَقُولُوٓا۟ أَهَٰٓؤُلَآءِ مَنَّ ٱللَّهُ عَلَيْهِم مِّنۢ بَيْنِنَآ ۗ أَلَيْسَ ٱللَّهُ بِأَعْلَمَ بِٱلشَّٰكِرِينَ ﴾

which means, "Thus We have tried some of them with others, that they might say: "Is it these (poor believers) that Allah has favoured from amongst us?" Does not Allah know best those who are grateful?" (Al-An'âm, 6:53)

He, the Almighty also says,

﴿ وَلَوْ عَلِمَ ٱللَّهُ فِيهِمْ خَيْرًا لَّأَسْمَعَهُمْ ... ﴾

which means, "Had Allah known of any good in them, He would indeed have made them listen." (Al-Anfâl, 8:23)

So, if Allah decrees misguidance and disobedience upon these souls, then it is just, like for example His decree that the serpent and the scorpion can be killed. All these decrees are just, for they have been created with such characteristics. We mentioned this subject in detail in the book, "**The Decree and the Destiny**."

In brief, the supplication, "Your judgment is executed on me and Your decree on me is just" is the best answer to both sects, the **Anti-Fatalists** who deny the decrees of Allah upon His servants and believe that man's actions are excluded from the destiny and the decree of Allah, and it is also a refutation against the other sect, "**The Jabriyyah**" who believe that every decree is just a concept which makes that supplication - namely, "Your decree on me is just" - of no value. According to them justice is every predetermined applicable action while injustice is inconceivable. **Invocation using the Names of Allah**

The expression, "I ask You by each Name of Yours ....etc", is an invocation with all the Names of Allah whether they are known or unknown. It is allowable in the Sight of Allah, as it is an invocation with the Attributes of Allah which refers to the connotations of His Names.

The expression, "to make the Qur'ân the spring (delight) of my heart, the light of my chest," the word 'spring' means the rain, which brings life to the earth. The Qur'ân is compared to rain because it revives the hearts. He makes a similarity between water, which is the cause of life, and between light, which is the cause of brightness. Allah, the Exalted, makes that similarity in the Qur'ânic verse in, which He says,

﴿ أَنزَلَ مِنَ ٱلسَّمَآءِ مَآءً فَسَالَتۡ أَوۡدِيَةٌۢ بِقَدَرِهَا فَٱحۡتَمَلَ ٱلسَّيۡلُ زَبَدٗا رَّابِيٗاۚ وَمِمَّا يُوقِدُونَ عَلَيۡهِ فِي ٱلنَّارِ ٱبۡتِغَآءَ حِلۡيَةٍ ... ﴾

which means, "He sends down water (rain) from the sky, and the valleys flow according to their measure, but the flood bears away the foam that mounts up to the surface, and (also) from that (ore) which they heat in the fire in order to make ornaments." (Ar-Ra'd, 13:17)

Allah, the Exalted, says,

$$\{ أَوْ كَصَيِّبٍ مِّنَ ٱلسَّمَآءِ ... \}$$

which means, "Or like a rainstorm from the sky." (Al-Baqarah, 2:19)

And the verse in which Allah says,

$$\{ ٱللَّهُ نُورُ ٱلسَّمَٰوَٰتِ وَٱلْأَرْضِ ... \}$$

which means, "Allah is the Light of the heavens and the earth...." (An-Nûr, 24:35)

And the verse in which Allah says,

$$\{ أَلَمْ تَرَ أَنَّ ٱللَّهَ يُزْجِى سَحَابًا ثُمَّ يُؤَلِّفُ بَيْنَهُۥ ... \}$$

which means, "See you not that Allah drives the clouds gently, then joins them together......." (An-Nûr, 24:43)

So the supplication implies that the heart is revived by the spring of the Qur'ân, for it is the light of the chest, a concept, which combines life and light.

Allah, the Almighty says,

$$\{ أَوَمَن كَانَ مَيْتًا فَأَحْيَيْنَٰهُ وَجَعَلْنَا لَهُۥ نُورًا يَمْشِى بِهِۦ فِى ٱلنَّاسِ كَمَن مَّثَلُهُۥ فِى ٱلظُّلُمَٰتِ لَيْسَ بِخَارِجٍ مِّنْهَا ... \}$$

which means, "Is he who was dead (without Faith by ignorance and disbelief) and We gave him life (by knowledge and Faith) and set for him a light (of Belief) whereby he can walk amongst men, like him who is in the darkness (of disbelief, polytheism and hypocrisy) from which he can never come out?" (Al-An'âm, 6:122)

Since the chest is broader than the heart, then enlightening it will surely affect the heart. The life of the body and organs are dependant on the life of the heart, which derives life from the chest and then gives life to the organs.

On the other hand, if grief, distress, and sorrow contradict the life of the heart and its brightness, the supplication involves the desire that they be totally removed by the Qur'ân.

However, if the previous feelings are to be removed by other than the Qur'ân, for example, enjoying health, this worldly life, status, a wife or children, then surely those feelings are temporary and will eventually dissipate. There are three kinds of passive feelings, which affect the heart and they are either related to the past, which causes sorrow, or related to the future so as to cause grief, or finally related to the present so as to cause distress.

A Precious Gem: The Throne and the Heart

Allah is the most Exalted from all that exists, and that is why He, the Almighty is the only One who deserves the Almighty throne. The closest thing to the throne that exists, is the brightest, the most honorable and the highest from all creation and that is the part of Paradise called al Firdaws.

Accordingly, the most distant place from the throne is the gloomiest and the narrowest place; it is the lowest of the low and is far distant from any blessing.

Allah, the Almighty created the hearts of man and made them the source of knowledge, love, and the desire to aspire to Him. Hence, the hearts of man are the pivot point of his existence.

Allah, the Exalted, says,

﴿ لِلَّذِينَ لَا يُؤْمِنُونَ بِٱلْءَاخِرَةِ مَثَلُ ٱلسَّوْءِ ۖ وَلِلَّهِ ٱلْمَثَلُ ٱلْأَعْلَىٰ ۚ وَهُوَ ٱلْعَزِيزُ ٱلْحَكِيمُ ﴾

which means, " For those who believe not in the Hereafter is an evil description, and for Allah is the highest description. And He is the All-Mighty, the All-Wise." (An-Nahl, 16:60)

Allah, the Almighty says,

﴿ وَهُوَ ٱلَّذِى يَبْدَؤُا۟ ٱلْخَلْقَ ثُمَّ يُعِيدُهُۥ وَهُوَ أَهْوَنُ عَلَيْهِ ۚ وَلَهُ ٱلْمَثَلُ ٱلْأَعْلَىٰ فِى ٱلسَّمَـٰوَٰتِ وَٱلْأَرْضِ ۚ وَهُوَ ٱلْعَزِيزُ ٱلْحَكِيمُ ﴾

which means, " And He it is Who originates the creation, then will repeat it (after it has been perished), and this is easier for Him. His is the highest description (i.e. none has the right to be worshipped but He, and there is nothing comparable unto Him) in the heavens and in the earth. And He is the Almighty, the All Wise." (Ar-Rûm, 30:27)

Allah, the Almighty says,

﴿ ...لَيْسَ كَمِثْلِهِۦ شَىْءٌ... ﴾

which means, "There is nothing like unto Him." (Ash-Shûrâ, 42:11)

In other words, loving, knowing and aspiring to Allah are the true definition of the heart of the sincere believer.

If the heart is not pure or honorable enough, and distant from every evil and malice, then it is unworthy to love, know and aspire to Allah. On the contrary, the lowest description of man's heart is that he loves and aspires to this worldly life instead of to Allah, the Almighty. When man's love, knowledge and aspiration is directed in this worldly way, the heart becomes narrow and gloomy as it is distant from the source of its revival and life.

Subsequently, the hearts of man can be divided into two kinds, the first of which is the heart of those, who incline to the Beneficent, which is the source of brightness, life, happiness, pleasure, delight and blessings. The second one is the throne of the devil where narrowness, darkness, death, sorrow, distress and grief are settled therein. This heart is obsessed by sorrow for the past, and grief and distress for the present.

At-Tirmidhy and others narrated, "The Prophet (peace be upon him) said, 'If the heart is overwhelmed by the brightness (of faith), surely it will be opened and delighted.' They said, 'O Messenger of Allah! What is the sign for that?' He replied, 'Resorting to the eternal dwelling (i.e. Paradise), being averted from the dwelling of deceit (i.e. the worldly life), and being prepared for death before its arrival.'"

In brief, the brightness, which overwhelms the heart is the impact of being close to Allah, the Almighty and obtaining His blessings of serenity and guidance. This fills the heart with pleasure, while lacking such feelings that come from knowing Allah and loving Him, makes it a gloomy and narrow place.

A Precious Gem: The Content of the Qur'ân

If we look closely at the words of the Qur'ân, we will find a Sovereign, to whom belongs all Dominion and all praise and thanks are due to Him, all affairs are in His grasp, and He is the source and the end of all affairs. He rose over His throne, and no secret of His kingdom shall ever be hidden from Him, as He is the Knower of the servants' souls. He Alone is the Planner of the kingdom's affairs. He hears, sees, grants, averts, rewards, punishes, honors, abases, creates, gives and takes life, provides estimates, judges, and conducts the affairs of man.

The decrees, whether minor or major, descend and ascend by His permission. Nothing can move, even equal to the weight of an atom, except by His permission; not a leaf falls, but He knows it.

Let's think about the way, in which He praises and glorifies Himself, and how He warns His servants and guides them to happiness and salvation, by directing their interest to the right path. He warns them against the way of destruction. He acquaints them with His Names and Attributes, and He gets closer to them by bestowing His blessings and grace upon them. He reminds them of His blessings, and orders them to the way of salvation. He warns them against His wrath, reminding them of the reward prepared for them if they are obedient, and also of the torment prepared for them if they are disobedient. He narrates the stories of the believers and the disbelievers as well as the end of both parties.

He praises the believers by virtue of their good deeds and qualities, and He dispraises His enemies by their wrong doings and evil qualities. He sets forth parables and provides evidence and proof. He refutes the lies of His enemies by portraying the best of answers, and believing the truthful and belying the liars. He says the truth and guides to the right path.

He calls to the dwelling of peace, mentioning its characteristics, and its bliss. He warns against the dwelling of destruction, mentioning its torment, awfulness and pain.

He mentions His servants and their need for Him at all times: there is never a time when they are not in need of Him, even for the twinkling of an eye. He states His richness above all creatures, and the fact the He is free of all needs and wants. He mentions the fact that all creatures stand in need of Him, and no one can attain the least blessing or more except by His Mercy and Grace, and no one can be afflicted by the least amount of evil or more except by His justice and wisdom.

The speech of Allah implies His gentle admonition to the believers, because in spite of everything He raises them from their falls, forgives and excuses them, reforms their corruption, and supports them. For them, He is the defender, the supporter, the sustainer, and the rescuer from every distress. He always fulfills His promises. They have no protector other than Him, for He is their true Master, and their Helper against their enemies, so what an excellent Protector and what an excellent Helper.

If the hearts witness through the Qur'ân, a glorious, great, bountiful, merciful sovereign like this, then how can these hearts stop loving Him, and how can they not compete in approaching Him and getting closer to Him? For them, that sovereign should be the most lovable of all, and His satisfaction should be sought more than the satisfaction of others.

Really, how can these hearts stop remembering Him, since loving and longing for Him are the source of power and remedy, to the extent that if the hearts do not have these things, then destruction and corruption would be their destiny, and their lives would be of no value.

A Precious Gem: No Place for Two Contradictions

In order for a place to contain something, it must be free from whatever contradicts it. This principle applies to mankind and all creation as well as to belief and desires.

So, if the heart is obsessed by belief in falsehood, there will be no place for truth. Accordingly, if the tongue is involved in trivial discourse, one shall be incapable of useful speech, unless falsehood is abandoned.

Hence, if the body is busy doing wrong actions, then acts of worship will be inapplicable unless these contradictory actions are abandoned.

This is how this principle is applied to concrete objects, and it is also applied to belief and religion. If the heart deviates from loving Allah, lacks yearning for Him and longing for His closeness, then the removal of contradictory feelings, like being related to other than Allah, is the only way for this heart to be overwhelmed by love for Allah.

For the tongue to remember Allah, and the body to serve Him, one should be free of the impact of others like being busy remembering and serving them.

Thus, if the heart is overwhelmed by the servants rather than the master, and is preoccupied with futile knowledge, surely there will be no place for being closer to Allah, or being acquainted with His Names, Attributes and judgments.

If the heart listens to trivial discourse, there will be no place for listening or understanding the words of Allah. Besides, if the heart is inclined to love others, there will be no room to love Allah, and if the heart remembers others rather than Allah, no place will be found to remember Him, and the same applies to the tongue.

Al-Bukhâry recorded that the Prophet (peace be upon him) said, "It is better for any of you that the inside of his body be filled with pus which may consume his body, than it be filled with poetry."[10]

This Prophetic tradition explained that it is possible that the inside of one's body may be filled with poetry, which means that it might be exposed to suspicion, doubts, illusions, uncertainties, futile knowledge, and trivial discourse.

So, if the heart is filled with such things, the facts of the Qur'ân and precious knowledge, which cause happiness and perfection in mankind, will find no room in that heart.

If a heart receives advice but it is filled with what contradicts it, there will be no place in that heart to accept this advice. The advice will simply pass over this heart and not be able to settle in it.

---

[10] Recorded by Al-Bukhâry, in His Sahih, Book of Al-Adab (Good Manners and Form), Chapter on not recommending poetry, no. (6154), and recorded by Muslim in His Sahih no. (2258).

Interpretation of Chapter At-Takâthur

In which Allah, the Almighty says,

$$﴿ أَلْهَاكُمُ التَّكَاثُرُ ۝ ﴾$$

which means, "The mutual rivalry for piling up of worldly things diverts you..." (At-Takâthur, 102:1)

Until the end of the chapter.

This chapter talks about promise, threat, and menace. It gives exhortation to whoever understands. Allah says,

$$﴿ أَلْهَاكُمُ ... ۝ ﴾$$

which means, "diverts you..." (At-Takâthur, 102:1)

That is to say, those matters divert you in a way that you are not to be excused. You are busy doing something else. If this diversion is intentional then the obligatory acts of worship have been violated, and if it was unintentional as when the Prophet (peace be upon him) said once about a Khamîsah, "....for it has just now diverted my attention from my prayer..."[11] its owner will be excused and it will be considered a form of forgetfulness. The heart can be diverted and the limbs can be misused and that is why they are gathered together. That is why Allah says which means, "The mutual rivalry for piling up of worldly things diverts you." (At-Takâthur, 102:1) and did not say, ".... busies you." A worker can use his body in his work while his heart is not diverted by his activity. 'Diversion' refers to distraction and avoidance. Allah did not mention the object of their competition

---

[11] Recorded by Al-Bukhâry in his sahîh, book of prayer, chapter on whoever performs prayer in a dress that has printed marks and looked at these marks, no. 373, and the book of Dress, chapter on garments and Khamâ'is, no. 5817. Muslim, book of Mosques and places of performing prayer, no. 556, and Abu Dâwûd in his Sunnah, no. 914, and An-Nasâ'y, no. 771.

in order to keep it general. Whatever the servants are mutually pilling up rather than obeying Allah and His Messenger and every matter that will be useful to him on the day of his Resurrection, is to be included in this mutual rivalry. Mutual rivalry could be money, power, authority, women, speech, or knowledge. This is especially true when the person is in need of this object. It could extend to those things that are not necessary, like further books, volumes, and unnecessary questioning and its branches. Mutual rivalry is when man seeks to acquire more than others and this is dispraised unless it is for something that will bring him close to Allah. Mutual rivalry includes competing in doing good deeds. Muslim recorded that 'Abdullâh bin Ash-Shikhkhîr (may Allah be pleased with him) narrated, "I came to the Messenger of Allah (peace be upon him) as he was reciting, "The mutual rivalry for piling up of worldly things diverts you..." (At-Takâthur, 102:1). He said, 'The son of Adam claims, 'My wealth, my wealth.' And he (the Holy Prophet) said, 'O son of Adam! Is there anything that really belongs to you, except that which you consumed, which you utilized, or which you wore and then it was worn out or you gave as charity and sent it forward for yourself?'"[12]

Note: Perfect Wisdom

- He, who did not make use of his eye, did not make use of his ear.

- The servant has a veil between him and Allah and another one between him and people. Whoever tore this veil between him and Allah, Allah will tear the veil between him and people.

- The servant has a Lord that he will stand in front of and a house that he will live in, so he must seek the pleasure

---

[12] Recorded by Muslim, book of Pertaining to piety and softening of hearts, no.2958,2959, At-Tirmidhy, no.2342,3354, and An-Nasâ'y, no.3613.

of Allah before meeting Him and he should furnish his house before moving into it.

- Loosing time is harder than death, as loosing time keeps you away from Allah and the Hereafter, while death keeps you away from the worldly life and your people.

- The whole world from its beginning until its end is not worth an hour of sadness, so what about the sadness of a whole life.

- What we love today will catch up with what we hate tomorrow, and what we hate today will catch up with what we love tomorrow.

- The most precious reward during life is to busy yourself with the most suitable and useful matters in their exact and suitable time.

How can he be rational who sells Paradise and what is in it, for one hour of passing pleasure?

- The Pious man will leave this worldly life while he did not obtain satisfaction in two matters: crying for himself and praising Allah.

- If you are afraid of any creature, you will run away from it. When you are afraid of Allah, you will love Him and seek to be close to Him.

- If knowledge is useful without actions, Allah, the Exalted would never have dispraised the people of the book, and if actions were useful without devotion, He would never have dispraised the hypocrites.

- Stand firm against evil thoughts, for if you fail to do so, they will become ideas, if you do not, they will become desires, so fight against them. If you do not, they will become a form of determination and intention, if you do not resist, they will become actions, and if you do not follow them up with their opposite, they will become habits that will be hard to quit.

- **Piety has Three Levels**

   One: protecting the heart and limbs against sin and forbidden actions.

   Two: protecting them against undesirable matters.

   Three: protection against curiosity and whatever is not of one's concern.

   The first will grant life to the servant, the second will grant him health and power, and the third will grant him happiness and joy.

- He whom Allah has predestined to enter Paradise, the reasons, which will cause his entrance shall spring from calamities; and he whom Allah has predestined to enter the Hellfire, the reasons which will cause his entrance shall spring from lusts.

- When Âdam (Adam, peace be upon him) sought immortality in Paradise by means of eating from the forbidden tree, he was punished by having to leave, and when Yûsuf (Joseph, peace be upon him) sought to get out of the prison by means of one of the two prisoners who had the vision, he remained in it for several years.

Reactions to Undesirable Destiny

If the servant experiences something that he hates, he should adopt six views:

One: to acknowledge monotheism. The Will of Allah should be done, and whatever He does not wish should never be done.

Two: to believe in the justice of Allah, and that the judgment of Allah is to be done and His judgment is just.

Three: to believe in mercy: that His mercy concerning this destiny will prevail more than His anger and vengeance.

Four: to believe in wisdom and that all destiny is according to His wisdom. He did not predestine anything without reason.

Five: to praise Allah. Indeed, to Allah all perfect praise is due.

Six: to be servants of Allah. The person is a mere servant of Allah. The orders and judgments of His Lord are to be done to him as he is His servant. He is under the authority and judgments of Allah as well as His religious judgments.

Consequences of Committing Sins

Lack of success, invalid views, absence of righteousness, corruption of the heart, failing to praise Allah, wasting time, avoidance of other creations, separation between the servant and his Lord, supplications not being answered, constriction of the heart, decaying of blessings in subsistence and age, prevention of attaining knowledge, humiliation, insults from enemies, a constricted breast, evil friends that will spoil one's heart and waste time, sadness and grief, a miserable life, and disappointment. All that results from sins and neglecting to praise Allah, as plants grow by being watered but are consumed by fire. The opposite of the above are the consequences of obedience to Allah, the Almighty.

Chapter on the Rights of Allah

The one who is just toward Allah will find true happiness. This is the same one who admits that he is ignorant, that his deeds are defective and that he himself is insufficient, and that he continually fails to give Allah His rights as He deserves. If Allah punishes him for his sins, he will know that this is just, and if such a person does a good deed, he will see it as a favor and charity from Allah and if Allah accepts it from him, it is another favor from Him and if He does not, it is because it is not suitable to be presented to Allah. If he did an evil deed, he will see it as a result of being abandoned by Allah, and that Allah had removed His protection from him and so he commits sins, and this is justice. He acknowledges his need for Allah and knows he is unjust toward himself. If Allah forgives him, it would be a generous favor from Him. The whole issue depends upon seeing Allah as the Well-Doer and seeing himself as the sinner and neglectful person. When something pleases him, he sees it as a favor from Allah and that it is He, who grants it to him, and whenever something displeases him, he knows that it is because of his sins and that Allah is being just toward him in every matter.

When the house of lovers are destroyed, they invoke Allah that the dwellers be able to return and find peace and goodness. When someone who loves Allah has stayed under the dust for several years, he would remember his obedience to Allah in this worldly life and would find the good he obtained.

A Precious Gem: Two Kinds of Jealousy

There are two kinds of jealousy: to be jealous for something and to be jealous of something. Being jealous for your lover means that you care for him/her and you do not want anything to come between that person and yourself or to compete with you. The feeling of jealousy for the lover always comes with the feeling of being jealous of whatever is in competition with you. The first kind of jealousy is praised, as the lover dislikes having partners in their love. This feeling is more likeable in loving the Messenger and the scholars, and even more likeable in loving the one, who most deserves our love, the Exalted! The idea of not wanting to have another compete with him/her in their love is envy. The desirable form of jealousy on His behalf is when the lover is jealous of his/her love for Him from being turned away to another one. Also, not wanting it to be known by others, thinking that others will spoil it, being jealous that his/her deeds may stem from parts that are not for his/her love, or being jealous because of hypocrisy. As a whole, jealousy requires that his/her condition, deeds, and actions all be for the sake of Allah. To be jealous that his/her time will be wasted in doing something else other than pleasing Allah is the state of the lover. This jealousy comes from the side of the servant and it is being jealous of his/her competitor who hinders and prevents the pleasure of his/her lover, the Exalted. While His lover, the Exalted is jealous for him/her through hating that the servant's heart should turn away from loving Him to love other than Him. That is why the jealousy of Allah is when the servant does whatever is forbidden. And out of His jealousy, He forbade shameful sins, illegal sexual intercourse, etc. whether committed openly or secretly. Because all mankind is His and He is jealous for them exactly as a master is jealous for his slaves. Allah is jealous for His servants to love other than Him in case this love will spur them on to commit sins.

- The person whose love and reverence for Allah in his heart prevents him from disobeying Him, Allah will venerate him in the hearts of creatures so that they will not humiliate him.

- If the roots of knowledge hold onto the heart, the tree of love will grow in it and if it becomes stronger it will bear the fruits of obedience and it will keep on giving its fruit at all times by the Leave of its Lord.

- The first ranks among people are those who do as Allah says,

﴿ ...ٱذۡكُرُواْ ٱللَّهَ ذِكۡرٗا كَثِيرٗا ۝ وَسَبِّحُوهُ بُكۡرَةٗ وَأَصِيلًا ۝ ﴾

which means, "Remember Allah with much remembrance. And glorify His Praises morning and afternoon [the early morning (*Fajr*) and *'Asr* prayers]." (Al-Ahzâb, 33:41-42)

The middle rank is as Allah says,

$$﴿ هُوَ ٱلَّذِى يُصَلِّى عَلَيْكُمْ وَمَلَٰٓئِكَتُهُۥ لِيُخْرِجَكُم مِّنَ ٱلظُّلُمَٰتِ إِلَى ٱلنُّورِ ... ﴾$$

which means, "He it is Who sends *Salât* (His blessings) on you, and His angels too (ask Allah to bless and forgive you), that He may bring you out from darkness (of disbelief and polytheism) into light (of Belief and Islamic Monotheism)." (Al-Ahzâb, 33:43)

The lowest rank is as Allah says,

$$﴿ تَحِيَّتُهُمْ يَوْمَ يَلْقَوْنَهُۥ سَلَٰمٌ ... ﴾$$

which means, "Their greeting on the Day they shall meet Him will be "*Salâm*: Peace (i.e. the angels will say to them: *Salâmu 'Alaikum*)!" (Al-Ahzâb, 33:44)

- The land of nature is wide and accepts whatever is going to be planted in it. If you plant a tree of faith and piety, it will give the sweetness of the Hereafter and if you plant a tree of ignorance and desire, it will give bitter fruit.

Return to Allah and seek Him in your eye, ear, heart, and tongue and do not forget to seek Him in these four ways. Whoever obeys Him is doing so concerning these four and whoever does not, is also doing so by means of these four. The fortunate one is he who hears, sees, speaks, and attacks while seeking the pleasure of Allah and the miserable one is the one who does so seeking his own pleasure and desires.

The example of obedience that grows and increases, is like a seed that you plant, which becomes a tree, then bears fruit, and you ate this fruit and planted their seeds again and whenever the tree bears fruit you eat it and plant its seeds. The exact example can be applied to sins and the way they increase. There is an old proverb and the wise will understand it. It means: the reward for good deeds is that they are followed by other good deeds, and the punishment for bad deeds is that they are followed by other bad deeds.

It is not strange that a servant lowers himself before Allah, worships, and does not become bored from serving Him because he needs Him. The strange matter is that Allah shows love to His servant by all means through granting blessings and rewards while He does not need him.

Chapter: More Wisdom

- You should keep away from committing sins as they humiliated Âdam (Adam, peace be upon him) after he had been honored and then he was driven out of Paradise.

- From the moment Âdam (Adam, peace be upon him) disobeyed his Lord, he suffered from great tension that lasted for a thousand years until Allah forgave him.

- Satan rejoiced when Âdam (Adam, peace be upon him) came out of Paradise but he did not know that when a diver sinks into the sea, he collects pearls and then rises again. The purpose beyond the existence of the sons of Adam is as Allah says,

$$\{ ...إِنِّي جَاعِلٌ فِي ٱلْأَرْضِ خَلِيفَةً... ﴾$$

which means, "Verily, I am going to place (mankind) generations after generations on earth." (Al-Baqarah, 2:30)

And He, the Almighty says,

﴿ ...اذْهَبْ فَمَن تَبِعَكَ مِنْهُمْ... ﴾

which means, " Go, and whosoever of them follows you." (Al-Isrâ', 17:63)

Whatever faced the sons of Adam during this worldly life is the purpose of their existence. They are humans and will follow Satan sometimes so they will have to repent. The Prophet (peace be upon him) said, "By Him in Whose Hand is my life, if you did not commit sin, Allah would sweep you out of existence and He would replace you with those who would commit sin and seek forgiveness from Allah, and He would pardon them."

- O Âdam (Adam, peace be upon him) do not be sad as I told you: come out from the Paradise, which I created for you and your descendants.

- O Âdam (Adam, peace be upon him) you used to come to Me like a king enters to another king. Today you enter like a servant when he comes to his king.

- O Âdam (Adam, peace be upon him) do not be discontent because of your slip, which caused you to err, for you are a human that commits sins. Allah says,

﴿ ...وَعَسَىٰ أَن تَكْرَهُوا شَيْئًا وَهُوَ خَيْرٌ لَكُمْ... ﴾

which means, "And it may be that you dislike a thing which is good for you." (Al-Baqarah, 2:216)

- O Âdam (Adam, peace be upon him)! I did not drive you out from Paradise in order to give it to others; I removed you in order to complete it for you. By Allah! Adam neither has good from his glory (Angels bowed to him) when he committed his sin, nor honor (knowing the names of all things), nor any characteristic (Allah created himwith His hands), nor pride (as Allah breathed into him from His spirit), instead he obtained benefit through humility to Allah. As Allah says that Adam said,

$$﴿ ...رَبَّنَا ظَلَمْنَا أَنفُسَنَا... ﴾$$

which means, "Our Lord! We have wronged ourselves." (Al-A'râf, 7:23)

As it was once said: when he obeyed in wearing the clothes of monotheism on his thankful body, the arrows of his enemies did not kill him, they wounded him but he mended, so it returned as it was and the wounded man stood up as if he had not had any pain.

Chapter: Salmân Al-Fârisy

There are several means of survival and they are destined in order to solve man's problems. Whoever is expelled feels like he is being tied, but when Allah wishes, destinies will be changed and good shall come, as people are different according to their deeds. Abu Tâlib, the uncle of the Messenger (peace be upon him) drowned in seas of evil and destruction. Salmân[13] was safe on the coast, Al-Walîd bin Al-Mughîrah[14] preceded his people toward straying, Suhaib[15]

---

[13] He is Salmân Al-Fârisy, who was a great companion. His roots went back to Magus of Asbahân. He was brought up in a village called Jiyân. He read the books of the Persians, the Romans, and the Jews. He traveled to Arab countries, met the Prophet (peace be upon him) in Qubâ' Mosque, embraced Islam, and the Muslims helped him until he freed himself from slavery. He died (may Allah be pleased with him) in 36 A.D. See *Usd Al-Ghâbah*, vol.2, p. 417, *Tajrîd Asmâ' As-Sahâbah*, vol.1, p.230, *Al-Istî'âb*, vol.2, p.634, *Al-Isâbah*, vol.3, p.141.

[14] Al-Walîd bin Al-Mughîrah bin 'Abdullâh bin 'Amr bin Makhzûm. He was from the judges of Arabia during the Pre-Islamic era and from the chiefs of Quraish. He showed enmity toward Islam and resisted it. He died three months after emigration. See *Al-Bidâyah wan-Nihâyah*, vol.3, p.246.

came in the Roman caravan, An-Najâshy was in Abyssinia saying: O my Lord! Here I am at Your service, Bilâl[16] calls, "Prayer is better than sleep", and Abu Jahl is with the disbelieving group.

Now we shall recount the story of Salmân Al-Fârisy, and we should start from the beginning. We mentioned that he was a Majian as were all his countrymen. He knew about Christianity and converted to it. He argued with his father and beat him with proofs so his father tied him up as punishment. This indeed, is the way of the people of evil. Fir'awn (Pharaoh) responded in the same way with Mûsâ (Moses, peace be upon him). Allah says that Fir'awn said,

$$\text{﴿ قَالَ لَئِنِ ٱتَّخَذْتَ إِلَٰهًا غَيْرِي لَأَجْعَلَنَّكَ مِنَ ٱلْمَسْجُونِينَ ﴾}$$

which means, "Fir'awn (Pharaoh) said: "If you choose an *ilâh* (god) other than me, I will certainly put you among the prisoners." (Ash-Shu'arâ', 26:29)

Al-Jahmiyyah[17] also did the same with Imam Ahmad and whipped him. The people of innovations imprisoned Ibn Taimiyah. Salman was persecuted like them. After escaping from his father's clutches, Salmân found a caravan that was

---

[15] Suhaib bin Sinân bin Mâlik, from Banu An-Namir bin Qâsit, who was agreat companion. He was from the first to embrace Islam. He died (may Allah be pleased with him) 38 A.H. See *Usd Al-Ghâbah*, vol.3, p. 36, *Tajrîd Asmâ' As-Sahâbah*, vol.1, p.268, *Al-Istî'âb*, vol.2, p.726, *Al-Isâbah*, vol.3, p.449.

[16] Bilâl bin Rabâh Al-Habashy, Abu 'Abdullâh. He was the Mu'adhin (caller to prayer) of the Messenger of Allah (peace be upon him) and the guardian of the public treasury. He witnessed all the battles and passed away in Damascus 20 A.H. See *Usd Al-Ghâbah*, vol.1, p.246, *Tajrîd Asmâ' As-Sahâbah*, vol.1, p.56, *Al-Istî'âb*, vol.1, p.178, *Al-Isâbah*, vol.1, p.326.

[17] They are a devious group that claim to be Muslims. Its principle is to deny the attributes of Allah. It claims that Hell and Paradise will perish and that faith means to know Allah while being ignorant. They are the followers of Jahm bin Safwân Ar-Râsiby. See Sharh Al-'Aqîdah At-Tahâwiyah, p.522.

about to leave, so he fled and traveled. He accompanied them hoping to find the truth and dedicated himself totally to serving monks. When the monks felt that their religion was about to end they told Salmân about the signs that would prove the prophethood of our Prophet and said that this religion was about to appear. They advised him to follow it. Later he was betrayed and was sold to a Jew in Medina. He waited for the new religion, until the news came while he was climbing a palm tree. He hurried to meet the Prophet (peace be upon him) His master cried out to him to take care of his work but he said how could he do so while he was busy with something else. When he met the Messenger (peace be upon him), he compared the two religions and embraced Islam. The Prophet (peace be upon him) said once, "Salmân is from us; (from my) family." O Muhammad! You want Abu Tâlib and we want Salmân; if Abu Tâlib was asked about his name, he would say, "'Abdumanâf". If he was asked about his relatives, he would say he is from a great family. If he is asked about wealth he would mention his camels, but if Salmân was asked about his name he would say, "'Abdullâh", and about his relatives he would say 'Islam', his wealth is poverty, his coffin is the mosque, and what he has won is patience. His clothing is piety and humility, his bed is staying up at night, his aim is to stand in front of Allah, and his path leads to Paradise.

Lessons and Warnings

- Sins are wounds and one wound may cause death.

- If your mind was free from the manipulation of your whims, the authority would return to it (mind).

- If you indulge in pleasure, you are gambling with your life.

- If you see a forbidden act, know that it will start a war, and you should protect yourself as Allah says,

$$\text{﴿ قُل لِّلْمُؤْمِنِينَ يَغُضُّوا۟ مِنْ أَبْصَـٰرِهِمْ وَيَحْفَظُوا۟ فُرُوجَهُمْ ۚ ذَٰلِكَ أَزْكَىٰ لَهُمْ ۗ إِنَّ ٱللَّهَ خَبِيرٌۢ بِمَا يَصْنَعُونَ ۝ ﴾}$$

which means, "Tell the believing men to lower their gaze (from looking at forbidden things), and protect their private parts (from illegal sexual acts, etc.). That is purer for them. Verily, Allah is All-Aware of what they do." (An-Nûr, 24:30)

If you do so you will be safe from the consequences. Allah says,

$$\text{﴿ ...وَكَفَى ٱللَّهُ ٱلْمُؤْمِنِينَ ٱلْقِتَالَ... ۝ ﴾}$$

which means, "Allah sufficed for the believers in the fighting." (Al-A<u>h</u>zâb, 33:25)

- The sea of pleasures may drown its owner and the swimmer fears to open his eyes under the water.

- Allah promised you the pleasures of the Hereafter, so do not be in a hurry and seek them in this worldly life as if you are cutting plants before their harvest time, while they are much better if you wait. Likewise, the pleasures of the Hereafter are so much better.

- Buy for yourself (through doing good deeds) while there is still a market and you have the ability to buy.

- Everyone will pass through times of sleep and neglect (following his lusts), but do not sink into sleep as the morning of the hereafter is close at hand.

- The truth will only be shown to perceptive people who will use the light of their minds to see the consequences of the matters they face.

- Get yourself out of this limited world of diseases to the wide world of the Hereafter, which has what the eyes have never seen. Nothing is impossible there, and love is not lost. O you who sold yourself for the sake of something that will cause you suffering and pain, and which will also lose its beauty, you sold the most precious item for the cheapest price, as if you neither knew the value of the goods nor the meanness of the price. Wait until you come to the Day of mutual loss and gain and you will discover the injustice of this contract. "There is no god but Allah" is something that Allah is buying. Its price is Paradise, and the Messenger is its agent, and you will be pleased to part with a small part of this worldly life to obtain it. The part you lose is a small part of something that as a whole is not worth a mosquito's wing.

- You have a weak will and the path of life is hard. Adam tired on this path, Nûh (Noah, peace be upon him) lamented for it, Ibrâhîm (Abraham peace be upon him) was thrown into the fire because of it, Ismâ'îl (Ishmael, peace be upon him) was about to be slaughtered in its cause, Yûsuf (Joseph, peace be upon him) was sold for a cheap price and was imprisoned for several years, Zakariyah (Zachary, peace be upon him) was sawed in half, Yahyâ (John, peace be upon him) was slaughtered, Aiyûb (Job, peace be upon him) suffered distress, Dâwûd (David, peace be upon him) cried, 'Îsâ (Jesus, peace be upon him) accompanied dangerous creatures, and Muhammad, (peace be upon him) suffered poverty and many kinds of harm. You say that you are enjoying yourself with pleasure and delight!

- War is breaking out and you are unarmed standing with those who are watching from a distance and if you are going to participate you will loose.

- If you do not work hard and face difficulties along your way in seeking glory, you will never taste honor and relief when you attain victory.

- It was said to one of the worshipers: You are tiring yourself so much! He said: I want to achieve comfort from it.

- The human being was honored with blessings of faith and good health, but he misused them, so they were justly taken away from him.

- The pleasures of life are similar to brides who are dressing for those who will prefer and choose; them or the brides (rewards) of the Hereafter, and whoever knows the significant difference between the two, will choose the best (the Hereafter).

- The intentions of pious people are like planets that move in towers without any obstacle.

- O you who have gone astray, make sure to catch the right way once again even from its end, as an Amir protects the end of his army.

- It was said to Al-Hasan: people that did good deeds preceded us (likened to those who are riding good horses) while we are as if riding donkeys. He said, "If you are walking on the right way, you will catch up with them quickly."

A Precious Gem: Lessons

- Whoever lacks amiability with people and finds it in seclusion, verily he is a truthful but feeble character and whoever finds it with people and lacks it in seclusion, surely he is an ailing one. Whoever lacks it both with people and in seclusion, surely, his character is dead.

And whoever finds it both in seclusion and with people, surely he is an affectionate, truthful and strong character. He, who finds delight in seclusion, cannot have more delight except with seclusion, and he, who finds delight with people by advising and guiding them, cannot have more delight except in their company. Finally, whoever finds delight with whatever Allah has willed for him, more delight will be granted to him both in seclusion and in the company of people. Thus, the most honorable condition is to submit to the will of Allah. The same light exists in the pure hearts that is found in nature, as it brightens from the laws of Allah. Allah, the Exalted, says,

﴿ ...يَكَادُ زَيْتُهَا يُضِيءُ وَلَوْ لَمْ تَمْسَسْهُ نَارٌ... ﴾

which means, "whose oil would almost glow forth (of itself), though no fire touched it." (An-Nûr, 24:35)

- Qiss[18] believed in Allah despite never having seen the Messenger (peace be upon him), however, Ibn Ubay disbelieved despite performing prayers in the mosque along with the Messenger.

- The prophecy of Mûsâ (Moses) and the faithfulness of Âsyah – the wife of Fir'awn (Pharaoh) - were predestined, he was put in the chest, and the chest was brought to her house. A tiny baby from a mother was given to a barren woman. Look! How many lessons can be derived from this story! And how many male infants were killed by Fir'awn (Pharaoh) in his attempt to reach Mûsâ (Moses)! However it was predestined that Mûsâ

---

[18] Qiss: He is Qiss bin Sâ'idah bin 'Amr bin 'Ady bin Mâlik Al-Âyâdy, and he belongs to Banu Âyâd. He was one of the Arab scholars and preachers in the pre-Islamic era. He was eloquent and well versed. The Prophet (PBUH) said that he will be resurrected alone as if he is a nation. He died in 23 A.H.

(Moses) would be brought up under the care of Fir'awn (Pharaoh) and would also be the means of his destruction.

- Dhul-Bijâdain was an orphan boy, whose uncle took care of him. But he was obsessed by the idea of following the Messenger (peace be upon him). Upon his decision to follow the Messenger, his was afflicted with a disease, so he waited for his uncle.

  When he was cured, he lost patience so he told his uncle, "O Uncle! I waited a long time hoping that you might embrace Islam but in vain." His uncle replied, "By Allah! If you embrace Islam, I shall deprive you of all that which I granted you." He (Dhul-Bijâdain) said, "Just one look at Muhammad is preferable to me than all this worldly life, and everything therein."

  When Dhul-Bijâdain decided to follow the Messenger

  (peace be upon him), his uncle deprived him of everything even his clothes, so his mother gave him a piece of cloth. He cut it in two pieces, one of which he wrapped himself with, and the other he used as a garment.

  When Jihad (fighting for the cause of Allah) was prescribed, he decided to join the believers, regardless of the long journey he would have to undertake.

  When he passed away, the Messenger (peace be upon him) descended to prepare his grave by himself, and he used to say, "O Allah! I am satisfied with him, so I beg You to be satisfied with him." Upon that, Ibn Mas'ûd (may Allah be pleased with him) said, "I wish I were him (he meant Dhul-Bijâdain)."

- Once, some wise men saw a non-Arab horse used for watering, in which they said, "If it were tame, it would have been ridden."

- Afflictions are but trials by which the faithful are distinguished from the unfaithful, and if you were to succeed therein, they would be turned to supporters by which you could attain your objective.

A Precious Gem: This Life of Deception

This worldly life is like an unchaste woman, who is not satisfied with one husband. So, be satisfied with whatever Allah grants you from this worldy life.

Walking thereon is like walking in a land that is filled with beasts, and water that teams with crocodiles. That which causes delight, turns to be the source of grief. Pain is found in the midst of pleasures, and delights are derived from its sorrows. As a bird sees the wheat, so does one's insight perceive polytheism, while vain desires render its holder blind.

Lusts were granted in abundance to humans, but those who believed in the unseen turned away from them, while those who follow their lusts were caused to regret.

The first category, are those, in which Allah says,

﴿ أُوْلَٰٓئِكَ عَلَىٰ هُدًى مِّن رَّبِّهِمْ وَأُوْلَٰٓئِكَ هُمُ ٱلْمُفْلِحُونَ ۝ ﴾

which means, "They are on (true) guidance from their Lord, and they are the successful." (Al-Baqarah, 2:5)

However, the other category, are those to whom Allah says,

﴿ كُلُواْ وَتَمَتَّعُواْ قَلِيلًا إِنَّكُم مُّجْرِمُونَ ۝ ﴾

which means, "(O you disbelievers)! Eat and enjoy yourselves (in this worldly life) for a little while. Verily, you are the Mujrimûn (polytheists, disbelievers, sinners, criminals, etc.)." (Al-Mursalât, 77:46)

When the successful ones are aware of the reality of this worldly life being sure of the inferiority of its degree, they overcame their vain desires for the sake of the Hereafter. They have been awakened from their heedlessness to remember what their enemies took from them during their period of idleness. Whenever they perceive the distant journey they must undertake, they remember their aim, so it appears easy for them. Whenever life becomes bitter, they remember this verse, in which Allah says,

﴿...هَـٰذَا يَوْمُكُمُ ٱلَّذِى كُنتُمْ تُوعَدُونَ ﴾

which means, "This is your Day which you were promised." (Al-Anbiyâ', 21:103)

Chapter: A Wondrous Reality

What a wonderful thing it is to know Him (i.e. Allah)! But how can one know Him and not love Him? How can one hear the caller but fail to respond? How can one know the profit that shall be gained in dealing with Him but still prefer others? How can one taste the bitterness of disobeying Him but still abstain from seeking the pleasure of obeying Him? How can one feel the severity of engaging in trivial speech, but fail to open your heart with His remembrance? How can one be tortured by being attached to others but not rush toward the bliss of turning to Him in repentance?

Perhaps it is most surprising to know that while you are in need of Him, you are still reluctant to move toward Him because you seek others.

A Precious Gem: Sources of Unlawfulness

No one can indulge in unlawfulness except for two reasons, the first of which is failing to trust in Allah, despite the fact that if one obeys Him, he will surely be granted the best of lawful gains. The second reason is knowing that whoever abandons anything for the sake of Allah, surely He will grant him something better than what he has abandoned. Unfortunately, his vain desires surpass his patience and his inclination overpowers his mind. The first one has poor knowledge, and the second one has poor insight.

Yahyâ bin Mu'âdh[19] said, "He whom Allah opens his heart with invocation, surely Allah will respond to him." I added, "but he whom Allah opens his heart, and feels in need of Allah, and his hope is strong, then Allah will respond to him."

A Precious Gem: Benefits

- When those, who are vigilant observe the influence of this worldly life upon those who seek it, the deceit of false hopes, the control of Satan, the domination of souls, and material fortune in the hands of evil ones, they resort to piety and submission, like a scared slave who seeks refuge in his master's house. The desires directed at this worldly life are simply deceptive enjoyment, and the insight of the ignorant is restricted to superficial matters, while the wise man perceives that which is hidden from the others.

- Once, two foxes were caught. While trapped in the net, one of them asked the other where he could meet him afterwards, and the other one replied that they would meet after two days in the tannery.

---

[19] He is called Yahyâ bin Mu'âdh bin Ja'far Ar-Râzy Abu Zakariyyâ, one of the ascetic preachers, who lived in Balakh and died in Nisapore in 258 A.H.

- By Allah! This worldly life is like a dream. After waking up, success may be one's destiny.

- Passing days are like dreams, the coming ones are wishes, and the time separating them is wasted.

- How can one feel secure, who has an unmerciful wife, an unforgiving son, a distrusting neighbor, a friend who gives no advice, a partner who misjudges him, an enemy whose hostility never ceases, a soul that is inclined to evil, an adorned world, vain desires, influential lusts, furious anger, the deception of Satan, and controlling weakness? If Allah rescued and guided him, all these problems would be under control, and if Allah deserted and abandoned him, leaving him on his own, all these distresses would cause his destruction.

- When the Glorious Qur'ân, and the Sunnah are abandoned, because it is thought that they are insufficient, and when human opinions, analogy, discretion, and the words of scholars are sought, people's natures are corrupted, their hearts become dark, their understandings become confused, and their minds become distorted. All the previously mentioned matters had a great impact on their lives to the extent that the young and the old lived under these circumstances, thinking them to be allowed. Alternative conditions prevailed, in which innovated matters replaced Prophetic traditions, inclination replaced wisdom, vain desires replaced reason, going astray replaced guidance, the wrong replaced the good, ignorance replaced knowledge, hypocrisy replaced devotion, the unlawful replaced the lawful, lying substituted truthfulness, flattery substituted advice, and injustice replaced justice, thus these evils reigned supreme, and their holders became privileged, despite the prevalence of their opposite in the past, where their holders were the privileged ones. If you see the superiority of such evils, and their slogans are set up where their armies are invading, surely the bottom of the earth would be much more desirable than its surface, the peaks of mountains would be more preferable than the plains, and accompanying beasts would be better than accompanying people.

- The earth trembles, the heavens have darkened, evil has appeared on land and on sea because of the injustice of the wicked, evil doers. Blessings have disappeared, good deeds are less, and the beasts have become powerless, life has become corrupted because of the wickedness of the wrong-doers. The morning light and the night's darkness shed tears, because of the awful deeds that are committed. Honorable writers among the angels and others from among them have complained to their Lord because of the prevalence of misdeeds and the supremacy of atrocities. By Allah! This is a warning of approaching torment, and forthcoming afflictions, so you have no resort except sincere repentance as long as repentance is still available. Do not wait until there is no escape in which Allah says,

$$﴿ ...وَسَيَعْلَمُ ٱلَّذِينَ ظَلَمُوٓا۟ أَىَّ مُنقَلَبٍ يَنقَلِبُونَ ۝ ﴾$$

which means, "And those who do wrong will come to know by what overturning they will be overturned." (Ash-Shu'arâ', 26:227)

- Buy success for yourself today, for the market still exists, and the price is affordable, and goods are low-priced, and do not wait until the market and the goods are inaccessible, in which Allah says,

$$﴿ ...ذَٰلِكَ يَوْمُ ٱلتَّغَابُنِ... ۝ ﴾$$

which means, "That will be the Day of mutual loss and gain." (At-Taghâbun, 64:9)

Allah says,

﴿ وَيَوْمَ يَعَضُّ ٱلظَّالِمُ عَلَىٰ يَدَيْهِ ... ۝ ﴾

which means, "when the Zâlim (wrong-doer, oppressor, polytheist, etc.) will bite at his hands." (Al-Furqân, 25:27)

- Insincere effort is like the traveler who fills his bag with sand, it just overburdens him for no good reason. If you have overburdened your heart with the grief and sorrows of this worldly life, neglecting prayers, which are the heart's provision and power, you would be like the traveler who overloaded his riding animal, while depriving it of its food, so it would not be able to continue on the journey.

- He who tastes the pleasure of good health, surely the bitterness of patience will become easy for him.

- The aim has the priority in estimation, it is the last in existence, it is the principle according to the mind, and it is the end of the journey.

- You have been powerless for a long time, so if your intention is highly elevated, the brightness of determination will loom above you.

- The disparity of people is based on their determination rather than their images.

- Feeling powerless is a deceptive excuse.

- The difference between you and the righteous people are the influence of vain desires, so if you want to approach the righteous, overpower your desires. This worldly life is like a racetrack, but the dust is overwhelming and the race cannot be seen. The people therein are either mounted or dismounted, or the owners of slaughtered beasts.

- There is evil in human nature, but enthusiasm is the best.
- Greed is not overcome except in overcoming vain desires.
- Being determined to reach your aim entails the exertion of your utmost effort, and being cautious for fear of losing hope.
- The stingy person is the poor one, whose poverty is unrewarded.
- Patience during distress is better than yielding to others.
- The noble woman prefers hunger rather than immorality.
- Resort to no one but your Lord, for resorting to others is a disgrace.
- Worshipping in solitude brings about pleasure.
- Resort to the eternal, but never resort to the mortal.
- The solitude of the ignorant is corruption while the solitude of the knowledgeable is fruitful.
- If wisdom and conviction are combined (in seclusion), and deep thought is gained, a fruitful conversation will take place.
- If your enemy abuses you, do not respond to his abuse for the result will be degradation.
- Avenging oneself is not wise, for if you know the reality of your soul, you might inadvertently help your enemy against yourself.
- If the blaze of revenge is derived from the blaze of wrath, the wrathful will burn first.

- Restrict your anger with tolerance, for anger is like a dog: if you set it free, it will cause damage.

- He, whose destiny is happiness, will be guided without having to inquire.

- If success is preordained to anyone, the seeds of good fortune would be implanted in his heart, and then they would be watered with hope and fear of Allah, then self-control will be granted, and knowledge will be the guardian that will protect him, and as a result, the plant will stand straight on its stem.

- If determination is adopted in the state of powerlessness, which is followed by strong resolution, surely the heart will be enlightened by the light of Allah.

- When night descends, sleep and sleeplessness struggle, fear of Allah and longing for Allah are the soldiers of wakefulness, while idleness and delaying are the soldiers of heedlessness. If determination is adopted, and negligence is defeated, then by the time day breaks, every party will take his share.

- A night rider undergoes hardship; in a marching army, the cavalry come in the front, while those who carry supplies are at the rear.

- Do not feel weary of standing by His door (i.e. Allah) even if you are driven away, and never stop asking His forgiveness even if you feel it is rejected. When the door is opened for the accepted ones, do not miss this chance and rush therein intruding, and stretch forth your hands saying,

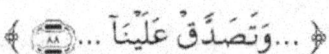

which means, " Be charitable to us." (Yûsuf, 12:88)

- O you who seeks provision without piety! How can you be satisfied with sins and still complain about your provision being straightened?

- If your aim is piety, other aims are never missed.

- Misdeeds stand as a block for earning. Surely, one can be deprived of provision by committing sins.

- Animals kept for reproduction are not on the same level as those meant for racing.

- The worker, who wants to know his degree in the master's eye, should first observe how much he works for him.

- Be the son of the Hereafter, and do not be the son of this worldly life, verily, the son follows his mother.

- This worldly life is not worth the movement of your footsteps thereon, so it is not wise to be misled by it.

- This worldly life is like the carrion, and indeed the lion hesitates to seize it.

- This worldly life resembles a passageway, and the Hereafter resembles the homeland, and indeed the wishes of pious men are directed toward the homelands.

- There are two kinds of meetings between friends:

The first kind is a meeting based on sociability and spending time, in which there are more disadvantages than advantages, the least of which is corruption of the heart, and wasting time.

The second kind is a meeting for the sake of supporting one another, and recommending one another to the truth and to patience. This is the best kind, yet there are still three disadvantages therein,

1) Flattering each other.

2) Being excessively talkative.

3) That such meetings become a habit or routine and they fail to achieve their aims.

In general, the result of social meetings will be derived from the source, which is either for the soul inclined to evil, or for the heart and the peaceful soul. If the source is good, surely the fruit will also be good. Pure souls derive their nature from their Lord, while evil ones derive their nature from the devil. Hence, Allah, the Exalted and Ever Majestic, renders good women for good men and bad men for bad women.

An Important Rule: There is no Power or Strength except with Allah

In this physical world, there is no force that can influence independently; and not only that, there is no force that has influence on its own, unless another force is joined to it and all that hinders its effect is gone. This is true of the forces that can be seen. Unseen and abstract forces depend on other forces, like the influence of the sun on animals and plants. In the same way, having a child depends on a number of forces other than sexual intercourse.

This is the truth of forces and their effects. Therefore, is anything is feared or hoped for from anything in creation, it must be remembered that the extent of its capacity is that it is a part of a force that does not alone possess the ability to influence. Moreover nothing possesses the ability to independently influence anything else, without depending on others, except Allah, the One, the Irresistible.

Therefore, we should not expect anyone or anything to benefit us nor should we fear anyone or anything except Allah. Surely depending on others or fearing them is worthless. If it is supposed that it is an independent force, capable of influencing alone, there would still be another force from something other than it. It has no ability that enables it to do anything by itself, for there is no power or strength except with Allah.

He is the only One Who has entire power and strength, and what mankind hopes and fears from the power and strength he sees in people are in reality owned and controlled by Allah alone. So, why should we hope for and fear that which does not possess either power or strength? The reality is that fearing anything in creation and hoping for it, are the causes that deprive and afflict the person who hopes for it or fears it. This is so according to the degree that you fear anything other than Allah, as you will be under its influence. And you will also be deprived according to the degree that you hope for other than Him. This applies to all people both in the levels of knowledge and status.

Therefore, that which Allah wills happens and that which He does not ordain, will never happen even if all the creatures agree upon it.

Monotheism Prevents Misfortunes

Monotheism is the refuge of its enemies and its supporters:

It saves its enemies from the distress and misfortunes of the life of this world:

﴿ فَإِذَا رَكِبُوا فِي الْفُلْكِ دَعَوُا اللَّهَ مُخْلِصِينَ لَهُ الدِّينَ فَلَمَّا نَجَّاهُمْ إِلَى الْبَرِّ إِذَا هُمْ يُشْرِكُونَ ﴾

which means, "And when they embark on a ship, they invoke Allah, making their Faith pure for Him only, but when He brings them safely to land, behold, they give a share of their worship to others." (Al-'Ankabût, 29:65)

It saves its supporters from the distress and misfortunes of this world and the Hereafter. That is why Yûnus resorted to it, and Allah saved him from the darkness of the whale's belly.

In the same way, the followers of the Prophets resorted to it and by it they were saved from that which the polytheists were tortured with in this world and that which is prepared for them in the Hereafter.

When Fir'aun (Pharoah) resorted to it at the time he saw death and he was about to drown, it was of no avail to him, because faith is of no avail at the time when the soul witnesses the reality. This is Allah's way with His servants. Nothing prevents the misfortunes of this world like Monotheism. That is why the supplication of distress is done with Monotheism, and as an example of this we remember the supplication of Dhun-Nûn, (Yûnus) [20] which no distressed person used to supplicate with but Allah drove his distress away. On the other hand, nothing causes great distress like polytheism, and nothing saves man from it except Monotheism. Therefore, it is the refuge and the fortress of all creation. And truly Allah is the only One who grants success.

A Precious Gem: Knowledge is Followed by Love

Love is followed by pleasure. It is either strong or weak according to the degree of love. Whenever the desire for the

---

[20] It is the supplication in the following words of Allah, the Exalted,

﴿ وَذَا ٱلنُّونِ إِذ ذَّهَبَ مُغَاضِبًا فَظَنَّ أَن لَّن نَّقْدِرَ عَلَيْهِ فَنَادَىٰ فِى ٱلظُّلُمَٰتِ أَن لَّآ إِلَٰهَ إِلَّآ أَنتَ سُبْحَٰنَكَ إِنِّى كُنتُ مِنَ ٱلظَّٰلِمِينَ ﴾

Which means "And (remember) Dhan-Nûn (Jonah), when he went off in anger, and imagined that We shall not punish him (i.e. the calamites which had befallen him)! But he cried through the darkness (saying): Lâ ilâha illa Anta [none has the right to be worshipped but You (O Allah)], Glorified (and Exalted) are You [above all that (evil) they associate with You]. Truly, I have been of the wrong-doers." (Al-Anbiyâ', 21: 87) cherished one is stronger, there is perfect pleasure. Love and yearning follow knowing Allah and appreciating His greatness. Whenever our knowledge of Allah is perfect, we will love Him more perfectly. Therefore, the perfection of blessing and pleasure in the Hereafter can be traced back to knowledge and love.

Whoever believes in Allah, His Names and Attributes, and knows them well, would love Him a great deal, and his feeling of pleasure, his being close to Him, looking at His Face and hearing His words would be complete when meeting Him on the Day of Judgment. Every pleasure, blessing, joy and delight would be like a drop of water compared to the sea. So how is it that an intelligent person can prefer weak and shortlived pleasure that is mixed with pain, to great, complete and eternal pleasure? The perfection of man is based on these two abilities: Knowledge and love. And the best knowledge is the knowledge about Allah, and the highest love is the love for His Sake. Surely, it is Allah's help that should be sought.

A Rule: Two Restraints that Rescue

Whoever performs a deed for the sake of Allah and the Hereafter, can only stay on the straight path by having two restraints: to let his heart continually seek Allah's Pleasure and the Hereafter, and restrain it from turning to anything other than that. And to restrain his tongue from that which is not beneficial, and constantly remember Allah and that which increases its faith and knowledge, and restrain his body from committing sins and indulging in lusts, and adhering to religious duties and recommendations. He should maintain these restraints until he meets his Lord to free him from restraint to enter the widest and best of places. And if he did not endure these two restraints, and indulges in lusts and desires, he will be punished with a horrible restraint while leaving this world. Therefore, all those who leave this world are either freed from this worldly restraint or are going to another kind of restraint in the Hereafter. And it is Allah Who Grants success.

Piety

Ibn 'Aun [21] was saying good bye to a man and said to him, "You should fear Allah, for he who fears Allah never feels loneliness. Zaid bin Aslam [22] said, "It used to be said, "Whoever fears Allah, people will love him even if they hated it. At-Thawry [23] said to Ibn Abu Dhi'b, "If you fear Allah, He will suffice you against people, and if you fear people, they will not avail you whatsoever against Allah."

Sulaimân bin Dâwûd said, "We have been given the same as that which people have been given as well as that which they have not been given. And we have been taught the same as that which people have been taught and that which they have not. However, we have not found anything better than the fear of Allah secretly and openly, and justice whether one is angry or pleased, and temperance whether one is rich or poor. In the book *Az-Zuhud*, by Imam Ahmad, he mentions a divine saying that goes as follows "If someone holds fast to someone

---

[21] He is 'Abdullah bin 'Aun bin Artaban Al-Mazniy. He was one of the memorizers of hadith. He was the sheikh of Al-Basra. Ath-Thawry and Yahya Al-Qattan learnt from him. Adopted from: Tahdhîb At-Tahdhîb (5\346), Târikh Al-Bukhâry Alkabîr (5\163), Aj-Jarh wat-Ta'dîl (1\145), (5\605) and Siyar A'lâmu-Nubalâ' (6\364).

[22] He is Zaid bin Aslam Al-'Adawy Al-'Amriy, Abu Usâmah. He was an Islamic jurist and an interpreter of the Qur'an from the people of Al-Madînah. He was an excellent memorizer, and had a group of students who used to attend his lectures in the Prophet's Mosque. He died (may Allah have mercy upon him) in 136 A. H. Adopted from Tahdhîb At-Tahdhîb (3\395), Târikh Al-Bukhâry Alkabîr (3\387), Aj-Jarh wat-Ta'dîl (3\2509).

[23] He is Sufyân bin Said bin Masrûq At-Thawry, Abu 'Abdullah, from the children of Thawr bin 'Abdu Manât, from Mudar. He was an amir of the believers in hadith. He died (may Allah have mercy upon him) in 161 A. H. Adopted from Tahdhîb At-Tahdhîb (4\111), Târikh Al-Bukhâry Alkabîr (4\92), Aj-Jarh wat-Ta'dîl (4\972), Mîzânul-I'tidâl (2\169) and Lisânul-Mîzân (7\233).

else other than Me, I would leave the person without any help. If he asks Me for anything I would not give it to him, and if the person supplicates Me, I would not answer him, and if he asks My Forgiveness, I would not forgive him. And if someone holds fast to Me without anything in My creation, I would guarantee his provision. If he asks Me for anything, I would give it to him, and if he supplicates Me, I would answer him, and if he asks My Forgiveness, I would forgive him."

A Precious Gem: Good Character is a Part of Piety

The Prophet (peace be upon him) established a relationship between the fear of Allah and good character, becausefearing Allah improves the relation between the servant and Allah, and good character improves the relation between a person and others. Therefore, fearing Allah makes it possible for Allah to love him, and good manners makes it possible for people to love that person.

A Precious Gem: Examples and Lessons

In order to be close to Allah and Paradise, the servant has to observe two important things: one concerning himself, and the other concerning people. That is to say he should pardon that which is between him and the people, and should not let people come between him and Allah. Therefore, he should not turn to anyone other than the person who guided him to Allah and the way that leads to Him.

O servant of Allah! The Companions of the Prophet (peace be upon him) are great examples.

﴿ اقْتَرَبَ لِلنَّاسِ حِسَابُهُمْ وَهُمْ فِي غَفْلَةٍ مُعْرِضُونَ ﴾

which means, "Draws near for mankind their reckoning, while they turn away in heedlessness." (Al-Anbiyâ', 21:1)

Their hearts were restless with fear, and tears ran down their cheeks due to fear of Allah just like water flows through the valleys according to their measure.

$$\{ ... \text{فَسَالَتْ أَوْدِيَةٌ بِقَدَرِهَا} ... \}$$

which means, "And the valleys flow according to their measure." (Ar-Ra'd, 13:17)

This worldly life adorned itself for 'Aly bin Abu Tâlib (may Allah be pleased with him), and he said to it, "I have divorced you three times and I will never return to you again." (using an allegory). One divorce was enough for him, as he followed the Sunnah, but he made it three to make it clear that he has not the slightest intention to return to it, for his good faith and good nature despise *Al-Muhalil* (One who marries a woman divorced thrice, with the intention of divorcing her so that the first husband may remarry her). And what is more, he is one of the narrators of the hadith, "Allah has damned *Al-Muhalil.*" [24]

Make a private place for yourself in this world, because fascinating things will be presented to you. Know them and be on your guard, and do not be harmed by withdrawing from preoccupations while you are among them.

The light of the truth is greater and brighter than that of the sun, therefore, there is no problem if those having insight are dim-sighted.

The road to Allah is free from those who have doubt, and those who give in to their lusts. It is full of those having certainty and patience. They are like guideposts along the road:

---

[24] Recorded by Abu Dâwûd in his Sunan. The book of marriage, the section of At-Tahlîl, no. (2076), and Ibn Mâjah. The book of marriage, the section of Al-Muhalil wal-Muhalil lahu, no. (1936).

$$\{ \text{وَجَعَلْنَا مِنْهُمْ أَئِمَّةً يَهْدُونَ بِأَمْرِنَا لَمَّا صَبَرُوا ۖ وَكَانُوا بِآيَاتِنَا يُوقِنُونَ} \}$$

which means, "And We made from among them (Children of Israel), leaders, giving guidance under Our Command, when they were patient and used to believe with certainty in Our Ayât (proofs, evidences, verses, lessons, signs, revelations, etc.)." (As-Sajdah, 32:24)

An Important Rule: Effect of "There is no god but Allah" at the Time of Death

The declaration of "There is no god but Allah" at the time of death has a great effect in expiating sins, as it is a testimony of he who believes in it, and knows its meaning. When reciting this declaration with certainty all his lusts come to an end. His rebellious self softens and yields after refusal and disobedience, proceeds after being turned away, humiliates after having given honor, and its desires and interests are released. This soul will go to its Lord seeking His forgiveness, completely certain that Allah is One, as he is cleansed from all the doubts of polytheism, and he is only concerned with the Almighty One that he will now meet. Whatever he has done secretly or privately has become one and he has faithfully said, "There is no god but Allah." His heart is no longer inclined to think of or turn to others. The whole world has been driven out of his heart. He is about to stand in front of Allah. He is only thinking about the Hereafter and has put the world behind him. This faithful declaration came as the last deed of his life in order to purify him from sins and take him to His Lord as he meets Him with this faithful and truthful declaration. If this kind of faithful and truthful declaration was said by him during his life, he would have hated this worldly life and its people, escaped to Allah, and deserted everything else other than Him. But he declared it with a heart full of the pleasures of this life, love for this life and seeking other than Allah. If it was as pure as at the time of his death, it would have provoked another, more sublime life.

We do not own ourselves! Allah owns us. He owns our souls, our hearts are between two fingers of His that turn them according to His wish. Our life, death, happiness, and sadness are in His hands; our moves, silence, words, and deeds are according to His will. If Allah gave us the power over ourselves He would be giving it to a failure, a sinner, and a wasteful creature, and if He gave power to other than Him, He would be giving authority to one who does not have any authority: neither good, bad, useful, death, life, nor resurrection. If Allah abandons us, our enemy will take authority over us and make us prisoners. We can never dispense with Allah, and although we need Him, we disobeyed Him and used to forget to remember Him.

As Long as One is Living, Subsistence is Guaranteed

- Concern yourself with that which you were ordered to take care of, and do not be concerned with something that was guaranteed for you. Subsistence and the moment of death are two matters whereof there is no doubt. As long as one is living, subsistence is guaranteed. And if Allah, according to His wisdom, closed the way to some means, He will, according to His mercy, open another means for you, which will be more useful. Let us consider the state of the embryo. It receives its nourishment, which is blood from one means which is the naval, and when it comes out of its mother's womb and this only means is closed, another two means are opened to it, which are better and sweeter than the first! This second means is pure and nourishing milk. When he finished his suckling period and these two means are closed because of weaning, Allah opens four more perfect means; two kinds of foods and two kinds of drinks. The two foods are from animals and plants and the two drinks are from water and milk, as well as whatever he likes from among other pleasures. When he passes away, his four means are closed, but Allah, the Exalted will open to him, if he was pious, eight doors of Paradise in order to enter Paradise from anyone of them according to his wish. So we notice that whenever Allah, the Exalted prevents His believing servant from something during this worldly life, He will bestow upon him something which is better and more useful to him. It should be noted that this is only granted to the believers. Allah preserves His servant from low and mean fortunes and is not pleased when such fortunes come to him, as He gives him a better and more valuable one. The servant does not always recognize the generosity of Allah, His wisdom and kindness, nor does he always know the significant difference between what he was granted and what he was protected from. He is fond of matters being decided immediately even if they are mean, and refuses the later ones even if they are better. If the servant could just treat Allah justly, he would have known that the pleasures of this world that Allah has protected him from are better for him than those things which Allah may have granted him from these pleasures. Allah prevented him from some of them in order to bestow upon him something that is better. He, the Almighty may have allowed him to be afflicted in order to protect him, tested to absolve him from sins, put him to death to resurrect him, and took him out of this world so as to stand in front of Him and follow the path that will bring him to Allah. Allah says,

﴿... جَعَلَ ٱلَّيۡلَ وَٱلنَّهَارَ خِلۡفَةً لِّمَنۡ أَرَادَ أَن يَذَّكَّرَ أَوۡ أَرَادَ شُكُورٗا ﴾

which means, "Has put the night and the day in succession, for such who desires to remember or desires to show his gratitude." (Al-Furqân, 25:62)

And He, the Almighty says,

﴿ ...فَأَبَى ٱلظَّٰلِمُونَ إِلَّا كُفُورًا ﴾

which means, "But the *Zhâlimûn* (polytheists and wrong-doers, etc.) refuse (the truth the Message of Islamic Monotheism, and accept nothing) but disbelief." (Al-Isrâ', 17:99)

- Whoever knows himself well, would keep himself busy reforming himself instead of talking about the faults of others. Whoever knows his Lord, would keep himself busy trying to please Him instead of trying to please himself.

- The most useful deed is the one that you did sincerely keeping far away from the sight of people and far away from any reproach.

Doors Leading to Hellfire and the Origin of Sin

There are three doors that lead people to Hellfire:

1. A suspicion, which causes one to doubt the religion of Allah.
2. A desire, which causes one to prefer the pleasures of this world more than obeying and pleasing Allah.
3. Anger, which causes aggression against Allah's creatures.

There are Three Causes of Sin

1. Pride: This caused Satan to fall.
2. Avarice: This drove Adam out of Paradise.

3. Envy: This encouraged the son of Adam to kill his brother.

Whoever has been preserved from the evil of these three things, would be protected against evil itself, because disbelief stems from pride, sin stems from avarice, and injustice grows out of envy.

The Wisdom of Allah in Creating the Human Body

Allah creates everything according to His wisdom. Every external and internal part of man's body has been created to fulfill a special purpose. The eye is for seeing, the ear is for hearing, the nose is for smelling, the tongue is for speaking, the private parts are for marriage, the hand is for attacking, the foot is for walking, the heart is for believing and knowing, the soul is for loving, and the mind is for thinking, knowing the consequences of religious and worldly matters, and preferring all that is supposed to be preferred, and neglecting all that is supposed to be neglected.

Whoever busies himself with other than Allah is the looser, and even more than him is the one who busies himself with people instead of himself.

Abu Sa'îd Al-Khudry (may Allah be pleased with him) narrated that the Prophet (peace be upon him) said, "When the son of Adam gets up in the morning, all the organs of his body submit to the tongue and say, 'Fear Allâh as our condition is according to you (i.e. our salvation or our destruction). If you are good, we will be good and if you were bad, we will be bad.'"[25] They submitted to the tongue because it conveys what the heart wants and it is an agent between it and the other organs.

---

[25] Recorded by At-Tirmidhy, book of asceticism, chapter on what was said about preserving the tongue, no.2407.

A Precious Gem: Fear Allah, follow His Orders, and Avoid What He has Forbidden

The Prophet (peace be upon him) said in the following hadith, "Fear Allah, follow His orders and avoid what He has forbidden." [26] In this hadith we find the interests of this worldly life and that of the Hereafter and its pleasures, whose reward will be gained by obeying Allah, and relieving the heart and body. Also, abandoning pain and hard work in seeking the pleasures of this worldly life is to be gained by following the orders of Allah and avoiding what He has forbidden. Whoever fears Allah will win the pleasure of the Hereafter and whoever follows His orders and avoids what He has forbidden will find rest from the pain and distress of this worldly life.

A Precious Gem: Sin and Debt

The Prophet (peace be upon him) referred to both sin and debt, as sin will cause loss in the Hereafter and debt will cause loss in this worldly life.

A Precious Gem: Fighting in the Cause of Allah

Allah, the Exalted says,

﴿ وَٱلَّذِينَ جَٰهَدُواْ فِينَا لَنَهْدِيَنَّهُمْ سُبُلَنَا ۚ وَإِنَّ ٱللَّهَ لَمَعَ ٱلْمُحْسِنِينَ ﴾

which means, "As for those who strive hard in Us (Our Cause), We will surely guide them to Our Paths (i.e. Allah's Religion - Islamic Monotheism). And verily, Allah is with the *Muhsinûn* (good doers)." (Al-'Ankabût, 29:69)

In this verse Allah made guidance dependent on fighting in His cause. Whoever acquires the most perfect guidance among people is the one who is better in fighting in the cause of Allah.

---

[26] Recorded by Ibn Mâjah, the book of trade, chapter on being provident in one's way of living, no.2144.

The most obligatory act among fighting is struggling against one's vain desires, fighting one's pleasures, fighting Satan, and fighting the world. Whoever fights these four matters seeking Allah in doing so, He, the Almighty will guide him to the means of gaining His pleasure, which means being granted Paradise. And whoever neglected fighting in the cause of Allah, will miss out on guidance to the extent that he neglected fighting in Allah's cause.

Al-Junaid[27] said, "Whoever strives hard against his lusts in Our Cause by means of repentance, We will guide them to paths of sincerity. We will never be able to fight our enemy in the outside except when we fight our enemies within ourselves. Whoever gains victory over himself will gain victory over his enemies and whoever is defeated within himself will be defeated by his enemies.

Chapter: Enmity between the Mind and Imagination

Allah, the Exalted placed enmity between Satan and the Angels, the mind and the imagination, and the soul prone to evil and the heart. Allah combined all these forms of enmity within man and provided every party with supporters. The war between the two parties will continue until one captures the other and subdues it. If the hearts, the minds, and the angels win, there will be happiness, pleasure, joy, relief, and victory. However, if the soul, imagination, and Satan win, there will be

---

[27] Al-Junaid bin Muhammad bin Al-Junaid Al-Baghdâdy Al-Khazzâz. His surname was Abu Al-Qâsim. He was Sufi from scholars of religion. He was born and brought up in Baghdad and known as Al-Khazzâz because he used to work in Al-Khaz, which is silk. He was the first to talk about theology in Baghdad. Scholars considered him a sheikh as he adjusted his principles according to Qur'ân and Sunnah. Among his letters is *Dawâ' Al-Arwâh*. He passed away (may Allah be merciful to him) in 297 A.H. in Baghdad. See his biography in *Al-A'lâm*, vol.2, p.141. See *Al-Bidâyyah wan-Nihâyah*, vol.11, p.121.

sadness, worry, distress, and suppression of all that is good. What do you think about the king (that is you) that was captured by his enemy who dethroned, captured, imprisoned, and prevented him from using his treasures, supplies, and slaves and took them over. In spite of all this, this king did not move to take revenge or ask for help. Above this king, there is another king that is Almighty, the Conqueror, and the most Honored, so he should ask Him. If you ask His help He will help you, if you ask for His support He will support you, if you ask for His protection He will take revenge for you, and if you run to Him, He will give you authority over your enemy and subdue him. If this captured king (human being) said that his enemy (his soul, imagination, and Satan) tied him strongly and prevented him from rising, running to You (Allah), and walking to Your door, He, the Almighty just has to send some soldiers to untie him and take him out of his prison, then he can come to His door, otherwise he would never be able to untie himself.

If he said this in order to refute the Mighty King, His message, and accept his state with his enemy, this mighty king (Allah) will leave him to whoever he chose to be his friend.

However, if he said this because he really needs Him, shows his weakness, and humiliation, and shows that he is too weak to walk to Allah or untie himself, it would be a blessing from Allah to support him. If Allah helps him He would bestow blessings on him and if He did not, He would not be unjust to him even if he had praised Him earlier. His wisdom requires that. When a human knows that the prison is that of Allah and the enemy is His servant, who has no power to do anything good nor bad, then armies of help will come to him.

Levels of Science

The highest ranks of intention in seeking knowledge is seeking knowledge of the Qur'ân and Sunnah and knowledge of the laws of Allah. The meanest intentions are those seeking the answers to hypothetical questions, that is neither divine nor real, or those who are hesitant and follow the words of others and do not have any intention to know what is right. It is rare if any of those obtain benefit from gaining knowledge.

The highest ranks of intention concerning 'will' is that intention should be attached to love for Allah and seeking His pleasure. The lowest is when one's intention is based on human aims against the aim of Allah. That is to say that the person worships Allah according to his aim without seeking the aim of Allah.

Corrupt Scholars

Corrupt scholars sit in front of the door to Paradise calling people to it through some words, while they are doing deeds that lead to Hellfire. Whenever their words call people to Paradise, their deeds do not conform with their words. If such words were true they would have been followed by them. They seem to be leaders while they are really highwaymen.

If Allah alone is your aim, then all favor and honor will be yours but if you aim at what you will gain from Him, then favor may not come to you as it is in His Hands. If your aim was favor, which you would gain from Allah, then it would not come to you. This is because it is in His Hands and a Deed of His Deeds. If you draw nearer from Allah, all favor would be yours. If favor was your aim, it would not come to you. If you knew Allah and tasted the pleasure of being near Him and then you degraded yourself to seeking favor, Allah would prevent you from gaining it as a punishment. This way, you lost being near Allah and gaining favor.

A Precious Gem: The Messenger's Victory

When the Messenger of Allah (peace be upon him) tasted victory after being constrained by the enemy, and his army enjoyed victory, and he became eminent, all mankind was divided into three categories: those who believed in him, those who made peace with him, and those who were fearful of him.

When he set the best examples of endurance, to which Allah says,

$$\left\{ \text{فَٱصْبِرْ كَمَا صَبَرَ أُوْلُواْ ٱلْعَزْمِ مِنَ ٱلرُّسُلِ} \ldots \right\}$$

which means, "Therefore be patient (O Muhammad) as did the Messengers of strong will." (Al-A<u>h</u>qâf, 46:35), the outcome was fruitful, to which Allah says,

$$\left\{ \ldots \text{وَٱلْحُرُمَٰتُ قِصَاصٌ} \ldots \right\}$$

which means, "and for the prohibited things, there is the Law of Equality (Qisâs)." (Al-Baqarah, 2:194)

Hence, he conquered Mecca in an unprecedented way, surrounded by the Muhâjirûn (the immigrants) and the An<u>s</u>âr (the supporters). He was also surrounded by various ranks of Companions, while Jibrîl (Gabriel) was ascending and descending in between the heavens and the earth. Allah made no one conquer His sanctuary except His Messenger.

The Messenger (peace be upon him) compared the day of conquering Mecca and the day in which Allah says,

$$\left\{ \text{وَإِذْ يَمْكُرُ بِكَ ٱلَّذِينَ كَفَرُواْ لِيُثْبِتُوكَ أَوْ يَقْتُلُوكَ أَوْ يُخْرِجُوكَ} \ldots \right\}$$

which means, "And (remember) when the disbelievers plotted against you (O Muhammad) to imprison you, or to kill you, or to get you out." (Al-Anfâl, 8:30)

to when the disbelievers drove him out the second of the two, he entered Mecca lowering his chin to his saddle, submitting and complying to the orders of Allah, Who had granted him victory; he was the one to whom mankind raised their heads, and to whom kings surrendered.

He entered Mecca victorious, supported and a conqueror, and Bilâl mounted the Ka'bah, after having been tortured in its precincts. In a high voice, he recited the Âdhân (the call for prayer), where all tribes came answering him from every place, entering the religion of Allah in crowds, while before they used to come individually.

When the Messenger (peace be upon him) ascended the pillar of glory, from which he never descended, all kings surrendered to him, and amongst them were those who granted him rulership in their countries, and others asked for peace and reconciliation, and those who consented to pay tribute, however, the fourth category gathered to be ready for war, as they were unaware of the fact that they were just gathering the booty and the prisoners of war to him.

Thus, when the Messenger's victory became obvious, along with conveying his message, and fulfilling his mission. Allah revealed to him,

﴿ إِنَّا فَتَحْنَا لَكَ فَتْحًا مُبِينًا ۝ لِيَغْفِرَ لَكَ اللَّهُ مَا تَقَدَّمَ مِن ذَنبِكَ وَمَا تَأَخَّرَ وَيُتِمَّ نِعْمَتَهُ عَلَيْكَ وَيَهْدِيَكَ صِرَاطًا مُسْتَقِيمًا ۝ وَيَنصُرَكَ اللَّهُ نَصْرًا عَزِيزًا ۝ ﴾

which means, " Verily, We have given you (O Muhammad) a manifest victory, that Allah may forgive you your sins of the past and the future, and complete His Favour on you, and guide you on the Straight Path; And that Allah may help you with strong help." (Al-Fath, 48: 1-3)

And Allah also revealed to him,

﴿ إِذَا جَاءَ نَصْرُ اللَّهِ وَالْفَتْحُ ۝ وَرَأَيْتَ النَّاسَ يَدْخُلُونَ فِي دِينِ اللَّهِ أَفْوَاجًا ۝ ﴾

which means, "When comes the Help of Allah (to you, O Muhammad) against your enemies) and the conquest (of Mecca), And you see that the people enter Allah's religion (Islam) in crowds." (Al-Fath, 110: 1-2)

After revealing these verses, the Angel of death descended upon the Messenger (peace be upon him) enabling him to choose between his rank in this worldly life and meeting his Lord, to which he chose the meeting with his Lord, for which he was longing. On that day, paradise was adorned for the honorable soul (of Muhammad), more than the celebrations for any king on his arrival to his homeland.

If the throne of the Beneficent shook due to the death of one of the Messenger's followers and rejoicing at his arrival, then what would be the case with the death of the best of all creatures. O you who are associated with this trivial worldly life, and are standing by another door, surely you will discover which secret will be yours on the day of gathering, in which Allah says,

$$﴿ يَوْمَ تُبْلَى ٱلسَّرَآئِرُ ۝ ﴾$$

which means, "The Day when all the secrets (deeds, prayers, fasting, etc.) will be examined (as to their truth)." (At-Târiq, 86:9)

Chapter: The Vanity of False Hopes

O you who are deceived by false hopes! Satan was cursed and descended from the glorious abode by neglecting one prostration he was ordered to perform. Adam descended from Paradise because of a mouthful he ate. The criminal was separated by a handful of blood. Moreover, the adulterer is supposed to be killed in the most awful way because he committed an unlawful act. Flogging is enjoined on him who says a word of slander, or drinks a drop of liquor. He (Allah) ordered that one of your hands should be cut in case theft is committed, so do not feel secure, for He might cast you into Hellfire because of only one sin.

Allah, the Almighty says,

﴿ وَلَا يَخَافُ عُقْبَٰهَا ﴾

which means, "And He (Allah) feared not the consequences thereof." (Ash-Shams, 91:15)

- A woman was cast into Hellfire because of a cat.[28] One may utter a word carelessly, which displeases Allah. This might be done without thinking about the gravity of the word, and then because of that he will be thrown into the Hellfire, like the distance between the east and the west.[29] And one may obey Allah for sixty years, and at his death he misjudges, and this will be the reason for his being thrown into Hellfire. The person's lifetime is judged by its end, and man's actions are regarded by their final deeds. Whoever breaks his ablution before the final salutation, surely his prayer becomes invalid, and whoever breaks his fast before sunset, surely his fast is invalid, and whoever is sinful at the end of his life, surely he will meet Allah in that state. If you give charity, surely you will find the blessing thereof, but beware of greed. How many times do you seek a good reward but it is rejected because of procrastination?

- Verily, no salvation is found when faith is incomplete, when false hope is overestimated, when a disease has no remedy or visitor, when one insists on vain desires, when a sleeping heedless mind wanders blindly in wild

---

[28] Narrated by Buhkâry, in his book, "Distribution of water", the Chapter of "the merits of distributing water" no. 2365. It was narrated by Muslim, in the Book of Al-Kusûf, the Chapter of "What is offered to the Prophet....no. (904).

[29] Narrated by Buhkâry, in his book, "To make the heart tender (Ar-Riqâq)", Chapter of keeping one's tongue.....no. 6478, narrated by Abu Hurairah.

intoxication, overwhelmed by its ignorance, feeling alienated from his Lord, and finding delight with his servants, and remembering people is his power and pleasure, while remembering Allah is his prison and death. To Allah he offers superficial acts of worship, and to people his devotion and trust are directed.

Chapter: Why Was Adam Considered the Last of Creatures?

The pen is considered the first thing to record the destiny of man before his existence. However, Adam is the last of creatures, due to several reasons:

One: Preparing the place before the dweller's arrival.

Two: Adam is the aim for which every other being is created, like the heavens, the earth, the sun, the moon, and the sea.

Three: The most proficient Creator ended His work with the best the same as He starts with its basis and origin.

Four: Souls usually aspire to the end and final stages, and that is why Mûsâ (Moses) told the sorcerers in the Qur'ânic verse in which Allah says,

﴿...أَلْقُوا مَا أَنتُم مُّلْقُونَ ۞﴾

which means, "Cast down what you want to cast!" (Yûnus, 10:80)

So when the people saw the sorcerers' actions, they inclined to the following one.

Five: Allah, the Exalted and Ever Majestic, adjourned the best of books, prophets, and nations to the latest period of time. He renders the Hereafter better than this worldly life, and the final stages to be more perfect than the earlier ones, and that is why there is a great difference between the Angel's saying,

"Read," to which the Prophet (peace be upon him) said, "I am not a reader," and Allah's saying,

$$... ٱلۡیَوۡمَ أَكۡمَلۡتُ لَكُمۡ دِینَكُمۡ ...﴿٣﴾$$

which means, "This day, I have perfected your religion for you." (Al-Mâ'idah, 5:3)

Six: Allah, the Exalted, gave the knowledge of all things to Adam.

Seven: Adam is the essence and fruit of existence, so it is correct that he is the last of all the entities.

Eight: Because Adam is honorable in the Sight of Allah, He prepared all his interests, requirements, necessities and means of life for him. As soon as he was created, he found the universe ready for him.

Nine: Allah, the Exalted, willed that His honor and grace would be manifested over other creatures, so He preceded their creation, and that is why the Angels said, "Even if Allah creates whatever He wills, no creatures will be more honorable to Him than us." Thus, when He created Adam and He commanded them to prostrate themselves before him, the honor and grace of Allah were manifested thereon by His knowledge, however, when Adam committed the sin, the Angels thought that the honor (bestowed upon Adam) was annulled, disregarding the fact that repentance is an act of worship. When Adam turned to Allah in repentance, performing that act of worship, the Angels knew that there is a secret in Allah's creation, which is known to no one but Him, the Almighty.

Ten: When Allah, the Exalted, started the creation of the world with the pen, it was magnificent to finalize His creation with the human being. Verily, the pen is the tool of knowledge, and the human is the knowledgeable entity. Accordingly, Allah manifested the honor of Adam over the angels by virtue of the knowledge bestowed upon him.

Satan's State with Adam

We contemplate the way in which Allah, the Exalted, has written the reason beyond Adam's descent on earth, wherein He preferred and honored him, as well as that He mentioned his name before his existence by saying,

$$\{ ...\text{إِنِّي جَاعِلٌ فِي ٱلْأَرْضِ خَلِيفَةً} ... \}$$

which means, "Verily, I am going to place (mankind) generations after generations on earth." (Al-Baqarah, 2:30)

We find that Allah described Adam as His vicegerent on earth before his existence, and He made the reason for his descent, by saying, "on earth." The lover used to excuse the beloved before committing his sin, so when Allah created Adam, He placed him in front of the gate of Paradise for forty years, because the lover used to stand by the beloved's door. Subsequently, Allah ordained subservience upon Adam,

$$\{ ...\text{لَمْ يَكُن شَيْئًا} ... \}$$

which means, "He was nothing." (Al-Insân, 76:1), in order not to feel haughty on the day in which Allah says, "Prostrate." However, Satan used to pass by Adam's body wondering, "You have been created for a certain reason." Then he used to enter Adam's body through his mouth and he used to come out through his back, saying, "If I empowered you, surely I would destroy you, but if you were to empower me, surely I would disobey you." Therein, Satan was ignorant about the fact that his destruction was at the hands of Adam. According to Satan, Adam was just pieces of clay combined together, which he despised.

When the clay was shaped, envy obsessed Satan, and when Adam received his soul, the envier was shocked. Adam was granted glory, and the creatures were presented to him. The angels were the plaintiffs and protested with Allah, the Judge while Adam was the attorney. The angels admitted and regretted what they had said earlier. Allah ordered them to bow to Adam, so they did and said that they did not know. Satan stood away and did not bow because it is evil and was covered by the color of evil and protest and its evil will never be purified.

O Adam! If you have been forgiven for the mouthful you ate, those who envy would have said, "How can one who fulfills his desires like you, who has no patience, be preferred by Allah?" O Adam! Your descent on earth was the reason beyond the ascent of supplications, and the (divine) messages in which Allah says, "Are there any supplicants (to whom I shall respond)?..." as well as the blessings of Allah that are bestowed upon those who are fasting, which is a fact which was included in the Prophetic tradition which starts by saying, "The smell coming out from the mouth of a fasting person..."[30]

O Adam! Your laughter in Paradise is yours, while your weeping in this worldly life is ours.

How can the one who submitted to Allah be harmed, while My Grace blesses him? Glory is compatible to him whose body is submissive. I am with them whose hearts are submissive to Me. However, sins are still overwhelming, until they affect the hearts, wherein the remedy was sent by the Most Kind and Courteous (to His slaves), All-Aware (of everything), illustrated by His Messengers. Allah says,

---

[30] Narrated by Al-Bukhâry in his Book, "Fasting", Chapter of the Merits of Fasting, no. 1894, narrated by Abu Hurairah in these words, "The smell coming out from the mouth of a fasting person is better in the sight of Allah than the smell of musk."

$$\{ ...فَإِمَّا يَأْتِيَنَّكُم مِّنِّي هُدًى فَمَنِ ٱتَّبَعَ هُدَايَ فَلَا يَضِلُّ وَلَا يَشْقَىٰ ۝ \}$$

which means, " Then if there comes to you guidance from Me, then whoever follows My Guidance shall neither go astray, nor fall into distress and misery." (Tâhâ, 20: 123)

Thus, the Messengers protected mankind by (divine) prohibitions, preserved their strength by Allah's commandments, and got rid of misdeeds by means of repentance, wherein righteousness was spread everywhere.

O you who wasted his strength without reserve, and transgressed in his illness without a shield, and who has no patience to repent! Do not deny the approach of destruction, for illness will cause corruption. If you were to follow the divine remedy so as to cure yourself, by having a shield from vain desires and lusts, you will have found salvation. Unfortunately, lusts blind your insight, to the extent that you think salvation means to abandon the promise of Allah in return for vain desires. What blind insight you have! It makes you impatient for one hour then you bear disgrace forever. You travel seeking this worldly life despite its transient nature, and you neglect to prepare for your journey to the Hereafter despite its eternity.

If you find a man, who is buying something worthless in return for something precious, and is selling something priceless in return for something of no value, verily he is a fool.

Chapter: Various Precious Gems

- When the origin of submission was manifested in Adam's nature, surely his sin was not significant.

- O son of Adam! If you meet me in the state that your sins fill the earth, but not associating anything with Me, I would meet you with the same vastness of mercy and forgiveness on My Behalf.

- When the Lord knew that His servant's sin was not committed on purpose, nor was done out of underestimating the wisdom of Allah, He taught him the way of turning to Him in repentance. Allah, the Exalted, says,

$$﴿ فَتَلَقَّىٰ ءَادَمُ مِن رَّبِّهِۦ كَلِمَٰتٍ فَتَابَ عَلَيْهِ ... ﴾$$

which means, "Then Adam received from his Lord Words. And his Lord pardoned him (accepted his repentance)." (Al-Baqarah, 2:37)

- By committing sins, the servant of Allah does not aim to disobey his Lord or to violate his prohibitions, but it was the result of an evil nature, the deceit of the soul and Satan, the strength of vain desires, and believing that one will be forgiven, however, according to Allah, the aim of committing sins is the reason behind passing judgments, manifesting the dignity of the Lord, and the submission of the servants, and their complete need for Allah. As well as this, the existence of the Attributes of Allah, like the Oft-Pardoning, the Oft-Forgiving, and the One Who accepts repentance, and the Clement to the repentant and remorseful. On the other hand, Allah is the Avenger, the Just, and the One with the Strongest Grasp on those who insist on disobeying. He, the Exalted, wants His servant to perceive His Perfection, and to feel absolute need of his Lord, moreover, He wants His servant to see the Perfection of His Power, Glory, Forgiveness, Mercy, and Patience, and that His Mercy is nothing but beneficence, for if Allah does not bestow His Mercy upon him, surely he will be destroyed. Estimating guilt by Allah has a great wisdom in it and a lot of benefit and mercy for that servant by offering him the way of repentance.

- Repentance is like the remedy for the ailing, and maybe an ailment is the reason beyond a good condition.
- Had it not been for committing sins, Adam would have been destroyed by arrogance.
- A sin causing submission is preferable in the Sight of Allah, than a good deed that causes pride.
- Submission to Allah is the path to salvation.
- There is no honor for one's soul except with submission (to Allah), no glory except with subservience (to Allah), no comfort except with weariness (for the sake of Allah), no satiation except with hunger (for the sake of Allah i.e. Fasting), no security except with fear (of Allah), no pleasure except with feeling alienated from everything but its Creator, and no life except with death.
- Vain desire brings about pleasure at first then it causes distress.
- He who remembers the consequence of sins, surely patience will become easy for him.
- Whatever you do to control things, be sure that divine predestination is applicable; therefore, hasten and peacefully submit yourself to Allah.
- To Allah belongs the kingdom of the heavens and the earth, yet He asks a loan from you (i.e. giving charity) but you are stingy. He created the seven seas, but He loved a tear from you (out of fear of Him) but your eyes were tearless.
- Abstaining from lowering one's gaze engraves the images (of the one who is seen) in the heart, and the heart is like the Ka'bah, and surely it will not be satisfied with idols.
- Worldly pleasures resemble an ugly woman who has controlled you, on the other hand the hour is (female fair

ones) wondered about your misdoing, however if vain desires dominate, they would blind your insight, so that righteousness will vanish.

- Glorified be Allah! Paradise has been adorned for its suitors; they exerted the utmost effort to attain the dowry. The sincere believers know Allah, the Exalted, by His Names and Attributes, so they prepare themselves for the Day of Resurrection, while you are still obsessed with vain desires.

- Knowledge resembles a carpet on which no one treads except the closest one (to Allah). Loving (Allah) resembles a chant, which no one is delighted with except the most loving and the most attached (to Allah).

- Loving Allah resembles a brook in a desert with no millstone, and that is why there are few water-drawers. The lover usually wants to be isolated with his lover in privacy in order to find delight, the same as the whale resorts to water, and a child seeks his mother.

- The worshipper has no resort except under the shade of Tûbâ (i.e. a tree in paradise), and the sincere servant of Allah has no abode except on the Day of Resurrection. So, do your best during your lifetime and it will suffice you in the Hereafter.

- O you who spends his lifetime in disobeying his Lord! No one amongst your enemies is wicked to you more than you are to yourself.

- The highest intention is that whose owner has prepared for the meeting with his Lord (i.e. the Day of Resurrection), to whom he offers all good deeds. On his arrival he will rejoice, and this is a situation in which Allah says,

﴿ وَقَدِّمُوا لِأَنفُسِكُمْ وَٱتَّقُوا ٱللَّهَ وَٱعْلَمُوٓا۟ أَنَّكُم مُّلَٰقُوهُ وَبَشِّرِ ٱلْمُؤْمِنِينَ ﴾

which means, "and send (good deeds, or ask Allah to bestow upon you pious offspring) before you for your ownselves. And fear Allah, and know that you are to meet Him (in the Hereafter), and give good tidings to the believers (O Muhammad SAW)." (Al-Baqarah, 2:223)

- By Allah! The enemy did not wrong you except after the Lord abandoned you, so do not think that Satan overpowers you, it is just the Maintainer (i.e. Allah) Who has forsaken you.

- Beware of your soul, for no misfortune has befallen you except because of it, so do not ever be reconciled with it. By Allah! Its honor is derived from its submission (to Allah), its dignity is derived from its subservience, its reform is derived from its breakdown, its comfort is derived from its hardship, its security is derived from its fear (of Allah), and its pleasure is derived from its sorrow.

- Glorified be Allah! Your outward self is adorned with the raiment of righteousness while your inward self submits to vain desires, so wherever your raiment is scented, the impact of vain desires emerge, from which the sincere believers divert themselves, and to which the wrong doers are inclined.

- Your own desires usually obsess you in places of worship, so if such desires control you, surely the end would be your departure from the mosque.

- Be sincere in your aim, and you will find the support of Allah surrounding you.

- Once a pious man was asked, "Teach me how to love Allah," to which he said, "Loving Allah is not brought about by teaching."

- There is a Qur'ânic verse in which Allah says, "Allah will bring a people whom He will love and they will love Him," it is not a wonder that He says, "They will love Him," but it is a wonder they He says, "Whom He will love."

- It is not a wonder that a poor, needy one loves the one who is charitable to him, but it is a wonder that the charitable one loves the poor.

Chapter: The Manifestation of the Lord

The Qur'ân is the words of Allah and He, the Almighty manifested His glory to His creatures through His attributes. When He shows His Greatness and Majesty, His creatures will submit and pride will melt away like salt in water. He manifests His attributes of beauty and perfection, which are the perfection of His names and the beauty of His deeds, which shows the perfection of His self. So the servant will love Him and his heart will be empty from any love other than love for Allah. And if the other wanted him to end this love, his heart and body will refuse. This love will remain as his innate nature and it is not artificial.

If Allah manifests His glory in the attributes of mercy, charity, and kindness, then the power of hope will emit from the servant and he will show his wish and resort to Allah and the more his hope increases the more he will work hard. It is exactly like the one who sows seeds in his land. The more his greed increases in what he will harvest, the more he will sow the seeds, but if his hope is weak, he will become stingy and careless in sowing them.

If Allah shows Himself through His attributes of justice, revenge, anger, wrath, and punishment, the evil soul will be repressed, stooped, and its power will be weakened from imagination, anger, and lust, and it will be afraid.

If He shows Himself through His attributes of commanding, forbidding, sending Messengers, revealing Books, and setting decrees, then the ability to obey, report, and follow these orders will be shown. People will follow His orders and will avoid whatever He has forbidden.

If He manifests Himself through His attributes of listening, seeing, and knowing, then the servant will be shy. He will be ashamed that his Lord sees and listens to him, as he does not want Him to see him doing what He hates, hear what He hates or hide what He hates. His thoughts, words and deeds will remain balanced according to the law of Islam not according to imagination and nature.

If Allah manifested Himself through His attributes of sufficiency, managing His servants' interests, insuring their subsistence, preventing distress, and supporting, protecting and accompanying His pious people, then the servant will show the ability to put his trust in Allah, be committed to Him, and will be satisfied with that and with all that Allah destined for him.

If He shows His attributes of glory and pride, the good soul will show humility to His power, submission to His pride, and his heart and limbs will submit to Him and all recklessness will vanish.

The essence of this is that Allah, the Exalted knows His servant through His attributes of both divinity and lordship. The attributes of Divinity provoke special love, longing to meet Allah, and pleasing Him by obeying, and remembering Him. And the attributes of the lordship of Allah induce trust in Him, resorting to Him, asking for His support, and showing humility and submission to Him. Perfection is when the servant knows the divinity and the lordship of Allah. It is also to see His power in His forgiveness, His wisdom in His Divine decree, His blessing in affliction, giving in preventing, justice in revenge, generosity in forgiveness, wisdom and blessing in commanding and forbidding, glory in anger and pleasure, patience in giving chances, generosity in advancing, and sufficiency in what He has forbidden. If you carefully consider the Qur'ân without any distortion or evil opinions you will see a dominating king over the Heavens, who manages His servants' affairs, sends Messengers, Books, and sometimes He is angry, or pleased, sometimes He rewards or punishes, sometimes He gives or prevents, sometimes He humiliates or honors, sometimes He lowers or raises, and sometimes He sees and hears from above the seven Heavens, and knows what is kept secret and what is broadcast. A leaf does not fall, nothing moves, and no one intercedes in His presence without His permission.

Chapter: The Merits of Abu Bakr

When the Messenger (peace be upon him) took the pledge of allegiance from the people of 'Aqabah, he ordered his Companions to immigrate to Medina. Quraish knew that his Companions had increased in number and that they would protect him, so they began to look for the solution. Some among them supported the idea of prison, others suggested banishment, and at the last they all agreed upon killing him. But Allah inspired His Messenger and ordered him to leave his bed and 'Aly slept in his place while Abu Bakr accompanied the Prophet (peace be upon him) on his journey. When they left the houses of Mecca, Abu Bakr feared for the Messenger (peace be upon him), so sometimes he walked in front of him and at other times he walked behind him. When he felt that the enemy might come from the sides, he sometimes walked on his right side and then went to his left side. until they reached the cave of Thawr. Abu Bakr insisted to be the first to enter the cave in case there was something harmful in it. And Allah placed a tree there that had not been there before. This tree cast a shadow over the cave and distracted the disbelievers from seeing them. Also, Allah sent a spider that spun its web around door of the cave, which misled the disbelievers and their guide. Allah also sent two pigeons that built a nest and it seemed to the onlooker that they had been there for a long time. All these things were miracles and were more than just resisting the enemy with soldiers.

When the disbelievers stood outside the cave and their talk was heard by the Prophet and his companion, Abu Bakr said, "O Messenger of Allah! If any of them should look under his feet, he would see us.' The Prophet (peace be upon him) replied, 'O Abu Bakr! What do you think of two (persons) the third of whom is Allah?'"[31] When the Prophet (peace be upon him) saw the sadness of Abu Bakr and his fear for the Messenger and none for himself, he consoled him and said what Allah says,

$$﴿ ... لَا تَحْزَنْ إِنَّ ٱللَّهَ مَعَنَا ... ﴾$$

which means, "Be not sad (or afraid), surely Allah is with us." (At-Tawbah, 9:40)

Abu Bakr accompanied the Messenger of Allah (peace be upon him) throughout his lifetime and when the Messenger died, he became his successor and used to be called the caliph of the Messenger of Allah (peace be upon him) and when Abu Bakr died, his successors used to be called the Emir of the believers.

They stayed in the cave for three days, then they left it, and continued their journey until Surâqah bin Mâlik followed them and when he was about to catch them, the Messenger of Allah (peace be upon him) invoked Allah against him, and his horse stumbled. When he realized that he would never be able to arrest them he offered them money to let him go in peace. He

---

[31] Recorded by Al-Bukhâry, book of interpretation of Qur'ân, chapter on the saying of Allah which means, "The second of two, when they (Muhammad SAW and Abu Bakr radhiallahu'anhu) were in the cave......." (At-Tawbah, 9:40), no.4663.

offered money to someone who had refused the keys of the treasures of the earth; he offered food to the one who is satisfied. The Prophet (peace be upon him) said, "My Lord gives me food and drink during my sleep."[32] Abu Bakr was the second to embrace Islam, to sacrifice himself, to live an ascetic lifestyle, to accompany him, to take over the caliphate, and they were both of like age, and both he and the prophet (peace be upon him) died due to the effects of poison.

Those who embraced Islam through him were among the ten and they are 'Uthmân, Talhah, Az-Zubair, 'Abdur-Rahmân bin 'Awf, and Sa'd bin Abu Waqqâs. During the time that he embraced Islam, he had forty thousand dirhams, which he spent seeking the pleasure of Allah.

The Prophet (peace be upon him) said, "I never benefited from any money as I benefited from the money of Abu Bakr."[33] He is better than the believing man of Fir'awn (Pharaoh), as he hid his Islam while Abu Bakr declared it openly. He is better than the believing man of Âl Yâsîn, as he fought in the cause of Allah for one hour while Abu Bakr did for several years. Although Abu Bakr was a poor man, he loved to spend his money for the sake of Allah, following the verse in which Allah says,

$$\text{﴿ مَّن ذَا ٱلَّذِى يُقْرِضُ ٱللَّهَ قَرْضًا حَسَنًا ... ﴾}$$

which means, "Who is he that will lend to Allah a goodly loan." (Al-Baqarah, 2:245)

And Allah says,

$$\text{﴿ وَسَيُجَنَّبُهَا ٱلْأَتْقَى ۝ ٱلَّذِى يُؤْتِى مَالَهُ يَتَزَكَّى ۝ ﴾}$$

---

[32] Recorded by Al-Bukhâry, in Kitâb As-Sawm, no.1965.
[33] Recorded by At-Tirmidhy, the book of Merits, chapter on merits of Abu Bakr As-Siddîq (may Allah be pleased with him), no.3661, and Ibn Mâjah, no.94.

which means, "And *Al-Muttaqûn* (the pious and righteous - see V.2:2) will be far removed from it (Hell). He who spends his wealth for increase in self-purification." (Al-Lail, 92:17-18)

The Qur'ân and history mention his virtues and the Muhâjirîn (emigrants) and the Ansâr (supporters) agreed that he should be the successor of the Prophet (peace be upon him). So you who hated him listen to his merits. Did they not hear what Allah says about him,

﴿ ...ثَانِىَ ٱثْنَيْنِ إِذْ هُمَا فِى ٱلْغَارِ... ۝ ﴾

which means, "The second of two, when they (Muhammad and Abu Bakr) were in the cave." (At-Tawbah, 9:40)

Abu Bakr answered the Prophet (peace be upon him) when he was called to Islam, and he neither denied nor hesitated. His adherence to Islam never wavered.

- Who was the companion of the Prophet (peace be upon him) during his youth? Who was the first among his companions to embrace Islam? Who was the one who gave legal opinion in his presence and was the fastest to answer? Who was the first to perform prayer with him? Who was the last to lead him in performing prayer? Who was the next after him to die and be laid next to him? The answer to all these questions, is Abu Bakr. He was very understanding and attentive during the days of apostasy and obtained legal opinion from the Qur'ân and Sunnah.

- He protected the Messenger with everything at his disposal. He accompanied the Prophet (peace be upon him) during his life and death. How could anyone deny his virtues? To do so would be to try to cover the sun in the middle of the day. He is the best among the Companions, and whoever loves him is a believer.

- Oh Rawâfid! Our love for him is based on the truth. We followed 'Aly when he said about him, "The Messenger of Allah (peace be upon him) was content with you in our religion, so why can't we be content with him in our lives?" By Allah! O 'Aly, you took our revenge from Ar-Rawâfid. We believe in and acknowledge his favors. Whoever was from Rawâfid, is not from us.

Warning: Great Pearls of Wisdom

- Beware of the one who is an enemy to the people of the Qur'ân and Sunnah, and do not let them infect you with enmity or you will be the loser.

- Beware of two enemies, which were the cause of the doom of many creatures: he who keeps away from Allah and acts on his suspicions, and he who is fascinated by this worldly life and the power he has obtained.

- Whoever was granted some kind of special power and readiness, will find his pleasure in using it in this worldly life. Whoever was granted the power to have sexual intercourse, will find his pleasure in utilizing this power, whoever was granted the power to get angry, will find pleasure in using his anger to get what he wants, whoever was granted the power of eating and drinking, will find pleasure in using his power, whoever was granted the power to gain knowledge, will find pleasure in using this power, and whoever was granted the power to love Allah and turn to Him, he will find his pleasure in using this power to gain closeness to Allah. Pleasures other than those will be less significant and rare.

Warning: Lessons and Warnings

- O You unarmed, having no good deeds in your account with Allah, beware of the sight of a pious man for he can see your defects from behind a veil. The Prophet (peace be upon him) said, "Beware of the insight of a believer."[34]

- Glory be to Allah: the soul has the pride of Satan, the envy of Cain, the insolence and impiety of 'Âd, the tyranny of Thamûd, the boldness of Nimrod, the tendency to attack violently like Fir'awn (Pharaoh), the injustice of Qârûn, the meanness of Hâmân, the fancy of Bil'âm[35], the trickery of the people of the Sabbath-breakers, the mutiny of Al-Walîd, and the ignorance of Abu Jahl. The soul of man also took some of the characteristics of the animals such as the greediness of the crow, the gluttony of a dog, the folly of a peacock, the lowness of a scarab, the disobedience of a lizard, the spite of a camel, the impulsive jumping of a cheetah, the power of a lion, the debauchery of a mouse, the malice of a snake, the frivolity of a monkey, the desire to collect and store like an ant, the cunning of a fox, the lightness of a butterfly, and the laziness of a hyena. But through taming and fighting this soul, all these traits will be removed, but whoever submits to these follies, will become their servant and his good self will not be bought by Allah, as Allah says,

---

[34] Recoded by At-Tirmidhy, book of interpretation of Qur'ân, no.3127.

[35] Bil'âm bin Bâ'ûrâ' whom Allah revealed the following verse in him, "And recite (O Muhammad SAW) to them the story of him to whom We gave Our Ayât (proofs, evidences, verses, lessons, signs, revelations, etc.), but he threw them away, so Shaitân (Satan) followed him up, and he became of those who went astray. (Al-A'râf, 7:175)

﴿ إِنَّ ٱللَّهَ ٱشْتَرَىٰ مِنَ ٱلْمُؤْمِنِينَ أَنفُسَهُمْ ... ﴾

which means, "Verily, Allah has purchased of the believers their lives." (At-Tawbah, 9:111)

Allah will never purchase any good (deed) that has not been refined by faith for without it, the good deed cannot enter the world of the pious worshippers of Allah. Hand your good deeds over to the buyer (Allah) before they are ruined through doing bad deeds. In this case the buyer will not accept them. The buyer knew what defects were present in this good deed before buying it, so hand it to Him and be assured that He will never return it.

- The value of the good person is estimated according to the buyer (Allah), and the price that will be paid for it (Paradise) is also allotted by Him. If the buyer is Great, then the price is significant, and whatever is sold will be considered precious.

- O you who evaluate matters, do you know the value of yourself? The universe was created for your sake.

- O you who were fed the milk of piety and changed by the will of Allah, all things are like a tree while you are the fruit; a picture and you are the meaning; a shell and you are the pearl, and buttermilk and you are the butter.

- Allah says to His servant, "Whenever you want Me, ask Me to come. Send for Me from yourself and you will find Me near you and do not ask Me to come through another servant, as I am more near to you than the other."

- If you knew the true value of yourself, you will never allow yourself to be humiliated by committing sins. Satan refused to bow to you when it refused to bow to your father Adam, so how come you reconciled with it and left us? If there is any love in your heart, its effect would appear on your body.

- If the heart is fed by love, greed for pleasure would disappear.

- If your love is true, you would feel an aversion for anything that does not remind you of the one you love. How odd! Whoever claims to love and needs someone to remind him of the lover, his love is not complete. The least thing that shows your love is that you never forget your lover.

- If a lover traveled to meet his lover, his solders will ride with him. Love will be the vanguard, hope will accompany them, longing will drive them, and fear will gather them on the road to the lover. When he will be about to reach the place of his lover, they will go together. So when he comes to the lover, gifts and rewards will be given to him from every direction in order to be examined whether he will dwell in tranquility and this will be his destiny or he will search for whoever bestowed them upon him.

- Their hearts were filled with good deeds and pure feelings for Allah, and when the time of early dawn came, these deeds were performed and by dawn they reached Allah.

- They walked seriously through this worldly life facing all kinds of pleasures and lusts. A little time passed and they returned from their travel and reached the Hereafter where they found reward and relief and they entered this world of the Hereafter and they were rewarded forever.

- People emptied their hearts from whatever distracted them, and replaced such things with love and appointed eyes to guard and care for them.

- Love is never found except in an empty and honest place.

- Know the value of what was lost and cry like someone, who knows the value of what has passed him by.

- If the human knew the pleasure of meeting Allah and being near Him, he would feel grief for being distant from Him.

- If you taste the pleasure of the Hereafter, your drunken heart would sober up.

- Whoever feels that the path of performing good deeds is long; his walk along that path will weaken.

- Whoever is true to his intention, will be granted resolution.

- The human being is always discontent; if August comes, he will long for March.

- All hard work is easy for those who believe in Allah, when they know that Allah hears them.

- Whoever tastes the pleasures of the Hereafter, it would be easy for him to leave this worldly life.

- O you who are patient! Bear a little more, just a little more remains.

- If one remembers the sweetness of meeting Allah, the difficulty of fighting in His cause will be made easy for him.

- You will know where your house is in the Hereafter, so prepare yourself for it and you will be happy there.

- The best intention is that of he who is preparing to meet his Lord.

- Prepare yourself with good deeds before going to the Hereafter and then you will obtain your reward there. Allah says,

$$﴿...وَقَدِّمُوا لِأَنفُسِكُمْ...﴾$$

which means, "And send (good deeds, or ask Allah to bestow upon you pious offspring) before you for your ownselves." (Al-Baqarah, 2:223)

- Paradise will be content if you performed obligatory acts of worship, Hellfire will be kept away from you if you avoid sins, and love cannot be satisfied with less than the sacrifice of your soul.

- The time in which you are obedient to Allah and you are longing for Him is the sweetest time.

- When people handed their souls over to the owner of Islamic law (Allah), He teaches them how to reach agreement in disputes so they learned to agree and obey.

Chapter

- Man taught his dog how to catch prey for him and the dog overcame his desire to eat the prey out of respect for his owner and fear of his power, and Allah taught you and you do not accept His teaching.

- Eating the game that is caught by an untrained dog is unlawful and likewise are the deeds of the ignorant who performed their deeds for their own sake and not for Allah.

- Man consists of the mind of an angel, the lust of an animal, and the fancy of Satan. One of them will prevail. If you could overcome your fancy and lust, you will be in a rank that is higher than an angel. And if your fancy and lust beat you, you will be in a rank that is less than a dog.

- It is lawful when a dog catches prey for its owner as Allah accepts deeds that are for His sake alone, while He refuses deeds that are done for others than Him, like when a dog catches prey for itself and not for its owner.

- The origin of all good and evil that is found in the servant and all that is praised or dispraised, are from Allah, the Donator and the Preventer. He, the Exalted manages His servants according to these two attributes. The true and sincere worshiper will praise Allah when He gives to him and will turn to Allah when He prevents him from something. Allah, the Exalted gives to him in order to be praised and prevents him in order to be asked. The sincere servant will always praise Allah and ask of Him.

And the Disbeliever is Ever a Helper (of the Satan) against his Lord

Allah, the Almighty says,

﴿ ...وَكَانَ ٱلْكَافِرُ عَلَىٰ رَبِّهِۦ ظَهِيرًا ۝ ﴾

which means, "And the disbeliever is ever a helper (of the Satan) against his Lord." (Al-Furqân, 25:55)

This is among the most honorable meanings of the Qur'ân. And similarly the believer is always with Allah and He is His helper against himself, his fancy, and his Satan. This is what is meant by the saying that someone is from the party of Allah and is from among His soldiers. He is a helper of Allah against his enemy. He fights them, hates, and makes them angry for the sake of Allah, the Exalted. He will also be accompanied by some of the characteristics of the angels in his war against His enemies, while others among those who neglect this war have none of these characteristics. The disbeliever is a helper of Satan, his soul, and his fancy against his Lord.

Ibn Abu Hâtim mentioned that 'Atâ' bin Dînâr reported that Sa'îd bin Jubair said, "He is helping Satan against Allah through enmity and polytheism." Laith said that Mujâhid said, "He is helping Satan against Allah by committing sins." Zaid bin Aslam said, "A helper is a supporter. He supports his enemy in his sin and by polytheism, so he is with his enemy, helping him against Allah." Allah says,

﴿ وَيَعْبُدُونَ مِن دُونِ اللَّهِ مَا لَا يَنفَعُهُمْ وَلَا يَضُرُّهُمْ ... ﴾

which means, "And they (disbelievers, polytheists, etc.) worship besides Allah, that which can neither profit them nor harm them." (Al-Furqân, 25:55)

This form of worship is helping, loving, and pleasing the enemies of Allah, but those who are the helpers of Allah are with Him against themselves, Satan, and fancies.

About those who, when they are reminded of the *Ayât* (proofs, evidences, verses, lessons, signs, revelations, etc.) of their Lord:

Allah says,

﴿ وَالَّذِينَ إِذَا ذُكِّرُوا بِآيَاتِ رَبِّهِمْ لَمْ يَخِرُّوا عَلَيْهَا صُمًّا وَعُمْيَانًا ﴾

which means, "And those who, when they are reminded of the *Ayât* (proofs, evidences, verses, lessons, signs, revelations, etc.) of their Lord, fall not deaf and blind thereat." (Al-Furqân, 25:73)

Muqâtil said, "If they were to be taught the Qur'ân, they will neither be deaf not to hear it nor blind not to see it, but they heard, saw, and believed in it. Ibn 'Abbâs said, "They were not deaf and blind toward it but were afraid and submissive." Al-Kalby[36] said, "They listen and see the Qur'ân." Al-Farrâ' said, "When the Qur'ân is being recited to them, they did not remain as they had been before hearing it, as if they had not heard it at all." Az-Zajjâj said, "The meaning is that when the verses of the Qur'ân were recited unto them, they fell down prostrating, weeping, hearing, and seeing as they were ordered to do." Ibn Qutaibah said, "They did not neglect the Qur'ân as if they were deaf and did not hear, and blind and did not see."

The Origin of Sin

There are three main origins of all sins, whether big and small: the heart is attached to someone or something other than Allah, obeying anger, power, and lust, which are polytheism, injustice, and adultery. To be attached to other than Allah and claim another god with Him is polytheism, the core of obeying one's anger is to kill, and the core of obeying one's lust r is to commit adultery. That is why Allah, the Exalted combined these three things when He says,

﴿ وَٱلَّذِينَ لَا يَدْعُونَ مَعَ ٱللَّهِ إِلَٰهًا ءَاخَرَ وَلَا يَقْتُلُونَ ٱلنَّفْسَ ٱلَّتِي حَرَّمَ ٱللَّهُ إِلَّا بِٱلْحَقِّ وَلَا يَزْنُونَ ... ﴾

---

[36] He is Ibrâhîm bin Khâlid bin Abu Al-Yamân, Abu Thawr Abu 'Abdullâh. Among the friends of Ash-Shâfi'y. He passed away (may Allah be merciful to him) 240 A.H. See *Tahdhîb At-Tahdhîb*, vol.1, p.118, *Al-Jarh wat-Ta'dîl*, vol.2, p.97, *Mîzân Al-I'tidâl*, vol.1, p.29, *Lisân Al-Mîzân*, vol.7, p.168.

which means, "And those who invoke not any other *ilâh* (god) along with Allah, nor kill such life as Allah has forbidden, except for a just cause, nor commit illegal sexual intercourse." (Al-Furqân, 25:68)

And these three are a cause and effect in each other; polytheism induces injustice and adultery, like sincerity and monotheism remove them. Allah says,

﴿ ...كَذَٰلِكَ لِنَصْرِفَ عَنْهُ ٱلسُّوٓءَ وَٱلْفَحْشَآءَ إِنَّهُۥ مِنْ عِبَادِنَا ٱلْمُخْلَصِينَ ﴾

which means, "Thus it was, that We might turn away from him evil and illegal sexual intercourse. Surely, he was one of Our chosen, guided slaves." (Yûsuf, 12:24)

Also injustice induces polytheism and adultery as polytheism is the biggest injustice of all just as the highest justice is monotheism. Justice is connected to monotheism and injustice is connected to polytheism. That is why Allah combined them:

One: Allah says,

﴿ شَهِدَ ٱللَّهُ أَنَّهُۥ لَآ إِلَٰهَ إِلَّا هُوَ وَٱلْمَلَٰٓئِكَةُ وَأُوْلُواْ ٱلْعِلْمِ قَآئِمًۢا بِٱلْقِسْطِ... ﴾

which means, "Allah bears witness that *Lâ ilâha illa Huwa* (none has the right to be worshipped but He), and the angels, and those having knowledge (also give this witness); (He is always) maintaining His creation in Justice."(Âl-'Imrân, 3:18)

Two: Allah says,

﴿ ...إِنَّ ٱلشِّرْكَ لَظُلْمٌ عَظِيمٌ ﴾

which means, "Verily! Joining others in worship with Allah is a great *Zhulm* (wrong) indeed. (Luqmân, 31:13)

And adultery induces polytheism and injustice, especially when it is strong and it occurs through injustice and by using the support of magic and Satan. Allah, the Exalted combined adultery and polytheism when He says,

﴿ ٱلزَّانِى لَا يَنكِحُ إِلَّا زَانِيَةً أَوْ مُشْرِكَةً وَٱلزَّانِيَةُ لَا يَنكِحُهَآ إِلَّا زَانٍ أَوْ مُشْرِكٌ ۚ وَحُرِّمَ ذَٰلِكَ عَلَى ٱلْمُؤْمِنِينَ ۝ ﴾

which means, "The adulterer marries not but an adulteress or a *Mushrikah* and the adulteress none marries her except an adulterer or a *Muskrik* [and that means that the man who agrees to marry (have a sexual relation with) a *Mushrikah* (female polytheist, pagan or idolatress) or a prostitute, then surely he is either an adulterer, or a *Mushrik* (polytheist, pagan or idolater, etc.) And the woman who agrees to marry (have a sexual relation with) a *Mushrik* (polytheist, pagan or idolater) or an adulterer, then she is either a prostitute or a *Mushrikah* (female polytheist, pagan, or idolatress, etc.)]. Such a thing is forbidden to the believers (of Islamic Monotheism)." (An-Nûr, 24:3)

So these three lead to and result in each other. That is why when the heart has more polytheism than monotheism, it will be more likely to be guilty of adultery and will attach significance to pictures and such things, instead of Allah.

Allah says,

﴿ فَمَآ أُوتِيتُم مِّن شَىْءٍ فَمَتَٰعُ ٱلْحَيَوٰةِ ٱلدُّنْيَا ۖ وَمَا عِندَ ٱللَّهِ خَيْرٌ وَأَبْقَىٰ لِلَّذِينَ ءَامَنُوا۟ وَعَلَىٰ رَبِّهِمْ يَتَوَكَّلُونَ ۝ وَٱلَّذِينَ يَجْتَنِبُونَ كَبَٰٓئِرَ ٱلْإِثْمِ وَٱلْفَوَٰحِشَ وَإِذَا مَا غَضِبُوا۟ هُمْ يَغْفِرُونَ ۝ ﴾

which means, "So whatever you have been given is but a passing enjoyment for this worldly life, but that which is with Allah (Paradise) is better and more lasting for those who believe (in the Oneness of Allah Islamic Monotheism) and put their trust in their Lord (concerning all of their affairs). And those who avoid the greater sins, and *Al-Fawâhish* (illegal sexual intercourse, etc.), and when they are angry, they forgive." (Ash-Shûrâ, 42:36-37)

Allah informed us that what He has is better for he who believed in Him and put his trust in Him. This is monotheism. Then He talked about those who avoid the power of lust and after that those who overcome the power of anger, so He combined monotheism, chastity, and justice, which are the means of all good.

A Precious Gem: Forms of Rejecting the Qur'ân and Uncertainty about It

Forms of rejecting the Qur'ân:

One: to refuse to listen to it, have faith in it and pay attention to it.

Two: to refuse to act according to it, abide by its lawful and unlawful commandments, even if the person reads it and has faith in it.

Three: to reject its arbitration and litigation according to its principles and branches of the religion, and to believe that its words are not meant to be indisputable, and that its proofs are verbal and does not reach the level of real knowledge.

Fourt: to reject careful consideration of it, and fail to understand it and learnthat which the Speaker intended.

Five: to reject seeking medication with it concerning all the diseases of the heart, by seeking the cure of such diseases from other than it.

All these are included in the following Qur'ânic verse:

﴿ وَقَالَ ٱلرَّسُولُ يَٰرَبِّ إِنَّ قَوْمِى ٱتَّخَذُوا۟ هَٰذَا ٱلْقُرْءَانَ مَهْجُورًا ﴾

which means, "And the Messenger (Muhammad) will say: "O my Lord! Verily, my people deserted this Qur'ân (neither listened to it, nor acted on its laws and orders)." (Al-Furqân, 25:30)

This is the case with people although some rejection is less than others.

Uncertainty in the hearts concerning the Qur'ân, is sometimes an uncertainty about whether it was really revealed by Allah or not, and whether it is really the truth from Allah. Sometimes this uncertainty is whether the Qur'ân is Sacred or not, whether it is the word of Allah or a part of His creation. Sometimes it is whether the Qur'ân is sufficient or not, whether it is necessary for people or that they are in need of some things other than it, like other reasonable things, analogies, opinions and policies.

Sometimes, it is about its meaning; its entirely clear meanings or interpreting it by leaving the entirely clear meanings and associating offensive interpretations. Sometimes, it is concerned with the entirely clear meanings, and whether or not they are meant to be practiced for their sake or for the sake of interest.

People have such uncertainties in their hearts about the Qur'ân. You will find that every innovator in the religion has some kind of uncertainty about the Verses that contradict his innovation in his heart. Every dissolute oppressor has some kind of uncertainty about the Verses that come in between him and his will. So consider this meaning carefully, then be pleased with that to which you are inclined.

A Rule: The Perfection of Oneself

The required perfection of oneself includes two things:

One: it should be a deep-rooted state and an indispensable part of one's character.

Two: it should be a character of perfection within himself.

If it is not in this way, it will not be perfection. Therefore, the person who tries to achieve perfection should compete for it and be sorry if he misses out on it. This is nothing else but learning about his True Creator and Lord, without whom there would be no righteousness, comfort and pleasure, which is only found in learning about Him, the Almighty, and wishing to see His countenance, and following the road that leads to Him and His Pleasure and Dignity. This should become a deep-rooted and indispensable state.

Apart from that, all other knowledge, will and deeds are considered to be either that which does not benefit him and does not perfect him, or that which prevents him from harm, especially if it becomes deep-rooted. In this case, it will torture and pain him according to its firmness within him.

The advantages that are separated from the self, such as clothing, vehicles. residence, high rank and wealth; they are in reality, something that is borrowed for some time, then the Lender will take them back. By then, and according to the degree of your attachment to these things, you will be in a state of pain and suffering because the Lender has taken back what He had lent you. And if they have become very dear to you, you will feel even greater pain and regret.

Therefore, anyone who wishes to attain happiness for himself should consider this point carefully. This is because most of creations are making every effort to deprive themselves, their own sufferance and regret, while thinking they are working for their happiness and comfort. They can only obtain real pleasure according to the degree of knowledge, love and good behavior they acquire. And their pain and regret will be according to the degree to which they miss these great targets. So, when they lack these qualities, they will only have physical and mental forces, with which they eat, drink, marry, get angry and obtain the rest of their pleasures and the facilities of their life.

They will not receive any honor or merit, but only lowliness, because these forces suit beasts better than people. They may be better than them and more distinguished, in the sense that they will be surer to bring harm upon themselves. Therefore, you should abandon a form of perfection that is shared by beasts, which may even surpass you in it, and which are more competent in it than you. You should abandon it so as to attain real perfection and there is no perfection except when Allah grants it.

A Precious Gem: The Reward of Being Busy in the Service of Allah

If the servant of Allah begins the day and the evening, without having any other concern except Allah, the Almighty, He will fulfill all his needs and relieve all his worries. He will empty the servant's heart for the sake of His Love, his tongue will constantly remember Him and he will have the strength to perform religious duties for His sake.

And if he begins the day and the evening, without having any other concern except the life of this world, Allah, the Almighty will cast worry and grief into his heart. He, the Almighty will leave him to himself, and keep his heart busy with things other than His Love. His tongue will not remember Allah but will only be concerned with the creation. He will use all his strength in things other than the sake of Allah, and he will remain busy in the service of creation. He will work very hard in the service of others. Just like a bellows that pumps itself up and then squeezes itself to the utmost in the service of others. Therefore, whoever refuses to submit to Allah, to obey and love Him, will be afflicted with the servitude, love and service of creation.

Allah, the Almighty says in the Qur'ân,

﴿ وَمَن يَعْشُ عَن ذِكْرِ ٱلرَّحْمَٰنِ نُقَيِّضْ لَهُۥ شَيْطَٰنًا فَهُوَ لَهُۥ قَرِينٌ ۝ ﴾

which means, "And whosoever turns away (blinds himself) from the remembrance of the Most Beneficent (Allah) (i.e. this Qur'ân and worship of Allah), We appoint for him Shaitân (Satan devil) to be a Qarîn (an intimate companion) to him." (Az-Zukhruf, 43:36)

Abu Sufyân bin 'Uyaynah [37] said, "You will never bring forward any famous proverb but I will bring the likeness of it from the Qur'ân." Thereupon someone said to him, "So where is in the Qur'ân "Give your fellow brother a date, and if he does not accept it then give him a firebrand." He then recited the previous Qur'ânic verse.

A Precious Gem: Elements of Knowledge

Knowledge is to transfer the image of a given thing and establish it in the heart. And action is to transfer the theoretical image from the heart and establish it in the world. Therefore, if the one, which is established in the heart corresponds to the reality, then it is true knowledge.

It is often true that some images that have no real existence remain within oneself, and the person who has adopted it in himself takes it to be true knowledge, whereas it has no reality. The knowledge of most people is of this kind.

---

[37] His full name is Sufyân bin 'Uyaynah bin Maymûn Al-Hilâly Al-Kûfy. He was a faithful memorizer, and the imam of the Sacred mosque of Mecca. He was one of the leaders of the study of hadith. He died (may Allah have mercy upon him) in 198 A. H. Adopted from Tahdhîb At-Tahdhîb (4\117), Târikh Al-Bukhâry Alkabîr (4\94), Aj-Jarh wat-Ta'dîl (4\973), Mîzânul-I'tidâl (2\170) and Siyar A'lâm An-Nubalâ' (8\454).

There are two kinds that conform with reality: the first one is used to accomplish the perfection of the self by understanding and knowing it, and that is done through knowing Allah, His Names, Attributes, Actions, Books, Commands and what He has forbidden.

The second one cannot make us perfect, and that is the knowledge that is not important, and therefore does not benefit when it is learned. The Prophet (peace be upon him) used to seek refuge with Allah from the knowledge that is not beneficial. And this is the case with most good knowledge, such as astronomy, its stages, the number of its stars, its quantities, and the knowledge of the number of mountains, their color, their measurements and so on.

Therefore, the honor of knowledge depends on its content and the level of its necessity, and surely that is nothing else except knowing Allah and everything related to Him.

The flaw of knowledge is when it is not in conformity with Allah's Will, which He loves and which pleases Him. That is when knowledge becomes corrupted. The corruption of knowledge occurs when people believe that something is lawful and pleases Allah, but in reality it is not the case, or to believe that it makes the person become closer to Allah even if it does not.

The corruption of one's intention is when deeds are not done for the sake of Allah and the Hereafter, but done for the sake of this worldly life. There is no way to be safe from these two flaws concerning knowledge and deeds, except by learning that which the Messenger (peace be upon him) brought from Allah, the Almighty concerning knowledge, learning, seeking Allah's Countenance and the Hereafter along with the subject of intention and will. Furthermore, faith and certainty bring about beneficial knowledge and good will, and both of them cause faith and increase it. Hence, it becomes clear that the deviation of the majority of people from faith is due to their deviation from beneficial knowledge and good will. And faith cannot be completed unless it is learnt from the light of Prophethood, by cleansing the will from the blemishes of vain desires and the will of the man.

His knowledge would then be adopted from the light of inspiration, his seeking of Allah's Countenance and the Hereafter. Therefore, this would be the best person in terms of knowledge and action, and he would be among the leaders who give guidance under Allah's Command and among the successors of His Messenger in his nation.

An Important Rule: The Apparent and Hidden Aspects of Faith

Faith has both apparent and hidden aspects. Its apparent aspect is when it is related by the tongue and acted upon by the body. The hidden aspect is the acknowledgment of the heart, and its submission and love. Therefore, the apparent aspect of faith will be of no use for someone who does not have the hidden aspect, though his blood is spared and his wealth and children are preserved by it. And no hidden aspect will be of any use, unless there is no fear that it will be weakened, coerced or in fear of being ruined. Therefore, the failure of apparent deeds without the existence of any real prevention, means the corruption of the hidden aspect and lack of faith. Its deficiency refers to its deficiency of faith and intensity refers to its intensity of faith.

Therefore, faith is the heart and core of Islam, and certainty is the heart and core of faith. Any piece of knowledge or deed that does not make faith and certainty stronger is abnormal, and any faith that does not urge one to perform good deeds is abnormal.

A Precious Gem: Trust in Allah

There are two kinds of trust in Allah:

One is: to trust in Him concerning one's needs and worldly interests or for the sake of removing worldly harms and misfortunes.

Two is: to trust in Him in order to obtain that which He loves and what pleases Him like faith, certainty, jihad and inviting people to Allah.

Between the two kinds, there is great excellence that cannot be counted by anyone but Allah. So when the servant puts his trust in Him as He should be trusted according to the second kind, this will suffice him without the first one. And when he puts his trust in Him according to the first kind without the second one, it will also suffice him, but he will not have the same blessed end. The greatest trust in Allah is that of guidance, adhering to Monotheism, following the example of the Messenger of Allah, and opposing the sinners and the wicked. This is the trust of the Prophets and that of their sincere followers.

Trusting in Allah is sometimes done out of necessity, in the sense that the servant does not have any other choice but to trust in Allah, like when life's circumstances become straitened for him, and he perceives that there is no fleeing from Allah, and no refuge but with Him.

And at other times, trusting in Allah is voluntarily, and that is in the existence of the means that leads to the purpose. If he leaves the recommended means, he will be dispraised for having done so. And if he makes use of the means and fails to trust in Allah, he will be dispraised for having done so, for it is a basic principle of Islam, and is mentioned in the Qur'ân, and it should be practiced.

If the means is forbidden, it will be unlawful for him to make use of it, and there will be no other way for him except to put his trust in Allah, for putting one's trust in Allah is the greatest means of attaining one's goal and removing harm. If the means is permissible, then you must ensure that it does not weaken your trust in Allah. If it does weaken your trust in Allah and your heart is confused, then it would better to leave it. And if it does not weaken it, then it would be better to engage in it, for the Wisdom of the Most Justs requires the effect to be connected to it.

You should never try to frustrate His Wisdom, especially when you are seeking to submit to Him. In that case, you will have performed the submission of the heart by putting your trust in Allah, and the submission of the body by performing the pious act.

To make use of the recommended means is to achieve trust in Allah. And whoever abandons them, his trust in Allah will not be sound. It is like using a means that leads to obtaining good and fulfills one's hope, so if it is not made use of, then the person's hope would become a mere wish, and quitting it would cause his trust to become weak.

The secret and the reality of trust in Allah is the reliance of the heart on Allah Alone. The person who relies on Allah, and not on any other person or thing, will not be harmed. Therefore, trusting in Allah in word only is totally different from trusting in Him with the heart. It is the same as repentence with the tongue while having the intention to commit sins again, and the repentance of the sincere heart even if the tongue has not said anything. For the statement of the servant: "I have put my trust in Allah" with the intention of something else in his heart is like the statement "I have repented to Allah" with the intention of committing sins.

The Complaint of the Ignorant

The ignorant people complain to people about Allah, and this is the highest degree of ignorance, for if he had known his Lord, he would not have complained about Him, and if he had known the people, he would not have complained to them.

One of the predecessors saw a man complaining to another man about his poverty and dire necessity. He said to him, "O you! By Allah, you have done nothing but complain about He Who has mercy for you, to the one who has no mercy for you.

The following verses have been mentioned about the meaning of the previous statement of the predecessor.

When you complain to a son of Adam

verily you complain about the Most Merciful

to the one who does not pity

On the contrary, the person who is profoundly knowledgeable about Allah complains to Allah Alone. And the most knowledgeable person about Allah is the one who complains about himself to Allah, and never to people. He complains about the causes that made people do wrong to him, for he knows the following Qur'ânic Verses,

﴿ وَمَآ أَصَٰبَكُم مِّن مُّصِيبَةٖ فَبِمَا كَسَبَتۡ أَيۡدِيكُمۡ وَيَعۡفُواْ عَن كَثِيرٖ ﴾

which means, "And whatever of misfortune befalls you, it is because of what your hands have earned. And He pardons much." (As-Shûrâ, 42:30)

﴿ ...وَمَآ أَصَابَكَ مِن سَيِّئَةٖ فَمِن نَّفۡسِكَ... ﴾

which means, "Whatever of good reaches you, is from Allah, but whatever of evil befalls you, is from yourself." (An-Nisâ', 4:79)

﴿ أَوَلَمَّآ أَصَٰبَتۡكُم مُّصِيبَةٞ قَدۡ أَصَبۡتُم مِّثۡلَيۡهَا قُلۡتُمۡ أَنَّىٰ هَٰذَاۖ قُلۡ هُوَ مِنۡ عِندِ أَنفُسِكُمۡۗ إِنَّ ٱللَّهَ عَلَىٰ كُلِّ شَيۡءٖ قَدِيرٞ ﴾

which means, "(What is the matter with you?) When a single disaster smites you, although you smote (your enemies) with one twice as great, you say: "From where does this come to us?" Say (to them), "It is from yourselves (because of your evil deeds)." And Allah has power over all things." (Âl-'Imrân, 3:165)

Therefore, there are three levels: the lowest one is to complain about Allah to His creatures, the highest one is to complain about yourself to Him and the middle one is to complain about His creatures to Him.

A Great and Important Rule: "O you who believe! Answer Allah (by obeying Him) and (His) Messenger"

Allah, the Almighty said,

﴿ يَٰٓأَيُّهَا ٱلَّذِينَ ءَامَنُواْ ٱسْتَجِيبُواْ لِلَّهِ وَلِلرَّسُولِ إِذَا دَعَاكُمْ لِمَا يُحْيِيكُمْ وَٱعْلَمُوٓاْ أَنَّ ٱللَّهَ يَحُولُ بَيْنَ ٱلْمَرْءِ وَقَلْبِهِۦ وَأَنَّهُۥٓ إِلَيْهِ تُحْشَرُونَ ﴾

which means, "O you who believe! Answer Allah (by obeying Him) and (His) Messenger when he calls you to that which will give you life, and know that Allah comes in between a person and his heart (i.e. He prevents an evil person to decide anything). And verily to Him you shall (all) be gathered." (Al-Anfâl, 8:24)

This Verse contains some instructions: one of them is that a prosperous life is only attained by obeying Allah and His Messenger (peace be upon him). Whoever has not obeyed will not have a real life, even though he would have the bestial life, which he shares with the animals.

The real and good life, therefore, is the life of the person who obeys Allah and His Messenger (peace be upon him) openly and secretly. They are those who are really alive, even if their bodies die. The others are dead even if they are alive physically, for it is simply a state of the heart.

That is why the person who is most alive is the one who perfectly obeys the call of the Messenger (peace be upon him), in every aspect of life. Therefore, whoever missed any part of it, has missed a part of life, and the person will have 'life' according to the level that he obeys the Messenger (peace be upon him).

According to Al-Mujâhid, the words "*Limâ yuhyîkum*" refer to the truth, meaning "that which will give you life for the truth." According to Qatâdah, they refer to the Qur'ân, for it contains life, trust, salvation and protection in this world and the Hereafter. And according to As-Saddiy, it refers to Islam, for He gave them life with it after having been dead due to disbelief.

According to Ibn Ishâq and 'Urwah bin Az-Zubair, and it is his wording: "*Limâ yuhyîkum*" refers to the battle that Allah made you powerful in after having been degraded. He made you powerful after being weak. He protected you from your enemy after being defeated by them. All these are expressions about one reality, which is to perform openly and secretly that which the Messenger (peace be upon him) brought from Allah, the Almighty.

According to Al-Wâhidy and the majority, these words refer to jihad, which is the opinion of Ibn Ishâq and the opinion of most knowledgeable people. According to Al-Farâ', the words mean: when he (peace be upon him) calls you to that which revives your standing by fighting your enemy, he means that their standing becomes stronger with struggle and jihad, and that if they abandon jihad, their standing will become weaker and their enemy will have the courage to challenge them.

I say, jihad is one of the greatest means that He avails them with in the life of this world, and the life in the grave after death until the Day of Resurrection and in the Hereafter. Concerning their life in this world, truly, they will have more power and be able to overcome their enemy by adopting jihad. The life in the grave is mentioned by Allah, the Almighty in the following Verse of the Qur'ân,

﴿ وَلَا تَحْسَبَنَّ ٱلَّذِينَ قُتِلُوا۟ فِى سَبِيلِ ٱللَّهِ أَمْوَٰتًۢا ۚ بَلْ أَحْيَآءٌ عِندَ رَبِّهِمْ يُرْزَقُونَ ﴾

which means: "Think not of those who are killed in the Way of Allah as dead. Nay, they are alive, with their Lord, and they have provision." (Âl-Imrân, 3:169)

The share of the Hereafter is for those who strive hard and fight, like the martyrs, and its great delight is greater than the share of anything in this worldly life. That is why Ibn Qutaibah said, "*Limâ yuḥyîkum*" means martyrdom. According to some commentators, "*Limâ yuḥyîkum*" means Paradise, for it is the home of life, and it is the eternal and good life. Narrated by Abu 'Aly Al-Jurjâny.

The Qur'ânic Verse examines all these aspects, for faith, Islam, the Qur'ân and jihad provide hearts with a good life, and the perfect life is in Paradise. And the Messenger (peace be upon him) is inviting man to faith and Paradise. Therefore, he is inviting to the life of this world and the Hereafter.

Moreover, man cannot maintain two kinds of life. One part is the life of his body, with which he perceives that which is useful and that which is harmful. Whenever this element of life is weakened within him, he feels pain and weakness. That is why the life of the patient, the sad person, the grieved, the distressed, the feared, the poor and the debased, their life is inferior to the person who does not suffer from these things.

The second kind of life is that of his heart and soul, with which he can differentiate between truth and falsehood, between transgression and righteousness, and between guidance and being astray. He chooses the truth and leaves falsehood.

Therefore, this life gives him more benefit and more ability to distinguish between that which avails and that, which is harmful concerning knowledge, will and deeds. And it avails him with the power of faith, will, the love of truth, and the power of hatred against falsehood.

His feeling, perception, love and reluctance exist according to his share of this life. Just as the body that is full of life feels and perceives that which is useful and that which is harmful. It also perceives its inclination to what is useful, and it is reluctant about what is harmful.

When the life of the heart comes to an end, its perception ceases to exist; it even cannot perceive that which is useful or harmful.

A man cannot live unless the angel breathes life into him in his mother's womb, and before that he was in a state like death. In the same way, there is no life for his spirit and heart unless the Messenger (peace be upon him) breathes into it the inspiration, which has been bestowed upon him.

Allah, the Almighty said,

﴿ يُنَزِّلُ ٱلْمَلَٰٓئِكَةَ بِٱلرُّوحِ مِنْ أَمْرِهِۦ عَلَىٰ مَن يَشَآءُ مِنْ عِبَادِهِۦٓ ... ﴾

which means, "He sends down the angels with inspiration of His Command to whom of His slaves..." (An-Nahl, 16:2)

He, the Almighty also said,

﴿ ... يُلْقِى ٱلرُّوحَ مِنْ أَمْرِهِۦ عَلَىٰ مَن يَشَآءُ مِنْ عِبَادِهِۦ ... ﴾

which means, "He sends the Inspiration by His Command to any of His slaves He wills." (Ghâfir, 40:15)

He, the Almighty also said,

﴿ وَكَذَٰلِكَ أَوْحَيْنَا إِلَيْكَ رُوحًا مِّنْ أَمْرِنَا ۚ مَا كُنتَ تَدْرِي مَا ٱلْكِتَٰبُ وَلَا ٱلْإِيمَٰنُ وَلَٰكِن جَعَلْنَٰهُ نُورًا نَّهْدِي بِهِۦ مَن نَّشَآءُ مِنْ عِبَادِنَا ... ﴾

which means, "And thus We have sent to you (O Muhammad) Ruhan (an Inspiration, and a Mercy) of Our Command. You knew not what is the Book, nor what is Faith. But We have made it (this Qur'ân) a light wherewith We guide whosoever of Our slaves We will." (As-Shûrâ, 42:52)

Allah, the Almighty said that His Inspiration is a spirit and a light. Therefore, life and illumination depend on the messenger, and whoever receives the breathe of life of this angel and the breathe of life of the Messenger (peace be upon him), then the person has received two forms of life.

Whoever receives the breathe of life of the angel, without that of the Messenger (peace be upon him), the person has then received one of the two lives. Allah, the Almighty said in the Qur'ân,

﴿ أَوَمَن كَانَ مَيْتًا فَأَحْيَيْنَٰهُ وَجَعَلْنَا لَهُۥ نُورًا يَمْشِي بِهِۦ فِي ٱلنَّاسِ كَمَن مَّثَلُهُۥ فِي ٱلظُّلُمَٰتِ لَيْسَ بِخَارِجٍ مِّنْهَا ... ﴾

which means, "Is he who was dead (without Faith by ignorance and disbelief) and We gave him life (by knowledge and Faith) and set for him a light (of Belief) whereby he can walk amongst men, like him who is in the darkness (of disbelief, polytheism and hypocrisy) from which he can never come out?" (Al-An'âm, 6:122)

In this Qur'ânic Verse, Allah, the Almighty made a connection between light and life (knowledge and faith) for the person who accepted Islam, just as He made a connection between death and darkness (disbelief, polytheism and hypocrisy) for the person who turns away from His Book (the Qur'ân).

According to Ibn 'Abbâs and all the commentators, the meaning of the verse is: the person was a straying disbeliever and then Allah guided him.

This verse contains some instructions:

The first one is that: he walks among people with light, while they are in darkness. His likeness and theirs is like some people who lost their way when the night fell upon them, as compared with someone else who has light and walks with it on the road. Such a person sees it and sees that which warns him.

The second one is that: he walks among them with his light, and they benefit from him, due to their need of it.

The third one is that: he walks with his light on the Straight Way on the Day of Resurrection, when the polytheists and hypocrites will remain in the darkness of their disbelief and hypocrisy.

Allah comes in between a person and his heart (i.e. He prevents an evil person from deciding anything).

﴿ ...وَٱعْلَمُوٓا۟ أَنَّ ٱللَّهَ يَحُولُ بَيْنَ ٱلْمَرْءِ وَقَلْبِهِۦ... ﴾

which means, "and know that Allah comes in between a person and his heart (i.e. He prevents an evil person from deciding anything). And verily to Him you shall (all) be gathered." (Al-Anfâl, 8:24)

What is well known about this verse is that Allah, the Almighty comes in between the believer and disbelief, between the disbeliever and belief, and He comes in between those who obey Him and their disobeying Him, and between those who disobey Him and their obeying Him. This is according to Ibn 'Abbâs and the majority of the commentators.

There is another comment about the verse, which is that Allah, the Almighty is near to the person's heart, and that no secret is hidden from Him, for He is in between him and his heart. This is what Al-Wâhidy narrated from Qatâdah, and it seems that this is the most suitable meaning, for response is originally made by the heart. Allah, the Almighty is in between the servant and his heart. He knows whether his heart has responded to Him or not, and whether he has hidden that response or not.

Referring to the first statement, the point of connection is that if you neglect to respond to Allah, then do not feel secure, for He would not make it easy for you to respond after that. He, the Almighty may choose to punish you for leaving it after the truth has been made clear to you. It would then be like the following verses,

﴿ وَنُقَلِّبُ أَفْـِٔدَتَهُمْ وَأَبْصَـٰرَهُمْ كَمَا لَمْ يُؤْمِنُوا۟ بِهِۦٓ أَوَّلَ مَرَّةٍ ... ﴾

which means, "And We shall turn their hearts and their eyes away (from guidance), as they refused to believe therein for the first time." (Al-An'âm, 6:110)

﴿ ...فَلَمَّا زَاغُوٓا۟ أَزَاغَ ٱللَّهُ قُلُوبَهُمْ... ﴾

which means, "So when they turned away (from the Path of Allah), Allah turned their hearts away (from the Right Path)." (As-Saff, 61:5)

﴿ ...فَمَا كَانُوا۟ لِيُؤْمِنُوا۟ بِمَا كَذَّبُوا۟ مِن قَبْلُ... ﴾

which means, "But they were not such as to believe in that which they had rejected before." (Al-A'râf, 7:101)

There is a clear warning not to leave the response with the heart, even if it is responded to with the body.

There is another message in the verse, which is that He, the Almighty combined the Revelation to the command to perform it for them, which is the response, and between destiny and one's faith in it. So it is like the following verses,

﴿ لِمَن شَاءَ مِنكُمْ أَن يَسْتَقِيمَ ۝ وَمَا تَشَاءُونَ إِلَّا أَن يَشَاءَ ٱللَّهُ رَبُّ ٱلْعَالَمِينَ ۝ ﴾

which means, "To whomsoever among you who wills to walk straight, And you will not, unless (it be) that Allah wills, the Lord of the 'Alamîn (mankind, jinns and all that exists)." (At-Takwîr, 81:28-29)

﴿ فَمَن شَاءَ ذَكَرَهُ ۝ وَمَا يَذْكُرُونَ إِلَّا أَن يَشَاءَ ٱللَّهُ ... ۝ ﴾

which means, "So whosoever will (let him read it), and receive admonition (from it)! And they will not receive admonition unless Allah wills." (Al-Muddaththir, 74:55-56)

And surely it is Allah alone Who knows best.

A Precious Gem: Jihad is Ordained for You

Allah, the Almighty says,

﴿ كُتِبَ عَلَيْكُمُ ٱلْقِتَالُ وَهُوَ كُرْهٌ لَّكُمْ ۖ وَعَسَىٰ أَن تَكْرَهُوا شَيْئًا وَهُوَ خَيْرٌ لَّكُمْ ۖ وَعَسَىٰ أَن تُحِبُّوا شَيْئًا وَهُوَ شَرٌّ لَّكُمْ ۗ وَٱللَّهُ يَعْلَمُ وَأَنتُمْ لَا تَعْلَمُونَ ۝ ﴾

which means, "Jihâd (fighting in the Cause of Allah) is ordained for you (Muslims) though you dislike it, and it may be that you dislike a thing which is good for you and that you like a thing which is bad for you. Allah knows but you do not know. (Al-Baqarah, 2:216)

And He, the Exalted and ever Majestic says,

﴿ ... فَإِن كَرِهْتُمُوهُنَّ فَعَسَىٰ أَن تَكْرَهُوا شَيْئًا وَيَجْعَلَ ٱللَّهُ فِيهِ خَيْرًا كَثِيرًا ۝ ﴾

which means, "If you dislike them, it may be that you dislike a thing and Allah brings through it a great deal of good." (An-Nisâ', 4:19)

The first verse is talking about Jihad, which is the perfection of the power of anger and righteous indignation, and the second is about marriage, which is the perfection of the power of lust. The servant hates to face his enemy using his power of anger fearing for himself while this hateful matter is good for him in his life and the next and he likes to make peace and forget about jihad while this matter is bad for him in his life and the next.

Also, the servant sometimes dislikes a woman because of one of her qualities while keeping her as his wife might grant him much good that he is not aware of and sometimes he loves a woman for one of her qualities and keeping her will bring him much evil that he is not aware of. The human being as Allah describes him is unjust and foolish. He should not make his criteria of what is harmful or beneficial for himself according to what he loves or hates, but the criteria should be what Allah has chosen for him in the form of orders and prohibitions.

The best and most useful thing for him is to obey Allah in secret and in public, and the worst and most harmful thing for him is to disobey Allah either secretly or publicly. If he sincerely obeys and worships Allah, every matter that he hates will be good for him but if he abandons obedience and worship, every matter that he loves will be evil and bad for him. Whoever truly knows Allah, His names, and His attributes, will surely know that any distress or harm that has happened to him bears interest and benefits that his mind cannot comprehend and may even benefit the servant in something that he hates.

If the Just Servant Knows the Truth

Generally, things that benefit mankind are found in things that are disliked while harm is found in what man loves. We can see clear examples in the one who is an expert in cultivating, and plants a garden and cares for the trees until they bear fruit and then he begins to cut the leaves and branches as he knows that this is for their good and if he leaves them in that state, their fruit would never be good again. He grafts the trees and clips them and cuts off the weak branches. He appears to be harming them but actually he is seeking their benefit and perfection. He never lets them drink as they want, but according to schedules because it is better for their leaves and it speeds up their growth. Then he cuts away a lot of their leaves although they are their decoration, because this decoration prevents the perfection of their growth. If these trees had a mind to think as animals do, they would think that all this is harmful and is spoiling them while actually it is for their benefit.

Loving parents do the same to their children because they understand the benefits. Sometimes the cure for the child is painful, but the parent will still do it and all this will be done for the sake of mercy and pity. Perhaps the parent will perceive some benefit for the child by not financing him, so he will not give to him, because he knows that these are the important causes of his decay. He also prevents him from many pleasures in order to protect him. The most just among judges, the most merciful among those who are merciful, and the most learned among those who have knowledge, who is more merciful to His servants than themselves, their fathers, and mothers, if He allows them to be inflicted with evil, that will be better for them than not inflicting them. If they had the chance to choose for themselves they would never be able to benefit by it. However, Allah, the Exalted manages their lives according to His knowledge, wisdom, and mercy, whether they like it or not. Only those who know and believe in His names and attributes do not accuse Him or doubt one of His judgments but only those who do not know His names and attributes argue with Him about His judgments and doubt His wisdom and fail to submit to His judgment. They even oppose it with their spoiled minds, false opinions and unjust policies. They neither knew their Lord nor obtain any benefit.

Whenever a servant has this knowledge, he will live in a Paradise on earth before he enters the Paradise of the Hereafter. He will be satisfied and pleased with his Lord and will be satisfied with the paradise in this worldly life. The servant will be pleased with whatever happens to him because he knows that it has been chosen by Allah and this is acceptance of Allah as his Lord, Islam as his religion, and Muhammad as his Messenger. The one who is not able to do this will never taste the sweetness of faith. This pleasure depends upon how much he comprehends the justice of Allah, His wisdom, mercy, and good choice. The more he knows, the more pleasure and satisfaction he will have. Allah judges His servants according to justice, benefit, wisdom, and mercy. The Prophet (peace be upon him) said in his famous invocation to Allah, "Whoever was afflicted with grief and distress and says, **'Allâhumma inny 'abduk, wa ibn 'abdik, wa ibn amatik, nâsiyaty biyadik, mâdin fiyya hukmuk, 'Adlun fiyya qadâ'uk, as'aluka bikul ism huwa lak, sammaita bihi nafsak, aw anzaltahu fy kitâbik, aw 'allamtahu ahadan min khalqik, aw ista'tharta bihi fy 'ilmil-ghaibi 'indik, an taj'ala al-qur'âna rabî'a qalby, wa nûra sadry, wa jalâ' huzny, wa dhahâba hammy** (O Allah! I am Your Servant, the son of Your Servant, the son of Your Maid servant. You have control over me. Your Judgment is executed on me. Your Decree on me is just. I ask You with each Name of Yours by which You have called Yourself, revealed in Your Book, taught to any of Your servants, or kept as a secret in the knowledge of the unseen with You, to make the Qur'ân the spring (delight) of my heart, the light of my chest, the eliminator of my sorrow, the remover of my worries and anxiety),' Allah, the Exalted and Ever-Majestic, will remove his grief and will change his sorrow into happiness." It was said, "O

Messenger of Allah! (Do) we have to learn these words?" He said, "Yes, whoever hears them should learn them."[38]

"Your Decree on me is just" means every judgment including what causes pain or is a punishment. And this judgment is good for the believer as the Prophet (peace be upon him) said, "By He who holds my soul in His hand, the decree of Allah on the believer is always good for him and this is not the case with anyone else except the believer."[39]

Ibn Al-Qaiyim said, "I asked our sheikh, 'Did that apply in the case of committing sins?' He said, 'Yes, with a condition.' By saying "with a condition", he meant that what will follow sins are acts that Allah loves like regretting, asking for forgiveness, being humble, crying, and etc."

A Precious Gem: Asceticism during this Worldly Life

Seeking the Hereafter will not be complete without asceticism in this worldly life, and asceticism during this worldly life will not be complete without two things:

One: recognizing the transitory, mortal, decaying, mean, and imperfect nature of this worldly life and thinking about the pain, which it causes. Whoever seeks this worldly life with all its pleasures, will suffer its pain and grief before gaining what he wished, for if he ever gains it he will suffer grief and sadness after its loosing it.

Two: knowing with certainty that the Hereafter is real and close at hand, and knowing that it is immortal, lasting, and that it contains pleasures and happiness, and that there is a huge difference between it and this worldly life. It is as Allah says,

---

[38] Mentioned above.
[39] Recorded by Muslim, book pertaining to piety and softening the hearts, chapter on every act of a believer is a blessing for him, no.2999.

﴿ وَٱلۡءَاخِرَةُ خَيۡرٞ وَأَبۡقَىٰٓ ﴾

which means, "Although the Hereafter is better and more lasting." (Al-A'lâ, 87:17)

It is perfect and its pleasures and blessings are eternal. These are just some of its characteristics. If man understands these two things he will prefer the next life and will neglect this worldly life. Everyone is naturally disposed to dislike leaving immediate benefits and present pleasures and waits for an expected benefit and longs for the absence of pleasure unless if he discovers the favor of the later one is more than the sooner one and has a strong wish for what is better and higher. But if he prefers this mortal and imperfect world it will be either because he did not realize what is better for him or because he did not want and long for what is better.

Each of these things indicates weakness of faith, mind, and insight. Whoever wants this worldly life and prefers it, he either believes that what is in the Hereafter is better and more lasting or he does not believe in it. If he does not believe, he will be lacking in faith but if he believes and does not prefer the Hereafter, his mind is ill and he is choosing evil for himself.

This is a present and necessary division that the servant must decide on. Preferring this worldly life instead of the Hereafter is either because of lack of faith or an ill mind. These two are the most common causes for preferring this worldly life and that is why the Messenger of Allah (peace be upon him) neglected it and his Companions kept their hearts away from it, abandoned it, and considered it as a prison, not a paradise. If they wanted it they would have gained all the pleasures it contained. The keys of treasures were offered to him (peace be upon him) and he refused and this worldly life presented all its wealth to his companions but they still preferred the Hereafter. They knew that life is only a crossing point and a passage that is not lasting, just like a cloud that will soon move, and a dream that they will soon wake up from.

The Prophet (peace be upon him) said, "What have I to do with this worldly life? I am exactly like a traveler who slept under the shade of a tree, then went and left it."[40] And he (peace be upon him) said, "This world (is so insignificant in comparison) to the Hereafter that it is like one of you dips his finger (and while saying this he pointed with his forefinger) in the ocean and then he sees what has stuck to it."[41] Allah, the Exalted says,

﴿ إِنَّمَا مَثَلُ ٱلْحَيَوٰةِ ٱلدُّنْيَا كَمَاءٍ أَنزَلْنَـٰهُ مِنَ ٱلسَّمَاءِ فَٱخْتَلَطَ بِهِۦ نَبَاتُ ٱلْأَرْضِ مِمَّا يَأْكُلُ ٱلنَّاسُ وَٱلْأَنْعَـٰمُ حَتَّىٰٓ إِذَآ أَخَذَتِ ٱلْأَرْضُ زُخْرُفَهَا وَٱزَّيَّنَتْ وَظَنَّ أَهْلُهَآ أَنَّهُمْ قَـٰدِرُونَ عَلَيْهَآ أَتَىٰهَآ أَمْرُنَا لَيْلًا أَوْ نَهَارًا فَجَعَلْنَـٰهَا حَصِيدًا كَأَن لَّمْ تَغْنَ بِٱلْأَمْسِ ۚ كَذَٰلِكَ نُفَصِّلُ ٱلْـَٔايَـٰتِ لِقَوْمٍ يَتَفَكَّرُونَ ۞ وَٱللَّهُ يَدْعُوٓا۟ إِلَىٰ دَارِ ٱلسَّلَـٰمِ وَيَهْدِى مَن يَشَآءُ إِلَىٰ صِرَٰطٍ مُّسْتَقِيمٍ ۞ ﴾

which means, "Verily the likeness of (this) worldly life is as the water (rain) which We send down from the sky, so by it arises the intermingled produce of the earth of which men and cattle eat until when the earth is clad with its adornments and is beautified, and its people think that they have all the powers of disposal over it, Our Command reaches it by night or by day and We make it like a clean-mown harvest, as if it had not flourished yesterday! Thus do We explain the *Ayât* (proofs, evidences, verses, lessons, signs, revelations, laws, etc.) in

---

[40] Recorded by At-Tirmidhy, book of asceticism, chapter on Akhdh Al-Mâl Bihaqihi, n.2377, and Ibn Mâjah, no.4109.
[41] Recorded by Muslim, book pertaining to paradise, its description its bounties, and its intimates, chapter pertaining to the destruction of the world and assembling on the day of resurrection, no.2858.

detail for the people who reflect. Allah calls to the home of peace (i.e. Paradise, by accepting Allah's religion of Islamic Monotheism and by doing righteous good deeds and abstaining from polytheism and evil deeds) and guides whom He wills to a Straight Path." (Yûnus, 10:24-25)

He told us about the meanness of this worldly life and urged man to avoid it while calling for the Hereafter.

Allah, the Almighty says,

﴿ وَٱضْرِبْ لَهُم مَّثَلَ ٱلْحَيَوٰةِ ٱلدُّنْيَا كَمَآءٍ أَنزَلْنَهُ مِنَ ٱلسَّمَآءِ فَٱخْتَلَطَ بِهِۦ نَبَاتُ ٱلْأَرْضِ فَأَصْبَحَ هَشِيمًا تَذْرُوهُ ٱلرِّيَـٰحُ ۗ وَكَانَ ٱللَّهُ عَلَىٰ كُلِّ شَىْءٍ مُّقْتَدِرًا ۝ ٱلْمَالُ وَٱلْبَنُونَ زِينَةُ ٱلْحَيَوٰةِ ٱلدُّنْيَا ۖ وَٱلْبَـٰقِيَـٰتُ ٱلصَّـٰلِحَـٰتُ خَيْرٌ عِندَ رَبِّكَ ثَوَابًا وَخَيْرٌ أَمَلًا ۝ ﴾

which means, "And put forward to them the example of the life of this world, it is like the water (rain) which We send down from the sky, and the vegetation of the earth mingles with it, and becomes fresh and green. But (later) it becomes dry and broken pieces, which the winds scatter. And Allah is Able to do everything. Wealth and children are the adornment of the life of this world. But the good righteous deeds (five compulsory prayers, deeds of Allah's obedience, good and nice talk, remembrance of Allah with glorification, praises and thanks, etc.), that last, are better with your Lord for rewards and better in respect of hope." (Al-Kahf, 18:45-46)

And He, the Almighty says,

﴿ ٱعْلَمُوٓا۟ أَنَّمَا ٱلْحَيَوٰةُ ٱلدُّنْيَا لَعِبٌ وَلَهْوٌ وَزِينَةٌ وَتَفَاخُرٌ بَيْنَكُمْ وَتَكَاثُرٌ فِى ٱلْأَمْوَٰلِ وَٱلْأَوْلَـٰدِ ۖ كَمَثَلِ غَيْثٍ أَعْجَبَ ٱلْكُفَّارَ نَبَاتُهُۥ ثُمَّ يَهِيجُ فَتَرَىٰهُ مُصْفَرًّا ثُمَّ يَكُونُ

﴿ حُطَٰمًا ۖ وَفِى ٱلْءَاخِرَةِ عَذَابٌ شَدِيدٌ وَمَغْفِرَةٌ مِّنَ ٱللَّهِ وَرِضْوَٰنٌ ۚ وَمَا ٱلْحَيَوٰةُ ٱلدُّنْيَآ إِلَّا مَتَٰعُ ٱلْغُرُورِ ۝ ﴾

which means, "Know that the life of this world is only play and amusement, pomp and mutual boasting among you, and rivalry in respect of wealth and children, as the likeness of vegetation after rain, thereof the growth is pleasing to the tiller; afterwards it dries up and you see it turning yellow; then it becomes straw. But in the Hereafter (there is) a severe torment (for the disbelievers, evil-doers), and (there is) Forgiveness from Allah and (His) Good Pleasure (for the believers, good-doers), whereas the life of this world is only a deceiving enjoyment." (Al-Hadîd, 57:20)

And He, the Almighty says,

﴿ زُيِّنَ لِلنَّاسِ حُبُّ ٱلشَّهَوَٰتِ مِنَ ٱلنِّسَآءِ وَٱلْبَنِينَ وَٱلْقَنَٰطِيرِ ٱلْمُقَنطَرَةِ مِنَ ٱلذَّهَبِ وَٱلْفِضَّةِ وَٱلْخَيْلِ ٱلْمُسَوَّمَةِ وَٱلْأَنْعَٰمِ وَٱلْحَرْثِ ۗ ذَٰلِكَ مَتَٰعُ ٱلْحَيَوٰةِ ٱلدُّنْيَا ۖ وَٱللَّهُ عِندَهُۥ حُسْنُ ٱلْمَـَٔابِ ۝ قُلْ أَؤُنَبِّئُكُم بِخَيْرٍ مِّن ذَٰلِكُمْ ۚ لِلَّذِينَ ٱتَّقَوْا۟ عِندَ رَبِّهِمْ جَنَّٰتٌ تَجْرِى مِن تَحْتِهَا ٱلْأَنْهَٰرُ خَٰلِدِينَ فِيهَا وَأَزْوَٰجٌ مُّطَهَّرَةٌ وَرِضْوَٰنٌ مِّنَ ٱللَّهِ ۗ وَٱللَّهُ بَصِيرٌۢ بِٱلْعِبَادِ ۝ ﴾

which means, "Beautified for men is the love of things they covet; women, children, much of gold and silver (wealth), branded beautiful horses, cattle and well-tilled land. This is the pleasure of the present world's life; but Allah has the excellent return (Paradise with flowing rivers, etc.) with Him. Say: "Shall I inform you of things far better than those? For *Al-Muttaqûn* (the pious - see V.2:2) there are Gardens (Paradise) with their Lord, underneath which rivers flow. Therein (is their) eternal (home) and *Azwâjun Mutahharatun* (purified mates or wives) [i.e. they will have no menses, urine, or stool, etc.], And Allah will be pleased with them. And Allah is All-Seer of the (His) slaves." (Âl-'Imrân, 3:14-15)

And He, the Almighty says,

﴿ ...وَفَرِحُوا بِٱلْحَيَوٰةِ ٱلدُّنْيَا وَمَا ٱلْحَيَوٰةُ ٱلدُّنْيَا فِى ٱلْأَخِرَةِ إِلَّا مَتَـٰعٌ ۞ ﴾

which means, "And they rejoice in the life of the world, whereas the life of this world as compared with the Hereafter is but a brief passing enjoyment." (Ar-Ra'd, 13:26)

Allah, the Exalted threatened those who seek this worldly life alone and neglect His verses. He, the Almighty says,

﴿ إِنَّ ٱلَّذِينَ لَا يَرْجُونَ لِقَآءَنَا وَرَضُوا بِٱلْحَيَوٰةِ ٱلدُّنْيَا وَٱطْمَأَنُّوا بِهَا وَٱلَّذِينَ هُمْ عَنْ ءَايَـٰتِنَا غَـٰفِلُونَ ۞ أُو۟لَـٰٓئِكَ مَأْوَىٰهُمُ ٱلنَّارُ بِمَا كَانُوا۟ يَكْسِبُونَ ۞ ﴾

which means, "Verily, those who hope not for their meeting with Us, but are pleased and satisfied with the life of the present world, and those who are heedless of Our *Ayât* (proofs, evidences, verses, lessons, signs, revelations, etc.), Those, their abode will be the Fire, because of what they used to earn." (Yûnus, 10:7-8)

And He, the Almighty reproached those who sought this worldly life from among the believers when He says,

﴿ يَـٰٓأَيُّهَا ٱلَّذِينَ ءَامَنُوا۟ مَا لَكُمْ إِذَا قِيلَ لَكُمُ ٱنفِرُوا۟ فِى سَبِيلِ ٱللَّهِ ٱثَّاقَلْتُمْ إِلَى ٱلْأَرْضِ أَرَضِيتُم بِٱلْحَيَوٰةِ ٱلدُّنْيَا مِنَ ٱلْأَخِرَةِ فَمَا مَتَـٰعُ ٱلْحَيَوٰةِ ٱلدُّنْيَا فِى ٱلْأَخِرَةِ إِلَّا قَلِيلٌ ﴾

which means, "O you who believe! What is the matter with you, that when you are asked to march forth in the Cause of Allah (i.e. *Jihâd*) you cling heavily to the earth? Are you pleased with the life of this world rather than the Hereafter? But little is the enjoyment of the life of this world as compared with the Hereafter." (At-Tawbah, 9:38)

The more the servant seeks this worldly life and is satisfied with it, the more he will slacken in obeying Allah and seeking the Hereafter. It is enough that Allah says,

﴿ أَفَرَءَيْتَ إِن مَّتَّعْنَٰهُمْ سِنِينَ ۝ ثُمَّ جَآءَهُم مَّا كَانُوا۟ يُوعَدُونَ ۝ مَآ أَغْنَىٰ عَنْهُم مَّا كَانُوا۟ يُمَتَّعُونَ ۝ ﴾

which means, "Tell Me, if We do let them enjoy for years, And afterwards comes to them that (punishment) which they had been promised! All that with which they used to enjoy shall not avail them." (Ash-Shu'arâ', 26:205-207)

And He, the Almighty says,

﴿ وَيَوْمَ يَحْشُرُهُمْ كَأَن لَّمْ يَلْبَثُوٓا۟ إِلَّا سَاعَةً مِّنَ ٱلنَّهَارِ يَتَعَارَفُونَ بَيْنَهُمْ ... ۝ ﴾

which means, "And on the Day when He shall gather (resurrect) them together, (it will be) as if they had not stayed (in the life of this world and graves, etc.) but an hour of a day. They will recognize each other." (Yûnus, 10:45)

And He, the Almighty says,

﴿ ... كَأَنَّهُمْ يَوْمَ يَرَوْنَ مَا يُوعَدُونَ لَمْ يَلْبَثُوٓا۟ إِلَّا سَاعَةً مِّن نَّهَارٍۭ بَلَٰغٌ فَهَلْ يُهْلَكُ إِلَّا ٱلْقَوْمُ ٱلْفَٰسِقُونَ ۝ ﴾

which means, "Therefore be patient (O Muhammad) as did the Messengers of strong will and be in no haste about them (disbelievers). On the Day when they will see that (torment) with which they are promised (i.e. threatened, it will be) as if they had not stayed more than an hour in a single day. (O mankind!

This Qur'ân is sufficient as) a clear Message (or proclamation to save yourself from destruction). But shall any be destroyed except the people who are *Al-Fâsiqûn* (the rebellious, disobedient to Allah)." (Al-A<u>h</u>qâf, 46:35)

And He, the Almighty says,

﴿ يَسْـَٔلُونَكَ عَنِ ٱلسَّاعَةِ أَيَّانَ مُرْسَىٰهَا ۝ فِيمَ أَنتَ مِن ذِكْرَىٰهَآ ۝ إِلَىٰ رَبِّكَ مُنتَهَىٰهَآ ۝ إِنَّمَآ أَنتَ مُنذِرُ مَن يَخْشَىٰهَا ۝ كَأَنَّهُمْ يَوْمَ يَرَوْنَهَا لَمْ يَلْبَثُوٓاْ إِلَّا عَشِيَّةً أَوْ ضُحَىٰهَا ۝ ﴾

which means, "They ask you (O Muhammad) about the Hour, - when will be its appointed time? You have no knowledge to say anything about it, to your Lord belongs (the knowledge of) the term thereof. You (O Muhammad) are only a warner for those who fear it. The Day they see it, (it will be) as if they had not tarried (in this world) except an afternoon or a morning." (An-Nâzi'ât, 79:42-46)

And He, the Almighty says,

﴿ وَيَوْمَ تَقُومُ ٱلسَّاعَةُ يُقْسِمُ ٱلْمُجْرِمُونَ مَا لَبِثُواْ غَيْرَ سَاعَةٍ ... ۝ ﴾

which means, "And on the Day that the Hour will be established, the *Mujrimûn* (criminals, disbelievers, polytheists, sinners, etc.) will swear that they stayed not but an hour." (Ar-Rûm, 30:55)

And He, the Almighty says,

﴿ قَٰلَ كَمْ لَبِثْتُمْ فِى ٱلْأَرْضِ عَدَدَ سِنِينَ ۝ قَالُواْ لَبِثْنَا يَوْمًا أَوْ بَعْضَ يَوْمٍ فَسْـَٔلِ ٱلْعَآدِّينَ ۝ قَٰلَ إِن لَّبِثْتُمْ إِلَّا قَلِيلًا ۖ لَّوْ أَنَّكُمْ كُنتُمْ تَعْلَمُونَ ۝ ﴾

which means, "He (Allah) will say: "What number of years did you stay on earth?" They will say: "We stayed a day or part of a day. Ask of those who keep account." He (Allah) will say: "You stayed not but a little, if you had only known!" (Al-Mu'minûn, 23:112-114)

And He, the Almighty says,

﴿ يَوْمَ يُنفَخُ فِي ٱلصُّورِ وَنَحْشُرُ ٱلْمُجْرِمِينَ يَوْمَئِذٍ زُرْقًا ۝ يَتَخَفَتُونَ بَيْنَهُمْ إِن لَّبِثْتُمْ إِلَّا عَشْرًا ۝ نَحْنُ أَعْلَمُ بِمَا يَقُولُونَ إِذْ يَقُولُ أَمْثَلُهُمْ طَرِيقَةً إِن لَّبِثْتُمْ إِلَّا يَوْمًا ۝ ﴾

which means, "The Day when the Trumpet will be blown (the second blowing): that Day, We shall gather the *Mujrimûn* (criminals, polytheists, sinners, disbelievers in the Oneness of Allah, etc.) *Zurqa*: (blue or blind eyed with black faces) In whispers will they speak to each other (saying): "You stayed not longer than ten (days)." We know very well what they will say, when the best among them in knowledge and wisdom will say: "You stayed no longer than a day!" (Tâhâ, 20:102-104)

Important Rule: The Basis of Goodness

The origin of goodness is to know that whatever Allah wills, will be and whatever He does not will, will not be. Then you will be sure that good deeds are blessings from Allah and you will praise Allah for them and invoke Him not to prevent you from them. You will know that sins are punishments, so you will invoke Him to protect you from committing sins and not to leave you with your own doings either good or bad. Those who know best agree that the origin of goodness is success from Allah and that the origin of evil is the result of being deserted by Allah. And they agree that success is when one is not abandoned by Allah and left to his own devices. So if every good is success from Allah and has nothing to do with the servant, , then its key is supplication, resorting to Allah, and sincere desire to please Him. Whenever the servant is given this key he will be welcomed and if the servant lost this key, the door to goodness will be closed on him.

- The Amir of the believers 'Umar bin Al-Khaṯṯâb said, "I do not care for answering my supplication, I care for the supplication, if you are inspired to supplicate the answer will come with it." According to the intention of the servant, his determination, aim, and desire in this matter, Allah will help and grant him success. Allah grants help to His servants according to their intentions, persistence, desires, and fear and also to extent to which they avoid evil. Allah, the Exalted is the most just of all judges and the best Knower among all those who know. He grants success in the suitable time. He is the All Knowing and the most Wise. Whoever Allah has deserted, it is because he neglected to praise and supplicate to Him and whoever has been granted success by Allah, it is because he praises, supplicates and resorts to Allah. And the base of all that is patience, and its place in faith is like the head in the body; if the head is cut, the body is useless.

Cruelty and Purity of the Heart

There is no harder punishment than when the servant has a cruel heart and moves away from Allah. Hellfire was created to melt such cruel hearts. The most remote heart from Allah is the cruel one. If the heart was cruel, the eye will never shed tears. Cruelty of the heart is caused by increasing four things over and above one's needs: excessive food, sleep, talk, and socializing. When the body is sick, food and drink is no use to it. Likewise when the heart is ill because of desires, advice is useless.

- Whoever wants to purify his heart, must prefer Allah over and above his own desires.

- The hearts that are attached to desires are far away from Allah according to the amount of attachment. The hearts are the vessels that hold the knowledge of the truth, and the most beloved to Him is the one that is most tender, firm, and pure.

- They busied their hearts with this worldly life, and if they had busied themselves with Allah and the Hereafter, they would think about His words and verses and would have returned to them with the most precious wisdom and benefits.

- If the heart was fed by remembering Allah, became satisfied by thinking about Allah, and purified from evil and desires, it would see wonders and be inspired with wisdom.

- Not everyone among those who claim to have acquired knowledge and wisdom, is from their people; the people of knowledge and wisdom are those who revive their hearts by overcoming their desires but those who controlled their hearts and revived their desires, knowledge and wisdom are just words on their tongues.

- Your heart will be ruined from feeling secure and being careless and will grow by remembering Allah and being pious.

- If the hearts neglect the tables (pleasures) of this worldly life they will sit at the tables of the Hereafter among the people of this invitation but if they are satisfied with the tables of this worldly life they will miss the others.

- Longing for Allah and the meeting with Him is like a breeze that blows through the heart and removes the blaze of this worldly life.

- The heart will rest and feel relief if it is settled with Allah and it will worry and be anxious if it is settled with people.

- It is as impossible for the love for Allah to enter the heart that is full of love for this worldly life, as it is for a camel to pass through the eye of a needle.

- If Allah loves His servant, He makes him for Himself, chooses him for His love, and selects him to worship Him. Allah will let His servant's tongue be busy in remembering Him and his limbs will be busy serving Him.

- The heart gets sick as the body does and its cure is in asking for forgiveness and protection. It also becomes rusty like a mirror does and it is polished by remembering Allah. The heart can also be naked like the body and can lose its dress and decoration, which is piety, and it can feel hungry and thirst like the body does and its nourishment is knowledge, love, trust, and offering service to Allah.

Precious Gems

Beware of being careless toward He who grants you life and allows you to breathe as well as providing you with everything, which you need.

- Whoever seeks more and more pleasures and power from this worldly life, and fears a loss in wealth and gains and fails to get rid of an enemy by trusting in Allah, in His arrangements, and good choice for him, has failed to hand all matters over to Allah and be satisfied with His judgments. He will not feel relief from grief and sadness. Whoever refuses to be satisfied with what Allah has decreed and chooses his own arrangements, he will live in distress, pain, and in a bad condition. Allah facilitates the way to Him for His creatures and covers it with a curtain of decree. Whoever is pleased with the arrangements and decree of Allah, His choice for him and willingly submits to His judgments, Allah will remove this curtain in order that the heart can be close to Him and the servant can learn to trust in Him.

- Whoever puts his trust in Allah, will neither ask other than Allah nor argue with Him, nor slacken his effort in the way of Allah.

- Whoever becomes busy with himself, will be distracted by others, and whoever becomes busy with his Lord, will become busy with himself.

- Sincerity is what is not known by any angel to write or by any enemy to spoil, and is that which will not spoil its owner by being proud.

- Satisfaction is when the heart submits to the judgments of Allah.

- People during this worldly life are to be punished according to their intentions. The heart has six places to wander about in: three are low and three are high. The low ones are the worldly life in order to beautify itself to him, a soul to talk to him, and an enemy to seduce him. These are places in which evil and debased souls are wandering. The high ones are knowledge that reveals itself to him, a mind that guides him, and the Lord that he worships.

- Following one's desires and having extended hope is the core of evil. Following one's desires blinds one from seeing what is right, and having extended hope makes one forget the Hereafter and prevents one from preparing for it.

- The servant of Allah cannot be true as long as he is flattering himself or others.

- If Allah wants good for His servant, He would make him admit his sins and prevent him from committing other sins, spend what he has for His sake and be ascetic in what he has, and endure the abuse of others. If Allah wants evil for His servant, He would do the opposite of all that.

- High intentions wander around and get attached to three things: gets to know an attribute that produces and increases love and will, notices a blessing that is the means of increasing praise and obedience, and remembers a sin that is the means of seeking and increasing forgiveness and submission. If one's intention is attached to something other than these three things it will wander in the valleys of seduction and temptation.

- Whoever loves this worldly life, will estimate its value, and he will make himself a slave to it, and it will humiliate him. And whoever neglects it, will notice his great value, and it will serve him, and it will humiliate itself for him.

- The traveler will reach his destination if he continues on his way, adheres to the right path, and wakes up at night. But he who strays from the right path and sleeps at night, how can he reach his destination?

A Precious and Valuable Gem: The (Religious) Scholar Whose Deeds are Inconsistent with his Knowledge

The religious scholars who prefer and love this worldly life shall surely speak other than the truth concerning their judgments and religious verdicts. Verily, the judgments of Allah usually contradict the desires of people especially the rulers and those who follow their whims, as their aims cannot be attained except by opposing the truth.

Accordingly, if the ruler and the religious scholar seek position and power and follow their desires, indeed they will not be able to fulfill their aims except by deviating from the truth, especially if there is a doubtful matter involved. The doubtful matter will agree with the desires of man, and vanity will prevail. As a result, righteousness will disappear, and truth will vanish.

However, there is no doubtful matter in the truth, so how can wrong doers dare to oppose it openly, assuming that they will be able to repent afterwards. Such behavior is mentioned in a Qur'ânic verse in which Allah says,

﴿ فَخَلَفَ مِنۢ بَعۡدِهِمۡ خَلۡفٌ أَضَاعُوا۟ ٱلصَّلَوٰةَ وَٱتَّبَعُوا۟ ٱلشَّهَوَٰتِ ... ﴾

which means, "Then, there has succeeded them a posterity who have given up As-Salât (the prayers) [i.e. made their Salât (prayers) to be lost, either by not offering them or by not offering them perfectly or by not offering them at their proper fixed times, etc.] and have followed lusts." (Mariam, 19:59)

They were also mentioned in another verse, in which Allah says,

﴿ فَخَلَفَ مِنۢ بَعۡدِهِمۡ خَلۡفٌ وَرِثُوا۟ ٱلۡكِتَٰبَ يَأۡخُذُونَ عَرَضَ هَٰذَا ٱلۡأَدۡنَىٰ وَيَقُولُونَ سَيُغۡفَرُ لَنَا وَإِن يَأۡتِهِمۡ عَرَضٌ مِّثۡلُهُۥ يَأۡخُذُوهُ أَلَمۡ يُؤۡخَذۡ عَلَيۡهِم مِّيثَٰقُ ٱلۡكِتَٰبِ أَن لَّا يَقُولُوا۟ عَلَى ٱللَّهِ إِلَّا ٱلۡحَقَّ وَدَرَسُوا۟ مَا فِيهِ وَٱلدَّارُ ٱلۡأٓخِرَةُ خَيۡرٌ لِّلَّذِينَ يَتَّقُونَ أَفَلَا تَعۡقِلُونَ ﴾

which means, "Then after them succeeded an (evil) generation, which inherited the Book, but they chose (for themselves) the goods of this low life (evil pleasures of this world) saying (as an excuse): "(Everything) will be forgiven to us." And if (again) the offer of the like (evil pleasures of this world) came their way, they would (again) seize them (would commit those sins). Was not the covenant of the Book taken from them that they would not say about Allah anything but the truth? And they have studied what is in it (the Book). And the home of the Hereafter is better for those who are Al-Muttaqûn (the pious). Do not you then understand?" (Al-A'râf, 7:169)

Allah, the Exalted, informs us that those wrong doers have chosen the goods of this low life (the evil pleasures of this world) despite being aware of its unlawfulness. Moreover, they say, as an excuse, "(Everything) will be forgiven to us." And if (again) the offer of the like (evil pleasures of this world) came their way, they would (again) seize them (would commit those sins), so they are insistent upon that, and that is the reason why they dare to utter falsehood against Allah, assuming that the judgment and the religion of Allah are implied therein.

Either they know the fact that the religion and the judgment of Allah contradict their claims, or they do not know. The result is that sometimes they utter falsehood against Allah, or else they say what is unlawful.

On the other hand, the pious know quite well that the Hereafter is better than this worldly life, so loving leadership and following one's desires would not be a temptation to them, so they would never prefer this worldly life to the Hereafter. They have only one path, which is abiding by the Glorious Qur'ân and the Sunnah. Besides, they seek help in patience and prayer, think deeply about this worldly life, its transient nature and its inferiority, and they compare it with the Hereafter, its greatness and the fact that it is eternal.

Following one's desires can blind the heart in a way that makes it confused between the Sunnah and innovation in religion. Sometimes, one may be confused whether or not an action is based on the Sunnah or on an innovation in religion. In fact, when misunderstandings like this occur, it is the fault of religious scholars as they prefer this worldly life and follow the rulers, and their vain desires. They are mentioned in these verses in which Allah says,

﴿ وَٱتْلُ عَلَيْهِمْ نَبَأَ ٱلَّذِىٓ ءَاتَيْنَٰهُ ءَايَٰتِنَا فَٱنسَلَخَ مِنْهَا فَأَتْبَعَهُ ٱلشَّيْطَٰنُ فَكَانَ مِنَ ٱلْغَاوِينَ ۝ وَلَوْ شِئْنَا لَرَفَعْنَٰهُ بِهَا وَلَٰكِنَّهُۥٓ أَخْلَدَ إِلَى ٱلْأَرْضِ وَٱتَّبَعَ هَوَىٰهُ ۚ فَمَثَلُهُۥ كَمَثَلِ ٱلْكَلْبِ إِن تَحْمِلْ عَلَيْهِ يَلْهَثْ أَوْ تَتْرُكْهُ يَلْهَث ۚ ذَّٰلِكَ مَثَلُ ٱلْقَوْمِ ٱلَّذِينَ كَذَّبُوا۟ بِـَٔايَٰتِنَا ۚ فَٱقْصُصِ ٱلْقَصَصَ لَعَلَّهُمْ يَتَفَكَّرُونَ ۝ ﴾

which means, "And recite (O Muhammad) to them the story of him to whom We gave Our Ayât (proofs, evidences, verses, lessons, signs, revelations, etc.), but he threw them away, so Shaitân (Satan) followed him up, and he became of those who went astray. And had We willed, We would surely have elevated him therewith but he clung to the earth and followed his own vain desire. So his description is the description of a dog: if you drive him away, he lolls his tongue out, or if you leave him alone, he (still) lolls his tongue out." (Al-A'râf, 7:175-176)

So, this is the likeness of the devious scholar of religion whose deeds contradict his knowledge.

The previous verses dispraised this behavior as follows:

One: He has gone astray after having been knowledgeable, and he has knowingly chosen disbelief over faith.

Two: He abandoned faith entirely with no return, so, he threw away the Ayât (proofs, evidences, verses, lessons, signs, revelations, etc.), like the serpent which throws away its skin.

So, if there was any remnant thereof, he could not throw it away.

Three: Satan controlled him and so he tempted and seduced him, and that is why Allah says, "So Satan followed him up," and He did not say, "pursue him", because following up means reaching and attaining him, which is much more eloquent than saying, "pursue him," as far as meaning and expression are concerned.

Four: He has erred after having been guided, which means that he has gone astray in knowledge and in intention, which is related to the corruption of his intention and deeds. Going astray is related to the corruption of knowledge and belief, and the corruption of one side entails the corruption of the other.

Five: If Allah, the Exalted, had so willed, He could have elevated him with knowledge, which would have prevented his destruction. In other words, if he was not knowledgeable, it would have been much better for him, and would have meant a lesser torment for him.

Six: Allah, the Exalted, informed us about his wicked intention, mentioning that he has preferred inferiority rather than the most honorable and the most righteous.

Seven: His inferior choice was not chosen because of an idea that crossed his mind, on the contrary, it was chosen due to his desire to cling to the earth. Clinging means permanent adherence, as if it was said, "He is sticking to the earth." The Qur'ânic expression described his inclination to this worldly life by referring to his clinging to the earth, because the worldly life is the earth, and those who are living therein, and everything that can be extracted thereof, either for adornment or enjoyment.

Eight: He deviated from the right path following his vain desires, so his own desire resembles a leader who should be followed.

Nine: He, the Almighty compared him to a dog, which is the most low amongst creatures, because of its greed.

Ten: He compares his covetousness to this worldly life and his impatience thereto and his grief of being deprived thereof by the lolling out of the dog's tongue, whether it is left alone or driven away. Accordingly, if that person is left alone, then he will be covetous of this worldly life, and if he is advised he will still be covetous of this worldly life. He clings to covetousness like the dog with its tongue lolling out. Ibn Qutaibiyah said, "Surely everyone pants because they are exhausted or thirsty, except dogs, for it is their habit to pant while lolling their tongues out in all cases, whether they are exhausted or not, and whether they are thirsty or not, and that is why the Qur'ânic expression compared it to the disbeliever, asserting that he has gone astray whether he is advised or left on his own. This is like the dog whether it is left alone or driven away.

A Precious Gem: The Ignorant Worshipper and the Immoral (Religious) Scholar

We have previously mentioned the case of the religious scholar who prefers this worldly life rather than the Hereafter. However, the mistake of the ignorant worshipper is rejecting knowledge, its verdicts, and his adherence to imagination and vain desires.

Sufyân bin 'Uyainah and others said, "Beware of the trial of the immoral (religious) scholar and that of the ignorant worshipper, for both are apparent trials. The latter avoids knowledge out of ignorance, and the former calls for wrong doings out of immorality.

Allah, the Exalted, sets the example of the ignorant worshiper in the Qur'ânic verse by saying,

﴿ كَمَثَلِ ٱلشَّيْطَٰنِ إِذْ قَالَ لِلْإِنسَٰنِ ٱكْفُرْ فَلَمَّا كَفَرَ قَالَ إِنِّى بَرِىٓءٌ مِّنكَ إِنِّىٓ أَخَافُ ٱللَّهَ رَبَّ ٱلْعَٰلَمِينَ ۞ فَكَانَ عَٰقِبَتَهُمَآ أَنَّهُمَا فِى ٱلنَّارِ خَٰلِدَيْنِ فِيهَا ۚ وَذَٰلِكَ جَزَٰٓؤُا۟ ٱلظَّٰلِمِينَ ﴾

which means, "Their allies deceived them) like Shaitân (Satan), when he says to man: "Disbelieve in Allah." But when (man) disbelieves in Allah, Shaitân (Satan) says: "I am free of you, I fear Allah, the Lord of the 'Alamîn (mankind, jinns and all that exists)! So the end of both will be that they will be in the Fire, abiding therein. Such is the recompense of the Zâlimûn (i.e. polytheists, wrong-doers, disbelievers in Allah and in His Oneness, etc.)." (Al-Hashr, 59:16-17)

His story is well known, for he has based his life on worshipping Allah unknowingly, so Satan seized the opportunity and seduced him causing his disbelief. So, this is the end of every ignorant worshipper who unconsciously disbelieves, and the other one is the final end of every immoral scholar who prefers this worldly life rather than the Hereafter.

Allah, the Exalted, made His servant's pleasure and satisfaction with this worldly life, besides his heedlessness of knowing the Ayât (proofs, evidences, verses, lessons, signs, revelations, etc.) of Allah, and acting thereupon, as a reason for the servant's misery and destruction. Those two attitudes (i.e. satisfaction with this worldly life and heedlessness of the Ayât of Allah) will not be found except in a heart, which disbelieves in the Hereafter, and does not yearn for the meeting with Allah.

If anyone sincerely believes in the Hereafter, he would never be satisfied with this worldly life nor would he be heedless of the Ayât of Allah.

If you think deeply about the human condition, you will find this trend prevalent amongst them; verily they are the inhabitants of the world. However, only a few of them contradict this trend, and that is why they are alienated from the majority. Every side has its own business, different knowledge, intentions and ways of life. Allah says,

﴿ إِنَّ ٱلَّذِينَ لَا يَرْجُونَ لِقَآءَنَا وَرَضُوا۟ بِٱلْحَيَوٰةِ ٱلدُّنْيَا وَٱطْمَأَنُّوا۟ بِهَا وَٱلَّذِينَ هُمْ عَنْ ءَايَٰتِنَا غَٰفِلُونَ ۝ أُو۟لَٰٓئِكَ مَأْوَىٰهُمُ ٱلنَّارُ بِمَا كَانُوا۟ يَكْسِبُونَ ۝ ﴾

which means, "Verily, those who hope not for their meeting with Us, but are pleased and satisfied with the life of the present world, and those who are heedless of Our Ayât (proofs, evidences, verses, lessons, signs, revelations, etc.), Those, their abode will be the Fire, because of what they used to earn." (Yûnus, 10:7-8)

Allah describes the opponents of this trend and their final end in another verse by saying,

﴿ إِنَّ ٱلَّذِينَ ءَامَنُوا۟ وَعَمِلُوا۟ ٱلصَّٰلِحَٰتِ يَهْدِيهِمْ رَبُّهُم بِإِيمَٰنِهِمْ تَجْرِى مِن تَحْتِهِمُ ٱلْأَنْهَٰرُ فِى جَنَّٰتِ ٱلنَّعِيمِ ۝ ﴾

which means, "Verily, those who believe [in the Oneness of Allah along with the six articles of Faith, i.e. to believe in Allah, His Angels, His Books, His Messengers, Day of Resurrection, and Al-Qadar (Divine Preordainments) - Islâmic Monotheism], and do deeds of righteousness, their Lord will guide them through their Faith; under them will flow rivers in the Gardens of delight (Paradise)." (Yûnus, 10:9)

The belief of such people in the meeting with Allah brings about an unsatisfied feeling toward this worldly life, and an ardent desire to remember Allah. Verily, this is the impact of the belief in the meeting with Him, while the previously mentioned is the impact of disbelief and heedlessness concerning the meeting with Him.

A Great and Precious Gem: The Best Acquirement for the Soul

Knowledge and faith are the best acquirements for the hearts and souls of man, by which the servant (of Allah) can be elevated in this worldly life and in the Hereafter. That is why Allah, the Exalted, mentioned them both in the Qur'ânic verse in which He says,

﴿ وَقَالَ ٱلَّذِينَ أُوتُوا۟ ٱلْعِلْمَ وَٱلْإِيمَٰنَ لَقَدْ لَبِثْتُمْ فِى كِتَٰبِ ٱللَّهِ إِلَىٰ يَوْمِ ٱلْبَعْثِ... ﴾

which means, "And those who have been bestowed with knowledge and faith will say: "Indeed you have stayed according to the Decree of Allah, until the Day of Resurrection." (Ar-Rûm, 30:56)

In another verse He, the Almighty says,

﴿ ...يَرْفَعِ ٱللَّهُ ٱلَّذِينَ ءَامَنُوا۟ مِنكُمْ وَٱلَّذِينَ أُوتُوا۟ ٱلْعِلْمَ دَرَجَٰتٍ... ﴾

which means, "Allah will exalt in degree those of you who believe, and those who have been granted knowledge." (Al-Mujâdalah, 58:11)

Such people are the most righteous and they deserve the highest degree. However, most people misinterpret the essence of knowledge and faith by which happiness and superiority are attained. Indeed, each sect claims that the knowledge and faith to which they belong are those that lead to happiness. On the contrary, most sects lack true faith that leads to salvation, as well as elevated knowledge, to the extent that they block the means to knowledge and faith that were revealed to the Messenger (peace be upon him) to which he called the nation, namely that knowledge which he and his Companions adhered to, and based their lifestyles on.

Maleficent Knowledge

Each sect believes that it has the correct knowledge by which it rejoices. Allah says,

﴿ فَتَقَطَّعُوٓاْ أَمْرَهُم بَيْنَهُمْ زُبُرًا ۖ كُلُّ حِزْبٍۭ بِمَا لَدَيْهِمْ فَرِحُونَ ۝ ﴾

which means, "But they (men) have broken their religion among them into sects, each group rejoicing in its belief." (Al-Mu'minûn, 23:53)

Indeed, every sect offers arguments, opinions and falsehood rather than pure knowledge, an idea which was asserted by Hammâd bin Zaid[42] when he said, "I asked Ayyûb[43] whether knowledge today is prevailing or if it was prevailing in previous periods," to which he said, 'Today argumentation prevails, while in the past, knowledge prevailed."

Thus, this well-versed scholar distinguished between knowledge and argumentation, for there were so many books and yet so much argumentation, and discussion and disputes, and the knowledge that had been revealed by Allah to the Messenger (peace be upon him) was neglected. Allah says,

﴿ فَمَنْ حَآجَّكَ فِيهِ مِنۢ بَعْدِ مَا جَآءَكَ مِنَ ٱلْعِلْمِ ... ۝ ﴾

---

[42] He is called Hammâd bin Zaid bin Dirham Al-Juhdamy. He was the most eminent Sheikh in Iraq. He was well-versed in Hadîth. He died in 179 A.H. Refer to: Tahdhîb At-Tahdhîb, vol. 3, p. 9, Al-Jarh wat-Ta'dîl, vol.3, p. 617, Târîkh Al-Bukhâry Al-Kabîr, vol. 3, p. 25, Sair A'lâm An-Nubalâ', vol. 7, p. 456.

[43] He is called Ayyûb bin Abu Tamîmah Kîsân As-Sikhtiyâny Al-Basry Al-'Anbary, Al-'Andhy, Al-Ghanwiy, Abu Bakr, the most eminent amongst religious scholars during his era. He was trustworthy. He died in 131 A.H. Refer to: Tahdhîb At-Tahdhîb, vol. 1, p. 397, Al-Jarh wat-Ta'dîl, vol.2, p. 257, Târîkh Al-Bukhâry Al-Kabîr, vol. 1, p. 409, Sair A'lâm An-Nubalâ', vol. 6, p. 15.

which means, "Then whoever disputes with you concerning him ['Iisa (Jesus)] after (all this) knowledge that has come to you." (Âl-'Imrân, 3:61)

Allah, the Almighty says also,

﴿ ...وَلَئِنِ ٱتَّبَعْتَ أَهْوَآءَهُم بَعْدَ ٱلَّذِى جَآءَكَ مِنَ ٱلْعِلْمِ... ﴾

which means, "And if you (O Muhammad) were to follow their (Jews and Christians) desires after what you have received of Knowledge (i.e. the Qur'ân)..." (Al-Baqarah, 2:120)

In another verse, He, the Almighty describes the Qur'ân saying,

﴿ ...أَنزَلَهُۥ بِعِلْمِهِۦ... ﴾

which means, "He has sent it down with His Knowledge." (An-Nisâ', 4:166)

Which means that the Qur'ân is the knowledge of Allah.

After a long period of time passed, most people adopted suspicious ideas, and false thoughts and concepts as if they were the core of knowledge, about which they wrote several books, leaving no stone unturned in such initiatives, to the extent that they wasted a lot of time in accumulating papers and darkening the hearts of man. They went beyond all limits by claiming that no knowledge is found in the Glorious Qur'ân and the Sunnah, assuming the their proofs are literal, while the truth is that they were lacking in knowledge and conviction.

Satan seized the opportunity to make them obsessed with these misconceptions, so he succeeded to drive the hearts away from knowledge and faith, the same as the serpent, which throws its skin away.

The eminent Imam Shamsud-dîn Ibn Al-Qaiyim said, "One of my companions was one of the followers of those so-called scholars, and he was studying one their books without memorizing the Glorious Qur'ân, so he told him, 'It is better for you to memorize the Qur'ân first.' The other one responded, 'There is no knowledge in the Glorious Qur'ân.'"

Ibn Al-Qaiyim added, "One of those who adopted this trend told me, 'We just listened to the Hadith in order to attain its blessings regardless of the knowledge implied therein, for others sufficed us in this task. We rely on their understanding and judgments.'"

He added, "Our Sheikh told me once in describing those people that they resorted to the chiefs of those sects and attained nothing but contemptible desires. To prove this fact, namely that their misconceptions are not considered the knowledge of Allah, is the contradictions and differences included therein. Allah says,

﴿ ...وَلَوْ كَانَ مِنْ عِندِ غَيْرِ ٱللَّهِ لَوَجَدُوا فِيهِ ٱخْتِلَٰفًا كَثِيرًا ﴾

which means, "Had it been from other than Allah, they would surely have found therein many contradictions." (An-Nisâ', 4:82)

This verse proves that within the knowledge of Allah, there is no contradiction, on the other hand, whatever is contradictory is surely not from Allah, for how can misconceptions, suspicions, and opinions be considered the religion revealed by Allah and sent to His Messenger? Glorified be Allah! Indeed this is a false charge.

On the other hand, the knowledge of the venerable Companions of which they used to study was something other than the misconceptions of those liars. Al-Hâkim narrated in the biography of Abu 'Abdullâh Al-Bukhâry that the Companions of the Messenger of Allah (peace be upon him) used to gather for the sake of learning the Glorious Qur'ân and the Sunnah regardless of personal views or analogy.

Chapter: Faith and Those Who Disagree with It

The majority of people abandon faith, as Allah says,

﴿ وَمَآ أَكۡثَرُ ٱلنَّاسِ وَلَوۡ حَرَصۡتَ بِمُؤۡمِنِينَ ۝ ﴾

which means, "And most of mankind will not believe even if you desire it eagerly." (Yûsuf, 12:103)

The faith of the majority of believers is incomplete but sure faith, which means to believe in what the Messenger (peace be upon him) was sent with, and to believe by knowing, learning, declaring, and loving, means to know its opposite and hate it. This is the faith of the pious of this nation and of the special ones of the Messenger and it is the faith of the great companion Abu Bakr and those like him. Most people merely declare the existence of the Creator and that He alone created the Heavens and the earth and what is between them. It is to be noted that even the idol worshippers from the Quraish and others like them believed in this.

To most people faith is simply reciting the two declarations of faith either accompanied by deeds or not, and whether the heart believes in them or not.

To others faith is just a heart that believes that Allah, the Exalted is the Creator of the Heavens and the Earth and that Muhammad is His servant and Messenger, even if a person did not say it with his tongue or perform any deeds. And even if he insults Allah and His Messenger and commits the gravest of sins, he is a believer as long as he believes in the oneness of Allah and the Prophethood of Muhammad (peace be upon him).

To others faith is denying the attributes of Allah, the Exalted like the fact that He established Himself on the throne, His words, books, hearing, sight, will, powers, wishes, love, hate, and other attributes that He described Himself with or His Messenger described Him with. To them, faith is to deny all these facts and they support their opinions by quoting those who deny and lie about these matters. Those who argue with each other and accuse each other of lying and those about whom 'Umar bin Al-Kha<u>tt</u>âb and Imam A<u>h</u>mad said, "They disagree in The Book, disagree with it, and agree on deserting it."

To others, faith is worshiping Allah according to their inclinations and desires without any restrictions from what the Messenger (peace be upon him) ordered us to do.

Faith to others is the state in which they found their fathers and ancestors, regardless of this state, and their faith is based upon two things:

One: This is the saying of our fathers and ancestors.

Two: Whatever they said is the truth.

Faith to others is simply maintaining high moral standards, good treatment, being cheerful, thinking good of others, and deserting people who commit sins.

To others faith is deserting this worldly life and its pleasures, emptying the heart of it and renouncing worldly pleasures. If they find a man like that they make him the best of the people of faith even if he is far away from faith in both knowledge and deeds. But worse than that, are those, who consider faith to be mere knowledge even if it is not accompanied by good deeds.

Faith is something other than all that. It is a compound reality that includes knowing what the Messenger came with, believing in it, declaring it verbally, following it out of love and submission, working and abiding by it both secretly and publicly, obeying it, and calling others to it as much as possible. To complete one's faith, you should seek Allah alone in love, hate, giving, and preventing, and Allah alone must be your Lord and the only One whom you worship. The path, which leads to that is by following His Messenger secretly and publicly and keeping your heart away from anything other than Allah and His Messenger.

- Whoever keeps himself busy seeking Allah instead of himself, Allah will save him from himself, and whoever keeps himself busy with Allah more than people, Allah will save him from people. Whoever keeps himself busy with himself rather than Allah, Allah will leave him to himself, and whoever busies himself with people rather than Allah, Allah will leave him to the people.

A Valuable and Precious Gem: The Origin of Happiness

Whoever abandons habits for the sake of someone or something other than Allah, will surely suffer hard and difficult times. However, whoever abandons habits for the sake of Allah sincerely from his heart, he will not suffer from leaving it except at the beginning so that his credibility will be examined. If he bears this pain it will be turned into pleasure. Ibn Sîrîn said, "I heard Shuraih swearing by Allah that a servant, when deserting something, for the sake of Allah never suffers from its loss." It was said, "Whoever abandoned anything for the sake of Allah; Allah will compensate him with what is better. And compensation is of different kinds and the best is to be compensated by Allah with His love, and satisfaction within his heart, its strength, activity, happiness, and contentment.

The most Foolish among People is he who Goes Astray at the End of his Journey while he was about to Reach his Destination

- The mind of man that is supported with success see that what the Messenger (peace be upon him) brought to us is right and that it agrees with reason and wisdom, but the ill minds see a contradiction between reason, wisdom, and Islamic law.

- The means to attain closeness to Allah is to follow the Sunnah secretly and publicly, resort to Allah, and seek Him alone in our words and deeds. No one reaches Allah except through these three and no one separates from Allah except through leaving these three, or one of them.

- The origins of happiness are based upon three things, and each one of them has an opposite and whoever lost one of these will get its opposite: monotheism and its opposite, which is polytheism, Sunnah and it opposite, which is innovation, and obedience and disobedience. All these three have one opposite, which is a heart that fails to seek Allah and the pleasures He promises, and fails to fear Allah and the punishments He promises for the wrong doers.

A Valuable and Important Rule: The People of Guidance and the People of Misguidance

Allah, the Exalted says,

﴿ وَكَذَٰلِكَ نُفَصِّلُ ٱلْآيَٰتِ وَلِتَسْتَبِينَ سَبِيلُ ٱلْمُجْرِمِينَ ﴾

which means, "And thus do We explain the *Ayât* (proofs, evidences, verses, lessons, signs, revelations, etc.) in detail, that the way of the *Mujrimûn* (criminals, polytheists, sinners), may become manifest." (Al-An'âm, 6:55)

And He, the Almighty says,

﴿ وَمَن يُشَاقِقِ ٱلرَّسُولَ مِنۢ بَعْدِ مَا تَبَيَّنَ لَهُ ٱلْهُدَىٰ وَيَتَّبِعْ غَيْرَ سَبِيلِ ٱلْمُؤْمِنِينَ نُوَلِّهِۦ مَا تَوَلَّىٰ ... ﴾

which means, "And whoever contradicts and opposes the Messenger (Muhammad) after the right path has been shown clearly to him, and follows other than the believers' way, We shall keep him in the path he has chosen." (An-Nisâ', 4:115)

Allah, the Exalted shows in detail, the paths of the believers and those of the sinners, as well as the consequences of both, the deeds of both, the friends and supporters of both, along with granting success to one of them, and the causes behind this success, and the causes of failure. Allah clarified the two matters in His Book, and revealed and explained them to the extent that we can see and differentiate between them as we see and differentiate between light and darkness.

Those who know Allah, His Book, and His religion know in detail the path of the believers and the path of the sinners. The two paths were revealed in front of them like as road, which reaches its destination and a road, which does not. Those who know the best are the most useful to people, and they have the most useful advice. That is why the Companions were distinguished more than all those who came after them until the Day of Resurrection. They were brought up amid the paths of polytheism and the ways that lead to destruction and they know it in detail, then the Messenger (peace be upon him) was sent to them. He led them out of this darkness to the path of light and to the straight way. They came out of darkness to complete light, from polytheism to monotheism, from ignorance to knowledge, from sin to goodness, from injustice to justice, and from blindness and confusion to insight and right guidance. They knew the value of what they received and what they had, as the goodness and benefit of matters becomes clear after knowing the opposite. They loved and their love increased for what they received and what they became. And their hate increased for what they left behind. They were the most loving people to monotheism, faith, and Islam and the most to hate its opposite. They knew the path in detail.

Preference

Some of those who came after the Companions were brought up in Islam and did not know its opposite, so some details were confusing to them concerning the path of the believers and the path of the disbelievers. This is because confusion occurs when one has only a little knowledge of one or both paths. As 'Umar bin Al-Khattâb said, "The ties of Islam decreased one by one with the people who were brought up in Islam and did not know the pre-Islamic era." This shows the perfect knowledge that 'Umar (may Allah be pleased with him) had. He knew the pre-Islamic era and its rules, which encompassed all that disagreed with what the Messenger (peace be upon him) was sent with, and all that is related to ignorance and that which contradicted the Messenger (peace be upon him).

Those, who do not know the path of the sinners and it is not obvious to him may consider the sinners to be believers, as has happened in this nation. Some people do not know the matters of belief, knowledge, or deeds and so take the disbelievers and enemies of the Messengers as friends. They considered matters as lawful while they are forbidden by Allah and His Messenger. This happened to the people of innovations from among Al-Jahmiyyah, Al-Qadariyah, Al-Khawârij, Ar-Rawâfid, and others from among those who created an innovation, called for it, and accused of disbelief whoever disagrees with it.

Such people belong to four groups:

Group One: those who know both the paths of the believers and that of the disbelievers in detail and prefer the path of the believers both in knowledge and deeds.

Group Two: those who neither know this or that and they are like animals and closer to the path of the disbelievers and they follow it.

Group Three: those who care more to know the path of the believers alone and not its opposite. He only knows its opposite through disagreeing with it and in a general way. Someone once wrote to 'Umar bin Al-Khattâb asking him about the best among two men: a man, who does not think about desires and a man who fights his desires seeking Allah. So 'Umar wrote that whoever longs for his desires and sins but abandons them seeking Allah is among those whom Allah had tested their hearts for piety and for them is forgiveness and a great reward.

So whoever knows about innovation, polytheism, and its paths, hated it for the sake of Allah, was cautious about them, warned others about them, pushed them away, did not let them harm his faith or cause doubts, and his insight increased by knowing them and his hate increased, is better than the one whose desires did not enter his heart. The more they came to the heart and tempted him, the more his love increased in the right and fought against them and the more his faith will become stronger. He who is tempted by these desires and sins, regardless of the way they came to him and he refused and fought against them, he will love their opposite more and long for it. Allah afflicts His believing servant with these desires and sins in order to make him love what is better than them and more useful and to fight against himself for the sake of Allah only. This struggle will bring him closer to Allah. Whenever his soul tempts him and he longs for it, he will change this longing and desire to another direction, which is the superior kind. Unlike the empty and cold soul even if it longs for what is superior it will differ from the other. There is a difference between he who travels to his beloved walking on a firebrand and thorns and he who rides fine animals on his way and between such a one and another who prefers his beloved while fighting against others. Allah, the Exalted afflicts His servants with desires either to be veil between them or to be a way to seek the pleasure of Allah and closeness to Him.

Group Four: those who know in detail the path of evil, innovations, and polytheism and the path of the believers. This is the case of many among those who compare nations and the people of innovations. , This is obvious for those who have read their books. Whoever knows the path of evil, injustice, and decay, was from among its people, but then repented, and returned to the path of the believers and was good, and his knowledge of this path will be general and he will not know its details like he who spent his life studying its ways.

The meaning is that: Allah, the Exalted and ever Majestic, likes that you know the path of His enemy so that you may avoid and hate it, as He likes you to know the path of His people in order to love and follow it. Such knowledge has a great deal of benefit that Allah alone knows because of His wisdom, and the perfection of His names and attributes. This is the greatest proof of the Might and Justice of Allah, His ownership, Divine power, love, hate, reward and punishment.

Those who are in need wait at the door of Allah asking for their needs, while the people who love Him are close to Him. If He wishes to fulfill the need of any of them, He would show mercy to them and give them honor. Surely to be far away from Allah is like being beaten and punished.

Chapter: Ten Useless Matters

There are ten useless matters; knowledge that is not acted on, the deed that has neither sincerity nor is based on following the righteous examples of others, money that is hoarded, as the owner neither enjoys it during this life nor obtains any reward for it in the Hereafter, the heart that is empty; has neither love nor longing for Allah, and does not want to be close to Him, a body that does not obey and serve Allah, loving Allah without following His orders or seeking His pleasure, time that is not spent in expiating sins or seizing opportunities to do good, a mind that thinks about what is useless, serving those who will not bring you close to Allah nor will benefit you in your life, hoping and fearing whoever is under the authority of Allah and is in His hand; has no authority over himself either to do good, bad, bring about death, life, or to resurrect himself.

However, the greater of these matters are wasting the heart and wasting time. Wasting the heart is done by preferring this worldly life more than the Hereafter, and wasting time is done by having incessant hope. Decay occurs by following one's desires and having incessant hope while all goodness is found in following the right path and preparing oneself to meet Allah.

How strange it is that when a servant of Allah has a problem, he seeks the help of Allah but he never asks Allah to cure his heart before it dies of ignorance, neglect, fulfilling one's desires and being involved in innovations. Indeed, when the heart dies, he will never feel the significance or impact of his sins.

Chapter: The Right to Submit to Allah

Allah, the Exalted gave His servant an order, wrote a judgment that He will fulfill, and a blessing that He will bestow. The servant will never escape from these three things. The judgment is of two kinds: either disasters or defects.

The individual is a servant of Allah during all these three and the most beloved to Allah among His creatures is he who knows his duties of being a servant of Allah and fulfills this right. Such people are those who are closest to Allah, while the farthest from Him is he who fails to be a true servant of Allah on all these three levels; and that rule becomes suspended for him in both deeds and knowledge. Being a servant of Allah in His order is to sincerely obey and follow the example of the Messenger of Allah (peace be upon him). Being a servant of Allah in His forbiddance is to avoid what He has forbidden while fearing, honoring, and loving Him. Being a servant of Allah in His judgment of disasters is to be patient, and to be satisfied with them, which is a higher rank, and moreover to praise Allah for them and this is even higher than satisfaction. He will be able to do that if love for Allah fills his heart, and if he knows that Allah chooses what is best for him. Surely, Allah is merciful to him, and even if he hates this disaster, it is for his good.

Being a servant in judgment (of defects) is to seek repentance, to place oneself in the position of giving apologies and to be humble and sure that Allah is the only One who is capable of removing such defects. No one can protect him from the evil of these defects except Allah, and if these defects continue they will keep him away from Allah and will expel him from the door of Allah. Defects that are manifested in committing sins are evil and only Allah can remove them and they are greater than the defects of the body.

The true servant of Allah seeks His pleasure and not His anger; he seeks His forgiveness not His punishment; he seeks the help of Allah against Allah, and resorts to Him from Him, and he knows that if Allah abandons him and leaves him to himself, all evil will appear, and he knows that there is no way to abandon sins and repent except with the help of Allah and His support. tAll this is in His hand, not in His servant's hand; the servant is weak and incapable to support himself or to praise his Lord without His support, and permission. He is just a poor and humble refugee throwing himself between the hands of Allah and in front of His door. He needs, seeks, longs for, and loves Allah; his body is busy in performing the orders of Allah, his heart is bowing between His hands, and he knows with certainty that there is no essential goodness in himself, and that all goodness is from Allah, and indeed He is the Lord of all blessings. He knows that Allah bestows blessings on His servant without his being worthy and He gives to him while he sins and disobeys. The share of Allah is praise and thanks but the share of the servant is dispraise and blame. Allah alone deserves all praise and the servant deserves all blame. All praise is to Him, all goodness is between His hands, all grace is to Him, all thanks is to Him, and all favor comes from Him.

Allah treats His servants well while His servants are ungrateful to Him. He becomes close to His servant by granting blessings and the servant strays away from Allah by committing sins, and He gives advice to His servant and His servant ridicules the truth in return.

Being servant of Allah in blessings is to know and acknowledge the blessings of Allah, to seek refuge in Allah and not to ascribe any share of worship to other than Him, even if this person is among the causes of having this blessing. Indeed if such a person is the cause of blessings, it is because Allah made him the cause. All blessings are from Allah alone and showing thanks and praise and love to Allah is through using His blessings and obeying Him.

Also being a servant of Allah in blessing is to perceive the great number of blessings one has, even if they are few. To know that all blessings come to him from His Lord without any price being paid by him, asking, or even deserving it. Actually this blessing increases his humility, submission, and love for Allah. The more Allah bestows blessings on His servant, the more the servant should submit to Him and love Him. The more Allah prevents, the more content the servant should be, and the more the servant commits sins, the more he will ask for forgiveness. This is the good servant.

Chapter: The Sweetness of Trusting in Allah

The sincere servant of Allah abandons an act while planning and hoping for more, fearing he will obtain less, asking for health, or escaping from disease, knowing that Allah has power over all things, that He alone has the choice and planning, that Allah knows what will benefit His servant more than he does, and that He, the Almighty is more capable to grant it to him. He is more useful to him than himself, more merciful than he is with himself, and more kind to him than he is to himself. If the servant of Allah knows that he cannot escape nor change the plan of Allah, he will commit all his affairs to Allah and throw himself between His hands as a humble servant throws himself between the hands of a mighty king who has authority over him and indeed the servant has no power of his own. When the servant knows all that, he will be relieved from all distress and sadness and will pass the burden to Allah who does not care or get tired. Allah will carry them; show him kindness and mercy without any tiredness. The servant has paid attention to Allah alone and Allah paid attention to the needs and benefits of his life and emptied his heart from them, and as a result, his life will be good and his heart will be happy. However, if the servant refuses and chooses to plan and chose for himself and cares more for his right than for the right of Allah, He will leave him with what he chose, and as a result he will live in distress, sadness, grief, fear, tiredness, and a bad condition, and his heart will never be pure, his work will not be suitable, and he will never find relief or pleasure. It will be as if there is a veil between himself and his pleasure and happiness. He works hard during this worldly life but he does not have any hope or reward in his resurrection. Allah, the Exalted gives His servant an order and gives him a guarantee. If the servant performs what he was ordered to do, like giving advice, being truthful, sincere, and diligent, Allah, the Exalted will fulfill what He promised like subsistence, sufficiency, victory, and fulfillment of one's needs. Allah, the Exalted guarantees subsistence to whoever worships Him, victory is for whoever trusts in Allah and asks His support, sufficiency is for whoever takes Allah as his only aim, forgiveness is for whoever asks for it, and Allah will fulfill the needs of whoever asks Him sincerely and trusts in Him. He, who is clever, cares for the orders of Allah and knows that Allah is true to His promise. Allah says,

﴿ ...وَمَنْ أَوْفَىٰ بِعَهْدِهِ مِنَ ٱللَّهِ... ﴾

which means, "And who is truer to his covenant than Allah?" (At-Tawbah, 9:111)

It is among the signs of happiness is that one pays attention to the orders of Allah without wishing for any guarantee, and it is among the signs of deprivation that the heart does not care for the orders of Allah.

Bishr bin Al-Hârith[44] said, "The people of the Hereafter are three: the worshiper, the ascetic, and the sincere ones. The worshiper worships Allah while seeking a reward whether in this worldly life or in the Hereafter. The ascetic worships Allah while neglecting that, and the sincere one worships Allah while being satisfied regardless of whether Allah gives to him or not.

Distance and Separation

Do not ever side against Allah and His Messenger. If one is ever guilty of this, it will lead him to distance and separation from Allah. Distance means having rival parties on opposite sides, and separation means to have both parties polarized. This is not an easy matter. The lesson to be learned here is to be on the side of Allah and His Messenger even if all the others are on the other side. The consequences of that are significant and long lasting. There is nothing more useful to the servant of Allah during his worldly life and the hereafter than being consistent on the side of Allah and His Messenger. It should be noted however that the majority of people cling to the other side, especially when desire and fear are intense. In such

---

[44] He is Bishr bin Al-Hârith bin 'Abdur-Rahmân bin 'Atâ', known as Bishr Al-Hâfy. He is among the greatest ascetics and worshipers. He lived in Baghdad and died in it in 227 A.H. See *Tahdhîb At-Tahdhîb*, vol.1, p.444, *Târîkh Al-Bukhâry Al-Kabîr*, vol.2, p.85, *Al-Jarh wat-Ta'dîl*, vol.2, p.356, *Mîzân Al-I'tidâl*, vol.1, p.238.

cases, you will hardly find any one on the side of Allah and His Messenger. Furthermore, it is usual for people to think that those who are on the side of Allah and His Messenger have defects in their minds and choose badly and may even be considered insane. Those who think in this way are the inheritors of the enemies of the Messengers. The enemies of the Messenger accused him of being insane when they were on one side and he was on the other. But whoever adapts himself to be in the good side will need deep knowledge of what the Messenger of Allah (peace be upon him) was sent with, in order to remove any doubts he may have and he will need complete patience in order to face the enmity of the enemies and the blame of the blamers. This will never be achieved without a strong will in seeking Allah and the Hereafter; he should love the Hereafter more than this worldly life and prefer it more and love Allah and His Messenger more than anything else. According to the nature of man, there is no harder deed than this. Himself, his desires, his nature, his Satan, his brothers, and his companions call him from one side to immediate pleasures and if he resists them, they will be against him. But if he is patient, Allah will help him and this difficult matter will become easy and pain will become pleasure. Allah praises His servant and He will make him taste the pleasure of being on the side of Allah and His Messenger and grant him honor in a way that will increase the happiness in his heart and which will empower him. All those who fought him before will be either afraid of him or peaceful and his helper. He will be stronger while his enemy will be weaker. Do not think it is difficult to confront people and take the side of Allah and His Messenger. If you are alone, Allah will be with you; you will be in His eyes, in His trust, and under His protection. He will only be testing your faith, belief, and patience. What can help you if Allah abandons you? Indeed, it is easier to take the side of Allah and His Messenger but if you suffer from greed and fear, you will not be able to. If you say, 'What will help me if I leave greed and fear?" You should answer yourself, 'Through monotheism, trust in Allah, and my knowledge that rewards are from Allah alone, sins are removed by Allah, and all matters are according to the will of Allah and not from anyone or anything else.

Advice: How to Set Your State Aright

Let's strive to be close to Allah. Let's long for the dwelling of peace wherein there is no toil, stress or weariness. The easiest way is to consider the fact that you are passing a period that lies between two other periods, namely your current life, which is the present one and it is between your past and your future.

The past can be set aright through repentance, regret and asking the forgiveness of Allah, and this is a way, which affords you no toil, weariness or hard work, as it is concerned with the heart.

The future can be set aright by abstaining from misdeeds, and this is a means of comfort and relief for you, for it is not a difficult act, but it is an intention that relieves your body, heart, and your mind.

In brief, your past is set aright through repentance; your future is set aright through abstention, determination and intention, which have nothing to do with overburdening the body.

However, our concern here is with the present time as it stands between the two other periods. If you waste it, then you are wasting your happiness and salvation. On the contrary, if you maintain it through setting your past and present aright, indeed you will attain success, salvation, relief, and pleasure.

Improving your present state is much more difficult than setting your past and your future aright, because it means that you should abide by the most deserving and beneficial deeds to achieve happiness. There are great differences between people in this regard. This is your chance to take the provision for your Hereafter, either Paradise or Hellfire. So, if you take this path to your Lord, you will attain glorious happiness and great success during this short period of time which has no value compared with eternity.

However, if you prefer vain desires, idleness, play and amusement, the period would pass quickly, followed by a permanent and great pain, the suffering of which is much more severe than the suffering of patience, the patience required to obey Allah.

Chapter: The Sign of Good Will

The sign of good will is when one seeks the pleasure of Allah, preparing for His meeting, feeling grief for any moment that passed in anything other than satisfying Him or keeping close to Him, and feeling delighted with Him, in other words, to have no interest in life except Allah all throughout the day.

Chapter: Asceticism in this Worldly Life

If people are satisfied with this worldly life, then they will be satisfied with Allah. If people are content with this worldly life, then they should be content with Allah. If people are delighted with their lovers, then they should be delighted with Allah. If people get acquainted with their masters and kings approaching them to attain dignity and glory, then they should know Allah and seek His pleasure, and then they will attain the utmost glory and dignity. One of the ascetics once said, "I can never imagine anyone who has heard about Paradise and Hellfire, and can still waste an hour with no prayers, supplications, recitation or charity." Someone told him, "I am weeping too much," to which he replied, "To laugh while confessing your sin is much better than to weep while feeling arrogant due to your knowledge. Indeed, the deeds of the arrogant are not accepted (by Allah)." Thereupon, he told him, "Advise me." The ascetic replied, "Abandon this worldly life leaving it to its seekers, as they have abandoned the Hereafter leaving it to its seekers. In this worldly life, imitate the bee, it eats good food, and provides good food for others. If it stumbles onto anything it never damages it."

Chapter: Kinds of Asceticism (Abstinence)

There are many kinds of asceticism (abstaining from things in this worldly life):

- Abstaining from unlawful things, which is an individual duty.

- Abstaining from doubtful matters. This is evaluated by the degree to which the doubtful matter relates; if the doubtful matter is major, then avoiding it will be a duty, and if it is minor, then avoiding it will be recommended.

- Abstaining from being overly curious.

- Abstaining from the matters, which do not concern you, either, speech, a look, a meeting, or anything else.

- Abstaining from one's self, which means feeling inferior for the sake of Allah.

- A general kind of asceticism, which means avoiding everything rather than Allah, or even anything that preoccupies you and keeps you away from Allah. The highest level of asceticism is concealing it, and the most difficult is overcoming one's desires. The difference between it and piety is that asceticism is abandoning whatever is not beneficial for the Hereafter, while piety is abandoning evil deeds for the sake of the Hereafter. The heart, which is overwhelmed with vain desires is incapable of either asceticism or piety.

Yahyâ bin Mu'âdh said, "I wondered at the cases of three people, one who performs acts of worship for the sake of people, and fails to perform them for the sake of Allah, and one who is greedy in giving charity, while he is asked by Allah to lend a goodly loan but in vain, and the last one is he who seeks the company of people, while Allah calls him to worship Him.

Disobeying a Command is Worse than Committing a Sin

Sahl bin 'Abdullah [45] said, "Abandoning the command of Allah is worse than committing a sin, for Adam was forbidden to eat from the Tree, but he ate from it, and Allah forgave him. Satan was commanded to prostrate before Adam, but he refused, and Allah did not forgive him."

I said, "This is a serious issue and is of great importance, which is, "Disobeying commands is worse in the sight of Allah than committing sins." There are several points concerning this.

Point one: that which Sahl mentioned about Adam and Satan, the enemy of Allah.

Point two: the cause of committing a sin is in most cases, lust and need. The cause of disobeying a command in most cases, is pride and love of glory. It is well known that whoever has the weight of an atom of pride in his heart will not enter Paradise, but whoever dies and has the Oneness of Allah in his heart will enter Paradise even if he had committed adultery and theft.

Point three: obeying a command is dearer to Allah than abandoning a sin, as has been indicated in many texts, such

---

[45] He is Sahl bin 'Abdullah bin Yûnus At-Tustary Abu Muhammad. He was born the year (200) A. H. He was an Imam and a scholar in the field of theology, mathematics and the flaws of deeds. He wrote a book called (fî Tafsîr Al-Qur'ân), and the book (Raqâiq Al-Muhibîn). He (may Allah have mercy upon him) died in (283) A. H. Adopted from Al-Bidâyah wa-Nihâyah (11\79).

as the words of the Messenger of Allah (peace be upon him), "The dearest deed to Allah is the performance of prayer at its due time."[46]

And his hadith, "Shall I inform you about the best of your deeds, the most virtuous and pure in the sight of the Owner, the heaviest in the (scale of) your grades and better for you than confronting your enemy while you fight them and they fight you?" Thereupon they said, "Yes, Messenger of Allah", then he said, "Remembering Allah." [47] And his hadith, "You should know that the best of your deeds is the performance of prayer..."[48] and so on.

Furthermore, abandoning a sin is a deed, which is refraining oneself from an action. That is why, Allah, the Almighty related love to the undertaking of commands by saying,

$$\{ \text{إِنَّ ٱللَّهَ يُحِبُّ ٱلَّذِينَ يُقَاتِلُونَ فِى سَبِيلِهِۦ صَفًّا} ... \}$$

which means, "Verily, Allah loves those who fight in His Cause in rows (ranks)..." (As-Saff, 61:4)

$$\{ ... \text{وَٱللَّهُ يُحِبُّ ٱلْمُحْسِنِينَ} \}$$

which means, "verily, Allah loves Al-Muhsinûn (the gooddoers)." (Âl-'Imrân, 3:134)

$$\{ ... \text{وَأَقْسِطُوٓا۟ إِنَّ ٱللَّهَ يُحِبُّ ٱلْمُقْسِطِينَ} \}$$

---

[46] Recorded by Al-Bukhary, Kitâb, Times of Prayers, Bâb, the Excellence of performing prayer at its due time, no. (527).
[47] Recorded by At-Tirmidhy. Kitâb Supplications, no. (3377), and Ibn Mâjah, no. (3377).
[48] Recorded by Ibn Mâjah. Kitâb Purification and its Sunnah practices, no. (277), and Ad-Dâramy (655).

which means, "And be equitable. Verily! Allah loves those who are equitable." (Al-Hujurât, 49:9)

$$﴿...وَٱللَّهُ يُحِبُّ ٱلصَّٰبِرِينَ ۝﴾$$

which means, "And Allah loves *As-Sâbirin* (the patient ones, etc.)." (Âl-1mrân, 3:146)

$$﴿...وَٱللَّهُ لَا يُحِبُّ ٱلْفَسَادَ ۝﴾$$

which means, "And Allah likes not mischief." (Al-Baqarah, 2:205)

$$﴿...وَٱللَّهُ لَا يُحِبُّ كُلَّ مُخْتَالٍ فَخُورٍ ۝﴾$$

which means, "And Allah likes not prideful boasters." (Al-Hadîd, 57:23)

$$﴿...وَلَا تَعْتَدُوٓا۟ إِنَّ ٱللَّهَ لَا يُحِبُّ ٱلْمُعْتَدِينَ ۝﴾$$

which means, "But transgress not the limits. Truly, Allah likes not the transgressors. [This Verse is the first one that was revealed in connection with *Jihâd,* but it was supplemented by another]." (Al-Baqarah, 2:190)

$$﴿لَّا يُحِبُّ ٱللَّهُ ٱلْجَهْرَ بِٱلسُّوٓءِ مِنَ ٱلْقَوْلِ إِلَّا مَن ظُلِمَ... ۝﴾$$

which means, "Allah does not like that the evil should be uttered in public except by him who has been wronged." (An-Nisâ', 4:148)

$$﴿...إِنَّ ٱللَّهَ لَا يُحِبُّ مَن كَانَ مُخْتَالًا فَخُورًا ۝﴾$$

which means, "Verily, Allah does not like such as are proud and boastful." (An-Nisâ', 4:36)

$$\left\{ \text{كُلُّ ذَٰلِكَ كَانَ سَيِّئُهُ عِندَ رَبِّكَ مَكْرُوهًا} \right\}$$

which means, "All the bad aspects of these (the above mentioned things) are hateful to your Lord." (Al-Isrâ', 17:38)

$$\left\{ \text{ذَٰلِكَ بِأَنَّهُمُ ٱتَّبَعُوا۟ مَآ أَسْخَطَ ٱللَّهَ} ... \right\}$$

which means, "That is because they followed that which angered Allah." (Muhammad, 47:28)

The previously mentioned verses lead us to understand that the deeds that please Allah, the Almighty are meant for the sake of their own virtue. That is why He preordains what He hates because it leads to what pleases Him.

He has also preordained wrongdoing, disbelief and wickedness due to what results from them like fighting in the Cause of Allah, martyrdom, repentance, invocation, submission, manifesting His Justice, Forgiveness, Revenge and Glorification, in addition to showing loyalty and hostility for His Sake, and other deeds. They are dearer to Him than removing their causes.

Therefore, it should now be clear that undertaking what pleases Him is dearer to Him than avoiding what He hates.

Point four clarifies that: obeying a command is meant for the sake of its own virtue, while abandoning a sin is meant to be done for the completion of the command. Allah, the Exalted, informed us that the prohibition of intoxicants and gambling is because they hinder man from remembering Allah and performing prayer. So, the prohibited acts are simply those that hinder man from obeying commands or perfecting them.

Point five clarifies that: obeying commands is a form of maintaining faith, while abandoning sins is a form of protecting faith from being disturbed. Maintaining faith is worthier than the act of protection, because the more the power of faith becomes stronger, the more it can push away evil elements, and when it becomes weak, the evil elements will prevail.

Point six: obeying commands is a revival, nourishment, adornment, joy, delight of the eye, pleasure and grace of the heart, while abandoning sins without obeying commands, would not benefit anything and shall abide in the Hellfire for ever.

Point seven: whoever undertakes both the prescribed and the forbidden deeds would either be saved if his good deeds exceed his sins, otherwise he would be saved after being punished for his misdeeds. Therefore, his abode would be salvation by virtue of obeying the commands.

On the contrary, whoever abandons both the prescribed and the prohibited deeds would be ruined, and would never be saved except by obeying the command, which is monotheism.

It could be argued that he would be ruined due to committing the prohibited, which is polytheism. This could be responded to by saying that it is enough to be ruined by abandoning monotheism, which has been commanded even if he does not commit polytheism, and moreover, when his heart becomes void of monotheism, and has not adopted monotheism, he would be ruined even if he does not worship anything with Allah. And if the worship of other than Him is added to that, he would be punished for abandoning monotheism, in addition to committing polytheism, which is prohibited.

Point eight: concerning he who is called to faith, if he says, "I neither believe nor disbelieve, I neither love nor hate and I neither worship Him (Allah) nor worship other than Him," he will be a disbeliever by virtue of abandonment and renunciation. However, if he says, "I believe in the Messenger, I love him, I have faith in him and do whatever he orders me, but my desires, will and nature are controlling me in such a way that I cannot abandon what he has prohibited me. I know quite well that he has prohibited me to do certain deeds, but I cannot quit them." In this case, he would not be considered a disbeliever, and his judgment is not like that of the first one, for he is obedient to some extent.

Point nine: both obedience and disobedience are basically related to the command and subsequently to the forbidden, in other words, the obedient one complies with the command while the disobedient one abandons it. Allah, Exalted be He, says,

﴿ ...لَّا يَعْصُونَ ٱللَّهَ مَآ أَمَرَهُمْ... ﴾

which means, "who disobey not, (from executing) the Commands they receive from Allah." (At-Tahrîm, 66:6)

And Mûsâ (Moses) said to his brother,

﴿ ...مَا مَنَعَكَ إِذْ رَأَيْتَهُمْ ضَلُّوٓا۟ ۝ أَلَّا تَتَّبِعَنِ ۖ أَفَعَصَيْتَ أَمْرِى ﴾

which means, "O Hârûn (Aaron)! What stopped you when you saw them going astray; "That you followed me not (according to my advice to you)? Have you then disobeyed my order?" (Tâhâ, 20:92-93)

On his death, 'Amr bin Al-'Âs said, "O Allah! I am the one whom You commanded, but unfortunately, I disobeyed (Your order), but (I testify that) there is no god but You."

The purpose of sending messengers is to obey them. By obeying the messengers we automatically comply with His orders. Abandoning what has been forbidden is the completion of obedience and accordingly, if the prohibited deeds are abandoned while the command is not obeyed, surely he would not be obedience. On one hand, he would be considered obedient as he obeyed the command, but on the other hand he would be considered disobedient because he performed a prohibited act. Thus he is completely different from the one who abandoned the command.

Point ten: complying with a command is an act of worship, a duty and a means of closeness to Allah, and that is the reason why man was created. Allah, Exalted be He, said,

﴿ وَمَا خَلَقْتُ الْجِنَّ وَالْإِنسَ إِلَّا لِيَعْبُدُونِ ﴾

which means, "And I (Allah) created not the jinns and humans except they should worship Me (Alone)." (Adh-Dhâriyât, 51:56)

In this verse, Allah, Exalted be He, informs mankind that the purpose of their creation is to worship Him and to know Him. In the same way, He sent them His Messengers and revealed His Divine Books so that they might know and worship Him. Therefore, worshipping Allah and Knowing Him is the purpose for which they have been created. Abandoning prohibited acts is not an end in itself, however, the act of complying with a command is required.

Point eleven: prohibition means that certain acts are not to be performed i.e., it is a not-to-do command; whereas a command requires an action to be followed, i.e., a to-do command. Therefore, the reality of prohibition returns to compliance to the command, and in this way the prohibition contains a 'to-do' command to be followed.

Point twelve: Muslim scholars have different views concerning the significance of performing a prohibited action. (1) The majority of scholars stated that the significance lies in keeping oneself away from the prohibited action and to maintain self-control. They based their argument on the premise that a 'to-do' command focuses on matters that exist while a 'not-do-command' focuses on matters that do not exist.

(2) The scholar Abu Hâshim and others viewed that abiding by prohibitions signifies avoiding an action. The result of this is to keep that action in a state of non-existence, even if the action has not yet occurred to him, as well as keeping his intention clear to keep away from it. If the significance of avoiding prohibited matters was just to keep away from the prohibition, the person would be a sinner if he did not undertake it.

(3) The judge Abu Bakr says that prohibitions are preordained and what is important here is to keep the act in a state of nonexistence.

(4) Another group of scholars say that a command to keep away from something basically means to do the opposite action, for it is a preordainment. Allah only prohibits man from depravity for the sake of abstinence, and that is what is commanded, and He prohibited him from wrongdoing for the sake of justice, which is necessary to be followed, and He prohibited him from lying for the sake of telling the truth. This is the case for all prohibitions.

According to them, the core matter of a prohibition is the command for the opposite of the prohibited act; the command has then returned to the fact that required a deed to be performed.

The correct view is that an ordainment can be classified into two categories: that which is sought for the virtue of its own self, and another that is pursued for the sake of something else. If the person did not feel like doing an evil deed or his own self did not urge him to do it, and the act remained in the original state of nonexistence, he would not be rewarded for keeping away from the prohibition.

However, if it occurred to him, and he kept himself away from it for the sake of Allah and abandoned it willingly, he would be rewarded for keeping away from it.

The reward is given for the 'to-do' command, whereas it is not given for an act that is in a state of absolute nonexistence. If the person abandons the act, while repressing a strong desire to do it he will be rewarded. However, if he abandons it because he is unable to do it, there is no reward. If he intended to do it but circumstances prevented him, he would not be punished like that of the doer, but he would be punished for his evil intention and desire to carry it out.

There are many texts concerning this issue, but it is not beneficial here to examine all the contradictory opinions.

Allah, the Almighty said,

﴿ ...وَإِن تُبْدُوا۟ مَا فِىٓ أَنفُسِكُمْ أَوْ تُخْفُوهُ يُحَاسِبْكُم بِهِ ٱللَّهُ ۖ فَيَغْفِرُ لِمَن يَشَآءُ وَيُعَذِّبُ مَن يَشَآءُ... ﴿٢٨٤﴾ ﴾

which means, "And whether you disclose what is in your ownselves or conceal it, Allah will call you to account for it. Then He forgives whom He wills and punishes whom He wills." (Al-Baqarah, 2:284)

﴿ ...فَإِنَّهُۥٓ ءَاثِمٌ قَلْبُهُۥ... ﴿٢٨٣﴾ ﴾

which means, "surely his heart is sinful." (Al-Baqarah, 2:283)

﴿ ...وَلَـٰكِن يُؤَاخِذُكُم بِمَا كَسَبَتْ قُلُوبُكُمْ... ﴿٢٢٥﴾ ﴾

which means, "But He will call you to account for that which your hearts have earned." (Al-Baqarah, 2:225)

﴿ يَوْمَ تُبْلَى ٱلسَّرَآئِرُ ﴿٩﴾ ﴾

which means, "The Day when all the secrets (deeds, prayers, fasting, etc.) will be examined (as to their truth)." (At-Târiq, 86:9)

The Messenger of Allah (peace be upon him) said, "When two Muslims fight (meet) each other with their swords, both the murderer as well as the murdered one will go to the Hell-fire.' They said, 'O Messenger of Allah! It is all right for the murderer but what about the murdered one?' The Messenger of Allah replied, "He surely had the intention to kill his companion." [49]

And in another hadith, "And a man said, if I had money, I would do (evil deeds) just like so and so. This person shares the same sin with him, due to his intention." [50]

Commentary on the above mentioned views:

Abu Hâshim viewed that one who avoids vice is praiseworthy even if he did not think of self-control (as the desire to undertake a vice was not originally there). If Abu Hâshim meant by the word praiseworthy, that such a person is not condemned. If he meant real praise, his view would be considered incorrect.

This argument is based on the fact that people never praise an impotent person for refraining from fornication; nor do they applaud a dumb person for avoiding slander and backbiting. People usually only praise those who keep away from vice while they have the ability to do it.

The judge Abu Bakr said that what is meant by prohibition is to keep the act in its original state of nonexistence, which is preordained. If he means by his statement to keep oneself away from the prohibited action and to have self-control, this

---

[49] Recorded by Al-Bukhary. The Book of Faith, bâb,

﴿ وَإِن طَآئِفَتَانِ مِنَ ٱلْمُؤْمِنِينَ ٱقْتَتَلُوا۟ فَأَصْلِحُوا۟ بَيْنَهُمَا ... ﴾

no. (31), and Muslim. The book of Jihad and Biographies. Bâb: Istihqâq Al-Qâtil salb Alqatîl, no. (1752).

[50] Recorded by At-Tirmidhy. The Book of Asceticism, no. (2325), and Ibn Majah no. (4228).

would be correct, but if he means mere nonexistence, then it would not be correct.

The group of scholars, who asserts that a command to keep away from something basically means to undertake the opposite action, are incorrect, because the basic concept here is to do both things: to keep away from a prohibition and to undertake its opposite command as well.[51] This is justified by the fact that the necessary means to undertake an obligation are not sought for their own virtue, as it is the preordained obligation that is sought for its virtue, and it is prohibited to hinder or weaken it. Thereupon, the prohibition is ordained only as a means to undertake the ends or help the desired end to come into existence.

Point thirteen: a command to undertake an action entails a prohibition to keep away from the opposite. This is true on the level of a logical necessity rather than a basic requirement. The significance of a command is to undertake it. Moreover, the aim of the Prohibitor when prohibiting an action, in the first place, is to put an end to that prohibited action. Being involved in its opposite comes on the level of logical necessity.

Therefore, He enacted a prohibition to keep away from the direct opposite of a command i.e. the command to act is the matter pursued for the sake of its own virtue.

The summary of the matter is that the command to do something is a command for the sake of its own virtue, and for its required necessity, and the prohibition of doing something is a command to avoid it, and the necessity to do so. Therefore,

---

[51] **Translator's Note:** To clarify this we take as an example the command to keep away from telling lies and to hold fast to telling the truth. According to the author, Ibn Al-Qayyim, the command to keep away from telling lies is meant for itself, though not in the first place, in addition to abide by the command to commit oneself to telling the truth.

what is required in both issues is an action and an abandonment, and both of them are a 'to-do' command.

Point fourteen: command and prohibition are on the level of an order. There is no praise where there is no affirmation, for negation, like its name, is a state of nonexistence that has no perfection or praise. If it contains an affirmation, there would be praise associated with it, like the negation of forgetfulness, which is essential for the perfection and manifestation of knowledge.

The negation of fatigue is essential for the perfection of strength and ability. The negation of sleep is essential for the perfection of life and the eternal state. The negation of child and wife is essential for the perfection of self sufficiency and sovereignty. The negation of partnership, support and intercession without leave is essential for the perfection of the Oneness of Allah and the uniqueness of His Perfection, Divinity and Sovereignty. The negation of oppression includes the perfection of justice. The negation of eyes to see Him includes His Majesty and that He is too Great to be seen, even if eyes will see Him (on the Day of Resurrection).

If this is understood, then we should know that if the prohibition does not include a confirmatory 'to-do' command, people would not be praised for abandoning it, and would not deserve to be rewarded or praised for abandoning it.

Point fifteen: Allah, the Almighty made the reward for obeying commands tenfold, and the reward for abstaining from prohibitions only one. This indicates that what He commanded to be undertaken is dearer to Him than abandoning what He prohibited. If it was the opposite, the evil deed would be tenfold and the good deed would be one reward or equivalent to the former.

Point sixteen: what is meant by the prohibited deed is to put an end to it so that it does not come into existence, whether he intended that or not and whether it occurred to him or not. The purpose of the commanded deed is to let it be; to let it exist and show love to Allah by one's intention and deed concerning it.

The core of the matter is that the existence of what He commanded to be done is dearer to Him than the nonexistence of what He commanded to be put to an end. Therefore, His love for the undertaking of what He commanded is greater than His hate for doing what He prohibited.

Point seventeen: It is from His infinite mercy that man does what pleases Him, helps in undertaking it, rewarding it and whatever follows. If man commits what He hates, then whatever follows that like dispraise, pain and punishment are part of His Anger. His Mercy precedes His Anger, and everything related to the attribute of mercy is dominant throughout creation compared to the attribute of anger, for Allah, the Almighty would not be anything else except Merciful, and His Mercy is part of His Self, like His Knowledge, Ability, Life, Hearing, Vision and Kindness. Therefore, it is impossible, with respect to Him, to be the opposite of these attributes.

His Anger is not necessary to His Self, and so He is not always angry to the extent that it is impossible to stop being so. Moreover, His Messengers, who are the most knowledgeable of all creation will say on the Day of Resurrection, "My Lord is more angry than He has ever been before and will never be in the future." [52] His Mercy encompasses all things, while His Anger does not. He, Exalted be He, has prescribed Mercy for Himself, whereas He has not prescribed Anger for Himself, and He has embraced all things with mercy and knowledge,

---

[52] Recorded by Al-Bukhary. Kitâb, Ahâdîth Al-Anbiyâ', bâb, the Word of Allah, the Exalted,

﴿ إِنَّا أَرْسَلْنَا نُوحًا إِلَىٰ قَوْمِهِ أَنْ أَنذِرْ قَوْمَكَ مِن قَبْلِ أَن يَأْتِيَهُمْ عَذَابٌ أَلِيمٌ ۝ ﴾

which means: "Verily, We sent Nûh (Noah) to his people" no. (3340), and Muslim, no. (194)

whereas He has not embraced all things with anger and revenge.

Therefore, mercy, and everything related to it, including its necessities and effects are predominant over anger and everything related to it and its effects. So, the means of mercy are dearer to Him than the existence of what necessitates anger. That is why mercy is dearer to Him than punishment, and pardoning is dearer to Him than revenge.

In this respect, the existence of what pleases Him is dearer to Him than neglecting what He hates, especially if the neglect of what He hates will prevent the existence of what pleases Him.

Point eighteen: Removing the effects of what He detests, i.e., prohibitions, by undertaking what He likes, i.e., the commands; could happen quicker than the effacement of what He likes, i.e., commands, by what He detests, i.e., the prohibitions. Allah, the Almighty might remove it with pardoning and overlooking. It might also be removed with repentance, forgiveness, righteous deeds, misfortunes that cause expiation of sins and intercession.

It is well known that righteous deeds remove evil deeds. Even if the sins of the servant reached the clouds, and then he turned to Allah for forgiveness, He would forgive him. And if he meets Him with sins the magnitude of the earth, while worshipping none besides Him, He would meet him with the likeness of it in forgiveness.

He, the Almighty, forgives sins even if they are as numerous as the waves of the sea. Allah is willing to cancel them and their effects with the slightest effort from His servant, who displays true repentance and remorse. That would happen because of the existence of what pleases Him like repentance, obedience and pure monotheism, and this fact indicates that the existence of such things are dearer to Him.

Point nineteen clarifies that: Allah, the Almighty preordained the existence of those things that He hates, due to the goodness that follows them. This is because He, the Almighty is more pleased with the repentance of His servant than the person who lost something dear and then found it; than the barren woman who has just given birth to a child, and the thirsty person who has just arrived at a watering place. The Messenger of Allah (peace be upon him) gave an excellent example about His Joy that goes beyond all measure when His servant repents. This does not mean that everything that pleases Him is dearer to Him than avoiding every deed that He hates, to extent that the two *rak'ahs* of forenoon Prayer become dearer to Him than not killing a Muslim, but what is meant is that the general concept of obeying His commands is better than the general concept of avoiding prohibitions.

The main issue here is the significance of repentance, which renders a deed beloved to Allah. Some people might say that Allah rejoices when His servant repents and that repentance occurs because of avoiding a prohibited act, then the joy was caused by abandonment.

To this we say that absolute abandonment is not the cause of joy, and moreover, it is not the cause of reward or praise.

Repentance is not essentially abandonment, although abandonment is one of its requirements. Rather it is a 'to-do' command, which means that the servant repents to his Lord and becomes dutiful to Him. To make this happen in reality it is necessary that the prohibited thing be abandoned. That is why the Exalted said,

﴿ وَأَنِ ٱسْتَغْفِرُواْ رَبَّكُمْ ثُمَّ تُوبُوٓاْ إِلَيْهِ ... ﴾

which means, "And (commanding you): "Seek the forgiveness of your Lord, and turn to Him in repentance." (Hûd, 11:3)

Therefore, repentance means turning away from what is hated to what pleases Him, and not just abandonment, because someone may merely abandon a sin, and not keep away from it for the sake of Allah and then adopt what pleases the Exalted. In this case, he would not be truly repentant, for repentance means refraining from something and turning in repentance to Allah with a sincere heart.

Point twenty: if someone fails to obey the commands of Allah he would be bereft of life, and that is what the Exalted said,

﴿ يَٰٓأَيُّهَا ٱلَّذِينَ ءَامَنُوا۟ ٱسْتَجِيبُوا۟ لِلَّهِ وَلِلرَّسُولِ إِذَا دَعَاكُمْ لِمَا يُحْيِيكُمْ ... ﴾

which means, "O you who believe! Answer Allah (by obeying Him) and (His) Messenger when he (SAW) calls you to that which will give you life." (Al-Anfâl, 8:24)

He, the Almighty also said,

﴿ أَوَمَن كَانَ مَيْتًا فَأَحْيَيْنَٰهُ وَجَعَلْنَا لَهُۥ نُورًا يَمْشِى بِهِۦ فِى ٱلنَّاسِ كَمَن مَّثَلُهُۥ فِى ٱلظُّلُمَٰتِ ... ﴾

which means, "Is he who was dead (without Faith by ignorance and disbelief) and We gave him life (by knowledge and Faith) and set for him a light (of Belief) whereby he can walk amongst men, like him who is in the darkness (of disbelief, polytheism and hypocrisy)?" (Al-An'âm, 6:122)

And He, the Almighty said about the unbelievers,

﴿ أَمْوَٰتٌ غَيْرُ أَحْيَآءٍ ... ﴾

which means, "(They are) dead, lifeless, and they know not when they will be raised up." (An-Na<u>h</u>l, 16:21)

And He, the Almighty said again,

﴿ إِنَّكَ لَا تُسْمِعُ ٱلْمَوْتَىٰ ... ﴾

which means, "Verily, you cannot make the dead to hear (i.e. benefit them and similarly the disbelievers)." (An-Naml, 27:80)

Doing a prohibited act, causes diseases of the heart, which is a living death.

Some of the prohibitions lead to polytheism, which is destruction in this life and the next.

It could be said that ruin comes about due to a lack of monotheism, and obeying Allah's commands brings about life, but when obedience is lacking destruction is imminent.

Point twenty one: failing to obey even some of Allah's commands brings about ruin and permanent misfortune.

Point twenty two: obeying Allah's commands requires abandonment of the prohibited deed if it is undertaken in its correct form with sincerity, following up and being done for the sake of Allah. The Exalted said,

﴿ ...إِنَّ ٱلصَّلَوٰةَ تَنْهَىٰ عَنِ ٱلْفَحْشَاءِ وَٱلْمُنكَرِ ... ﴾

which means, "Verily, As-Salât (the prayer) prevents from Al-Fahshâ' (i.e. great sins of every kind, unlawful sexual intercourse, etc.) and Al-Munkar (i.e. disbelief, polytheism, and every kind of evil wicked deed, etc.)" (Al-'Ankabût, 29:45)

The mere abandonment of prohibited deeds does not require performing the commanded deed.

Point twenty three: the deeds that He commanded are related to His attributes, and the prohibitions that He hates are related to the results of His Actions. This is a difficult point that needs to be illustrated. Therefore, we say that prohibitions are evil deeds that lead to more evil deeds, and commands are righteous deeds that lead to more righteous deeds. The righteous deed lies in His Hand, whereas the evil deed is not related to Him. This is because evil does not belong to His attributes, His actions or His Beautiful Names, but it belongs to the results and consequences of actions, though it is evil with respect to the servant, but with respect to the Creator, the Almighty, it is not evil (it does not affect Him).

Therefore, the purpose of allowing the servant to commit a prohibited deed is to produce an evil result on the servant, though it is not necessarily essentially evil for the servant. Failing to obey Allah's commands means that a righteous deed is missed, and whenever the command is more pleasing to Allah, the Exalted, like monotheism and faith, the evil that occurs by missing it is greater.

The core of these points is that obeying His command is what pleases Him, and He hates the prohibited acts.

Chapter: Remembering Allah and Being Grateful to Him

Islam is based on two fundamental concepts: remembering Allah and being grateful to Him. Regarding this Allah, the Exalted, says,

﴿ فَاذْكُرُونِي أَذْكُرْكُمْ وَاشْكُرُوا لِي وَلَا تَكْفُرُونِ ﴾

which means, "Therefore remember Me (by praying, glorifying, etc.) I will remember you, and be grateful to Me (for My countless Favours on you) and never be ungrateful to Me." (Al-Baqarah, 2:152)

The Prophet (peace be upon him) once told Mu'âdh, "By Allah! I love you so much so do not forget to say at the end of each prayer, **'Allâhumma a'inny 'alâ dhikrika wa shukrika wa** ḥusni 'ibâdatik (O Allah! Help me to remember You, to feel grateful to You, and to worship You perfectly).'"[53]

It is worth mentioning here that remembering Allah does not include only remembering Him verbally (with one's tongue) but it also includes remembering Him within one's heart. However, the mode of remembering Him includes remembering His Names, His Attributes, His commandments, His prohibitions, as well as remembering Him by uttering His words, which entails knowing Him, believing in Him, and believing both in the Attributes of His Perfection, and the qualities of His Majesty. It also entails glorifying Him in various ways of praising, which is not applicable except through monotheism, for true remembrance requires the previously mentioned aspects, as well as the remembrance of His bounties, blessings and beneficence.

On the other hand, gratefulness to Allah means obeying Him and getting closer to him by performing those deeds that have been ordained by Him, both the inner and the outer ones.

Those two fundamentals are considered the core of religion, for remembering Allah entails knowing Him, and being grateful to him entails obeying Him, which is the reason behind the creation of all things. It is also the reason for which punishment and reward are founded, divine books are revealed, and messengers are sent. That is the truth by which the heavens, the earth, and all that is between them are created, and the contrary is falsehood above which He is Exalted, and this is the misconception adopted by His enemies.

Allah, the Exalted says,

﴿ وَمَا خَلَقْنَا ٱلسَّمَآءَ وَٱلْأَرْضَ وَمَا بَيْنَهُمَا بَٰطِلًا ۚ ذَٰلِكَ ظَنُّ ٱلَّذِينَ كَفَرُوا۟ ... ﴾

---

[53] Narrated by Abû Dâwûd, in his book "Prayers", Chaper of "Seeking the forgiveness of Allah", no. .1522. Narrated also by An-Nasâ'y.

which means, "And We created not the heavens and the earth and all that is between them without purpose! That is the consideration of those who disbelieve!" (Sâd, 38:27)

And He, the Almighty says,

$$\text{﴿ وَمَا خَلَقْنَا ٱلسَّمَٰوَٰتِ وَٱلْأَرْضَ وَمَا بَيْنَهُمَا لَٰعِبِينَ ۝ مَا خَلَقْنَٰهُمَآ إِلَّا بِٱلْحَقِّ ...﴾}$$

which means, "And We created not the heavens and the earth, and all that is between them, for mere play, We created them not except with truth." (Ad-Duhkân, 44: 38-39)

And He, the Almighty says,

$$\text{﴿ وَمَا خَلَقْنَا ٱلسَّمَٰوَٰتِ وَٱلْأَرْضَ وَمَا بَيْنَهُمَآ إِلَّا بِٱلْحَقِّ وَإِنَّ ٱلسَّاعَةَ لَءَاتِيَةٌ ... ۝ ﴾}$$

which means,"And We created not the heavens and the earth and all that is between them except with truth, and the Hour is surely coming." (Al-Hijr, 15:85)

After mentioning His blessings in the Chapter of Yûnus, Allah says,

$$\text{﴿ ... مَا خَلَقَ ٱللَّهُ ذَٰلِكَ إِلَّا بِٱلْحَقِّ ... ۝ ﴾}$$

which means, "Allah did not create this but in truth." (Yûnus, 10: 5)

And He, the Almighty says,

$$\text{﴿ أَيَحْسَبُ ٱلْإِنسَٰنُ أَن يُتْرَكَ سُدًى ۝ ﴾}$$

which means, "Does man think that he will be left Suda [neglected without being punished or rewarded for the obligatory duties enjoined by his Lord (Allah) on him]?" (Al-Qiyâmah, 75:36)

And He, the Almighty says,

﴿ أَفَحَسِبْتُمْ أَنَّمَا خَلَقْنَاكُمْ عَبَثًا وَأَنَّكُمْ إِلَيْنَا لَا تُرْجَعُونَ ﴾

which means, "Did you think that We had created you in play (without any purpose), and that you would not be brought back to Us?" (Al-Mu'minûn, 23:115)

And He, the Almighty says,

﴿ وَمَا خَلَقْتُ الْجِنَّ وَالْإِنْسَ إِلَّا لِيَعْبُدُونِ ﴾

which means, "And I (Allah) created not the jinns and humans except that they should worship Me (Alone)." (Adh-Dhâriyât, 51:56)

And He, the Almighty says,

﴿ اللَّهُ الَّذِي خَلَقَ سَبْعَ سَمَاوَاتٍ وَمِنَ الْأَرْضِ مِثْلَهُنَّ يَتَنَزَّلُ الْأَمْرُ بَيْنَهُنَّ لِتَعْلَمُوا أَنَّ اللَّهَ عَلَىٰ كُلِّ شَيْءٍ قَدِيرٌ وَأَنَّ اللَّهَ قَدْ أَحَاطَ بِكُلِّ شَيْءٍ عِلْمًا ﴾

which means, "It is Allah Who has created the seven heavens and the earth the like thereof (i.e. seven). His Command descends between them (heavens and earth), that you may know that Allah has power over all things, and that Allah surrounds (comprehends) all things in (His) Knowledge." (At-Talâq, 65:12)

And He, the Almighty says,

﴿ جَعَلَ اللَّهُ الْكَعْبَةَ الْبَيْتَ الْحَرَامَ قِيَامًا لِلنَّاسِ وَالشَّهْرَ الْحَرَامَ وَالْهَدْيَ وَالْقَلَائِدَ ذَٰلِكَ لِتَعْلَمُوا أَنَّ اللَّهَ يَعْلَمُ مَا فِي السَّمَاوَاتِ وَمَا فِي الْأَرْضِ وَأَنَّ اللَّهَ بِكُلِّ شَيْءٍ عَلِيمٌ ﴾

which means, "Allah has made the Ka'bah, the Sacred House, an asylum of security and Hajj and 'Umrah (pilgrimage) for mankind, and also the Sacred Month and the animals of offerings and the garlanded (people or animals, etc. marked with the garlands on their necks made from the outer part of the stem of the Makkah trees for their security), that you may know that Allah has knowledge of all that is in the heavens and all that is in the earth, and that Allah is the All Knower of each and everything." (Al-Mâ'idah, 5:97)

The previous verses prove that the aim of creation is to remember Allah and be grateful to Him; remembrance without forgetfulness, and gratefulness without disbelief. Allah, the Exalted, remembers the one who remembers Him, and He is grateful to the one, who is grateful to Him. So remembering Allah is the reason behind Allah's remembrance and being grateful to Allah is the reason behind increasing the blessings of Allah.

In brief, remembering Allah should be done with both the tongue and the heart. However, being grateful to Allah is done out of love and repentance from the heart, and out of praise and glorification from the tongue, and out of obedience and servitude from the body.

Chapter: Guidance Leads to More Guidance and Aberration Leads to More Aberration

It has been repeated in the Qur'ân that deeds that are performed in the hearts and the body are the cause of guidance and aberration. Therefore, deeds that are done in the hearts and the body require guidance, just like the way an effect is attached to a cause, and the same thing applies to aberration. So righteous deeds produce guidance, and whenever there is an increase in them, there would be an increase in guidance. When evil deeds are performed, they will increase. That is because Allah, the Almighty loves righteous deeds and that is why He rewards them with guidance and success. And He hates evil deeds, so He rewards them with aberration and distress.

Also, because He loves righteous deeds and righteous people, He brings their hearts close to Him according to the amount of righteous deeds they perform. And because He hates evil deeds and evil people, He keeps their hearts far away from Him according to the degree of evil that they are guilty of.

According to the first principle, Allah, the Almighty said,

﴿ الٓمٓ ۝ ذَٰلِكَ ٱلْكِتَٰبُ لَا رَيْبَ ۛ فِيهِ ۛ هُدًى لِّلْمُتَّقِينَ ۝ ﴾

Alif-Lâm-Mîm. [These letters are one of the miracles of the Qur'ân and none but Allah (Alone) knows their meanings]. This is the Book (the Qur'ân), whereof there is no doubt, a guidance to those who are *Al-Muttaqûn* [the pious and righteous persons who fear Allah much (abstain from all kinds of sins and evil deeds which He has forbidden) and love Allah much (perform all kinds of good deeds which He has ordained)]." (Al-Baqarah, 2:1-2)

This contains two instructions:

Instruction One is that He guides the person who abstains from prohibited things that cause His Displeasure for it is known by all people that Allah, the Almighty hates oppression, adultery, mischief on the earth, and that He hates those who do these deeds. In the same way, He loves justice, kindness, generosity, truthfulness and spreading goodness on earth, and He loves those, who do these deeds. When the Book was revealed, Allah, the Almighty rewarded the righteous people by making it easy for them to believe in it as an act of recompense to them for their righteous deeds and obedience. And He forsook the evil oppressors by coming in between them and guidance.

The Stages of Guidance

Instruction Two is that after the servant believes in the Book, and is guided by it in general, accepts its orders and believes in what it contains, there would be more guidance for that servant, for there is no end to guidance, regardless of how far the servant reaches; there would always be above him guidance upon guidance, and after that guidance more guidance. Whenever the servant fears his Lord, he would receive more guidance, and he would always be increased in guidance as long as he fears Allah, the Almighty. And whenever he neglects a chance to be pious, he would be missing a chance to receive guidance, and whenever he fears Allah, the Almighty his guidance would increase, and whenever he accepts guidance, his piety would increase. To illustrate this fact, consider the following verses from the Glorious Qur'ân,

﴿ يَٰٓأَهْلَ ٱلْكِتَٰبِ قَدْ جَآءَكُمْ رَسُولُنَا يُبَيِّنُ لَكُمْ كَثِيرًا مِّمَّا كُنتُمْ تُخْفُونَ مِنَ ٱلْكِتَٰبِ وَيَعْفُوا۟ عَن كَثِيرٍ ۚ قَدْ جَآءَكُم مِّنَ ٱللَّهِ نُورٌ وَكِتَٰبٌ مُّبِينٌ ۝ يَهْدِى بِهِ ٱللَّهُ مَنِ ٱتَّبَعَ رِضْوَٰنَهُۥ سُبُلَ ٱلسَّلَٰمِ وَيُخْرِجُهُم مِّنَ ٱلظُّلُمَٰتِ إِلَى ٱلنُّورِ بِإِذْنِهِۦ وَيَهْدِيهِمْ إِلَىٰ صِرَٰطٍ مُّسْتَقِيمٍ ۝ ﴾

which means, "Now has come to you Our Messenger (Muhammad) explaining to you much of that which you used to hide from the Scripture and passing over (i.e. leaving out without explaining) much. Indeed, there has come to you from Allah a light (Prophet Muhammad) and a plain Book (this Qur'ân)." (Al-Mâ'idah, 5:15-16)

﴿ ...ٱللَّهُ يَجْتَبِىٓ إِلَيْهِ مَن يَشَآءُ وَيَهْدِىٓ إِلَيْهِ مَن يُنِيبُ ۝ ﴾

which means, "Allah chooses for Himself whom He wills, and guides unto Himself who turns to Him in repentance and in obedience." (As-Shûrâ, 42:13)

And Allah, the Almighty said,

$$\text{﴿ سَيَذَّكَّرُ مَن يَخْشَىٰ ﴾}$$

which means, "The reminder will be received by him who fears (Allah)." (Al-A'lâ, 87:10)

And He, the Exalted said,

$$\text{﴿ ...وَمَا يَتَذَكَّرُ إِلَّا مَن يُنِيبُ ﴾}$$

which means, "And none remembers but those who turn (to Allah) in obedience and in repentance (by begging His Pardon and by worshipping and obeying Him Alone and none else)." (Ghâfir, 40:13)

And He, the Exalted said,

$$\text{﴿ إِنَّ ٱلَّذِينَ ءَامَنُوا۟ وَعَمِلُوا۟ ٱلصَّٰلِحَٰتِ يَهْدِيهِمْ رَبُّهُم بِإِيمَٰنِهِمْ... ﴾}$$

which means, "Verily, those who believe [in the Oneness of Allah along with the six articles of Faith, i.e. to believe in Allah, His Angels, His Books, His Messengers, Day of Resurrection, and Al-Qadar (Divine Preordainments) - Islâmic Monotheism], and do deeds of righteousness, their Lord will guide them through their Faith." (Yûnus, 10:9)

First, He guided them to faith, and then when they accepted that guidance and believed in it, He rewarded them by guiding them to more faith as an act of guidance after guidance. The likeness of this is in the following verses of the Glorious Qur'ân,

$$\text{﴿ وَيَزِيدُ ٱللَّهُ ٱلَّذِينَ ٱهْتَدَوْا۟ هُدًى... ﴾}$$

which means, "And Allah increases in guidance those who walk aright [true believers in the Oneness of Allah who fear Allah much (abstain from all kinds of sins and evil deeds which He has forbidden), and love Allah much (perform all kinds of good deeds which He has ordained)]." (Maryam, 19:76)

Allah, the Almighty also said,

﴿ يَٰٓأَيُّهَا ٱلَّذِينَ ءَامَنُوٓاْ إِن تَتَّقُواْ ٱللَّهَ يَجْعَل لَّكُمْ فُرْقَانًا... ﴾

which means, "O you who believe! If you obey and fear Allah, He will grant you *Furqân* a criterion [(to judge between right and wrong), or (*Makhraj*, i.e. making a way for you to get out from every difficulty)]." (Al-Anfâl, 8:29)

As a part of this criterion, is that Allah, the Almighty grants them some light, with which they can differentiate between truth and falsehood, and He also grants them victory and glory that enable them to establish truth and destroy falsehood. The Qur'ân has commented on this point. Allah, the Almighty said,

﴿ ...إِنَّ فِى ذَٰلِكَ لَءَايَةً لِّكُلِّ عَبْدٍ مُّنِيبٍ ﴾

which means, "Verily, in this is a sign for every faithful believer that [believes in the Oneness of Allah], and turns to Allah (in all affairs with humility and in repentance)." (Saba', 34:9)

He, the Almighty said,

﴿ ...إِنَّ فِى ذَٰلِكَ لَءَايَٰتٍ لِّكُلِّ صَبَّارٍ شَكُورٍ ﴾

which means, "Verily, in this are indeed signs for every steadfast grateful (person)." (Saba', 34:19)

This is in Chapters Luqmân, Ibrahîm, Saba' and As-Shûra.

He revealed these verses to benefit those who have patience and are grateful. Just as He revealed His Glorious Qur'ânic verses to benefit the pious, those, who fear Allah and return to Him in repentance, those whose intentions are to seek His Pleasure, and that it is only observed by those who fear Allah, the Almighty. Allah, the Almighty said in the Qur'ân,

﴿ طه ۝ مَا أَنزَلْنَا عَلَيْكَ ٱلْقُرْءَانَ لِتَشْقَىٰٓ ۝ إِلَّا تَذْكِرَةً لِّمَن يَخْشَىٰ ۝ ﴾

which means, "_T_âHâ These letters are one of the miracles of the Qur'ân, and none but Allah (Alone) knows their meanings.] We have not sent down the Qur'ân unto you (O Muhammad) to cause you distress, but only as a Reminder to those who fear (Allah)." (_T_âhâ, 20:1-3)

He, the Almighty also said about the Hour,

﴿ إِنَّمَآ أَنتَ مُنذِرُ مَن يَخْشَىٰهَا ۝ ﴾

which means, "You (O Muhammad) are only a warner for those who fear it." (An-Nâzi'ât, 79:45)

If someone does not believe in it, and does not hope for it or fear it, the Qur'ânic Verses will not benefit him. That is why Allah, the Almighty mentioned the punishment of the nations who falsely denied the Messengers and that which happened to them. He said,

﴿ ... إِنَّ فِى ذَٰلِكَ لَءَايَةً لِّمَنْ خَافَ عَذَابَ ٱلْءَاخِرَةِ ۝ ﴾

which means, "Indeed in that (there) is a sure lesson for those who fear the torment of the Hereafter." (Hûd, 11:103)

He mentioned that there is a lesson for those who fear the torment of the Hereafter in His punishment of those who reject faith.

It would not be a lesson for the person who does not believe in it and does not fear its torment. That is why when such a person hears its verses, he says, "There is still good and bad in the world. There is comfort and distress, happiness and unhappiness." And they may attribute that to astronomic and psychological causes. But in reality, it was due to the patience and gratefulness of the person concerned.

Faith is founded on both patience and gratefulness. Therefore, the servant's faith will be strong according to his patience and gratefulness. The verses of Allah will only benefit those who believe in Him and His verses, and faith is granted through patience and gratefulness. The main part of gratefulness is monotheism, and the main part of patience is not to yield to vain desires. If the person is a polytheist who follows his vain desires, he would not be patient or grateful, therefore, the verses would neither be beneficial for him nor be a means of him being granted faith.

Chapter

The second principle is the consistency of evil, arrogance and falsehood along with aberrance; and there are many examples of that in the Qur'ân, like the following verses,

﴿ ...يُضِلُّ بِهِ كَثِيرًا وَيَهْدِي بِهِ كَثِيرًا ۚ وَمَا يُضِلُّ بِهِ إِلَّا ٱلْفَٰسِقِينَ ۝ ٱلَّذِينَ يَنقُضُونَ عَهْدَ ٱللَّهِ مِنۢ بَعْدِ مِيثَٰقِهِۦ وَيَقْطَعُونَ مَآ أَمَرَ ٱللَّهُ بِهِۦٓ أَن يُوصَلَ وَيُفْسِدُونَ فِى ٱلْأَرْضِ ۚ أُو۟لَٰٓئِكَ هُمُ ٱلْخَٰسِرُونَ ۝ ﴾

which means, "By it He misleads many, and many He guides thereby. And He misleads thereby only those who are Al-Fâsiqûn (the rebellious, disobedient to Allah). Those who break Allah's Covenant after ratifying it, and sever what Allah has ordered to be joined (as regards Allah's Religion of Islamic

Monotheism, and to practice its legal laws on the earth and also as regards keeping good relations with kith and kin), and do mischief on earth, it is they who are the losers." (Al-Baqarah, 2:26-27)

Allah, the Almighty also said,

﴿ يُثَبِّتُ ٱللَّهُ ٱلَّذِينَ ءَامَنُواْ بِٱلْقَوْلِ ٱلثَّابِتِ فِي ٱلْحَيَوٰةِ ٱلدُّنْيَا وَفِي ٱلْأَخِرَةِ ۖ وَيُضِلُّ ٱللَّهُ ٱلظَّالِمِينَ ۚ وَيَفْعَلُ ٱللَّهُ مَا يَشَآءُ ﴾

which means, "Allah will keep firm those who believe, with the word that stands firm in this world (i.e. they will keep on worshipping Allah Alone and none else), and in the Hereafter. And Allah will cause to go astray those who are *Zhâlimûn* (polytheists and wrong-doers, etc.), and Allah does what He wills." (Ibrâhim, 14:27)

He, the Almighty Allah, said,

﴿ فَمَا لَكُمْ فِي ٱلْمُنَٰفِقِينَ فِئَتَيْنِ وَٱللَّهُ أَرْكَسَهُم بِمَا كَسَبُوٓاْ ... ﴾

which means, "Then what is the matter with you that you are divided into two parties about the hypocrites? Allah has cast them back (to disbelief) because of what they have earned." (An-Nisâ', 4:88)

He, the Exalted, said,

﴿ وَقَالُواْ قُلُوبُنَا غُلْفٌۢ ۚ بَل لَّعَنَهُمُ ٱللَّهُ بِكُفْرِهِمْ فَقَلِيلًا مَّا يُؤْمِنُونَ ﴾

which means, "And they say, "Our hearts are wrapped (i.e. do not hear or understand Allah's Word)." Nay, Allah has cursed them for their disbelief, so little is that which they believe." (Al-Baqarah, 2:88)

He, the Exalted said,

﴿ وَنُقَلِّبُ أَفْـِٔدَتَهُمْ وَأَبْصَٰرَهُمْ كَمَا لَمْ يُؤْمِنُوا۟ بِهِۦٓ أَوَّلَ مَرَّةٍ... ﴾

which means, "And We shall turn their hearts and their eyes away (from guidance), as they refused to believe therein for the first time." (Al-An'âm, 6:110)

He, the Exalted, announced that He punished them due to their disbelief when the Prophets came to them with the message. They knew it well, but they just turned away from it, so Allah, the Almighty turned their hearts and their eyes away from guidance, and came in between them and faith. Just as the Almighty said,

﴿ يَٰٓأَيُّهَا ٱلَّذِينَ ءَامَنُوا۟ ٱسْتَجِيبُوا۟ لِلَّهِ وَلِلرَّسُولِ إِذَا دَعَاكُمْ لِمَا يُحْيِيكُمْ ۖ وَٱعْلَمُوٓا۟ أَنَّ ٱللَّهَ يَحُولُ بَيْنَ ٱلْمَرْءِ وَقَلْبِهِۦ... ﴾

which means, "O you who believe! Answer Allah (by obeying Him) and (His) Messenger when he calls you to that which will give you life, and know that Allah comes in between a person and his heart (i.e. He prevents an evil person to decide anything)." (Al-Anafâl, 8:24)

He, the Exalted, ordered them to obey Him and His Messenger (peace be upon him) when He called them to that which will give them life. Then He warned them not to fail to obey Him, for this would be the reason for Him to come in between them and their hearts. Allah, the Exalted said,

﴿ ...فَلَمَّا زَاغُوٓا۟ أَزَاغَ ٱللَّهُ قُلُوبَهُمْ ۚ وَٱللَّهُ لَا يَهْدِى ٱلْقَوْمَ ٱلْفَٰسِقِينَ ﴾

which means, "So when they turned away (from the Path of Allah), Allah turned their hearts away (from the Right Path). And Allah guides not the people who are Fâsiqûn (rebellious, disobedient to Allah)." (As-Saff, 61:5)

Allah, the Almighty also said,

$$\text{﴿ كَلَّا ۖ بَلْ ۜ رَانَ عَلَىٰ قُلُوبِهِم مَّا كَانُوا۟ يَكْسِبُونَ ۝ ﴾}$$

which means, "Nay! But on their hearts is the *Rân* (covering of sins and evil deeds) which they used to earn." (Al-Mutaffifîn, 83:14)

Allah, the Exalted said that their sins and evil deeds covered their hearts and came in between them and faith in His verses, therefore, they said that these verses were nothing but tales of the ancients.

Allah, the Almighty said about the hypocrites,

$$\text{﴿ ...نَسُوا۟ ٱللَّهَ فَنَسِيَهُمْ... ۝ ﴾}$$

which means, "They have forgotten Allah, so He has forgotten them." (At-Tawbah, 9:67)

He rewarded them for their indifference to Him by forgetting (neglecting) them, and did not mention any guidance or mercy concerning them. He also said that He made them forget themselves, therefore, they did not try to make themselves perfect by means of good knowledge and righteous deeds, which are guidance and the religion of truth (Islam). He made them forget to seek after that, to love it, learn it and aspire after it, as a punishment for their indifference to Him. The Almighty said the following verses concerning them,

$$\text{﴿ ...أُو۟لَـٰٓئِكَ ٱلَّذِينَ طَبَعَ ٱللَّهُ عَلَىٰ قُلُوبِهِمْ وَٱتَّبَعُوٓا۟ أَهْوَآءَهُمْ ۝ وَٱلَّذِينَ ٱهْتَدَوْا۟ زَادَهُمْ هُدًى وَءَاتَىٰهُمْ تَقْوَىٰهُمْ ۝ ﴾}$$

which means, "Such are men whose hearts Allah has sealed, and they follow their lusts (evil desires). While as for those who accept guidance, He increases their guidance, and bestows on them their piety." (Muhammad, 47:16-17)

He combined following one's vain desires with aberration, which is its outcome and its cause, just as He connected piety and guidance for those who are guided.

Chapter: Guidance is the Partner of Mercy and Aberration is the Partner of Misery

Just as Allah, the Almighty connects guidance and piety, and aberration and transgression, in the same way, He connects guidance, mercy, aberration and distress. Concerning the first, Allah, the Almighty said,

﴿ أُولَٰئِكَ عَلَىٰ هُدًى مِّن رَّبِّهِمْ ۖ وَأُولَٰئِكَ هُمُ ٱلْمُفْلِحُونَ ۝ ﴾

which means, "They are on (true) guidance from their Lord, and they are the successful." (Al-Baqarah, 2:5)

And He, the Almighty said,

﴿ أُولَٰئِكَ عَلَيْهِمْ صَلَوَاتٌ مِّن رَّبِّهِمْ وَرَحْمَةٌ ۖ وَأُولَٰئِكَ هُمُ ٱلْمُهْتَدُونَ ۝ ﴾

which means, "They are those on whom are the *Salawât* (i.e. blessings, etc.) (i.e. who are blessed and will be forgiven) from their Lord, and (they are those who) receive His Mercy, and it is they who are the guided-ones." (Al-Baqarah, 2:157)

And He, the Almighty said concerning the believers,

﴿ رَبَّنَا لَا تُزِغْ قُلُوبَنَا بَعْدَ إِذْ هَدَيْتَنَا وَهَبْ لَنَا مِن لَّدُنكَ رَحْمَةً ۚ

إِنَّكَ أَنتَ ٱلْوَهَّابُ ﴾

which means, "(They say): "Our Lord! Let not our hearts deviate (from the truth) after You have guided us, and grant us mercy from You. Truly, You are the Bestower." (Âl-'Imrân, 3:8)

And the people of the cave said,

$$ ...رَبَّنَآ ءَاتِنَا مِن لَّدُنكَ رَحْمَةً وَهَيِّئْ لَنَا مِنْ أَمْرِنَا رَشَدًا $$

which means, "Our Lord! Bestow on us mercy from Yourself, and facilitate for us our affair in the right way!" (Al-Kahf, 18:10)

And He, the Almighty said,

$$ لَقَدْ كَانَ فِى قَصَصِهِمْ عِبْرَةٌ لِّأُوْلِى ٱلْأَلْبَٰبِ ۗ مَا كَانَ حَدِيثًا يُفْتَرَىٰ وَلَٰكِن تَصْدِيقَ ٱلَّذِى بَيْنَ يَدَيْهِ وَتَفْصِيلَ كُلِّ شَىْءٍ وَهُدًى وَرَحْمَةً لِّقَوْمٍ يُؤْمِنُونَ $$

which means, "Indeed in their stories, there is a lesson for men of understanding. It (the Qur'an) is not a forged statement but a confirmation of the Allah's existing Books [the Taurât (Torah), the Injeel (Gospel) and other Scriptures of Allah] and a detailed explanation of everything and a guide and a Mercy for the people who believe." (Yûsuf, 12:111)

And He, the Almighty said,

$$ وَمَآ أَنزَلْنَا عَلَيْكَ ٱلْكِتَٰبَ إِلَّا لِتُبَيِّنَ لَهُمُ ٱلَّذِى ٱخْتَلَفُوا۟ فِيهِ ۙ وَهُدًى وَرَحْمَةً لِّقَوْمٍ يُؤْمِنُونَ $$

which means, "And We have not sent down the Book (the Qur'an) to you (O Muhammad), except that you may explain clearly unto them those things in which they differ, and (as) a guidance and a mercy for a folk who believe." (An-Nahl, 16:64)

And He, the Almighty said,

﴿ ...وَنَزَّلْنَا عَلَيْكَ ٱلْكِتَٰبَ تِبْيَٰنًا لِّكُلِّ شَىْءٍ وَهُدًى وَرَحْمَةً وَبُشْرَىٰ لِلْمُسْلِمِينَ ۞ ﴾

which means, "And We have sent down to you the Book (the Qur'an) as an exposition of everything, a guidance, a mercy, and glad tidings for those who have submitted themselves (to Allah as Muslims)." (An-Nahl, 16:89)

And He, the Almighty said,

﴿ يَٰٓأَيُّهَا ٱلنَّاسُ قَدْ جَآءَتْكُم مَّوْعِظَةٌ مِّن رَّبِّكُمْ وَشِفَآءٌ لِّمَا فِى ٱلصُّدُورِ وَهُدًى وَرَحْمَةٌ لِّلْمُؤْمِنِينَ ۞ ﴾

which means, "O mankind! There has come to you a good advice from your Lord (i.e. the Qur'ân, ordering all that is good and forbidding all that is evil), and a healing for that (disease of ignorance, doubt, hypocrisy and differences, etc.) in your breasts, - a guidance and a mercy (explaining lawful and unlawful things, etc.) for the believers." (Yûnus, 10:57)

Then Allah, the Almighty mentioned it again,

﴿ قُلْ بِفَضْلِ ٱللَّهِ وَبِرَحْمَتِهِۦ فَبِذَٰلِكَ فَلْيَفْرَحُواْ ۞ ... ﴾

which means, "Say: he "In the Bounty of Allah, and in His Mercy (i.e. Islam and the Qur'ân); -therein let them rejoice." (Yûnus, 10:58)

Verily, there are various expressions of the predecessors concerning the interpretation of the words (Bounty) and (Mercy). But the truth is that they refer to guidance and grace. His Bounty is His Guidance, and His Mercy is His Grace. That is why He connects guidance and grace, just like in Al-Fâtihah,

﴿ ٱهْدِنَا ٱلصِّرَٰطَ ٱلْمُسْتَقِيمَ ۞ صِرَٰطَ ٱلَّذِينَ أَنْعَمْتَ عَلَيْهِمْ ۞ ... ﴾

which means, "Guide us to the Straight Way. The Way of those on whom You have bestowed Your Grace." (Al-Fâtihah, 1:5-6)

The likeness of this is His word to His Messenger (peace be upon him) while reminding him of His Grace upon him.

﴿ أَلَمْ يَجِدْكَ يَتِيمًا فَـَٔاوَىٰ ۝ وَوَجَدَكَ ضَآلًّا فَهَدَىٰ ۝ وَوَجَدَكَ عَآئِلًا فَأَغْنَىٰ ۝ ﴾

which means, "Did He not find you (O Muhammad (Peace be upon him)) an orphan and gave you a refuge? And He found you unaware (of the Qur'ân, its legal laws, and Prophethood, etc.) and guided you? Asnd He found you poor, and made you rich (self-sufficient with self-contentment, etc.)?" (Ad-Duhâ, 93:6-8)

He gathered His guidance and Grace upon him, by giving him refuge and helping him.

And the likeness of this is also found in the word of Nûh (peace be upon him),

﴿ ...أَرَءَيْتُمْ إِن كُنتُ عَلَىٰ بَيِّنَةٍ مِّن رَّبِّي وَءَاتَىٰنِي رَحْمَةً مِّنْ عِندِهِۦ... ۝ ﴾

which means, "Tell me, if I have a clear proof from my Lord, and a Mercy (Prophethood, etc.) has come to me from Him." (Hûd, 11:28)

And the word of Shu'aib,

﴿ ...أَرَءَيْتُمْ إِن كُنتُ عَلَىٰ بَيِّنَةٍ مِّن رَّبِّي وَرَزَقَنِي مِنْهُ رِزْقًا حَسَنًا... ۝ ﴾

which means, "Tell me, if I have a clear evidence from my Lord, and He has given me a good sustenance from Himself (shall I corrupt it by mixing it with the unlawfully earned money)." (Hûd, 11:88)

And He, the Almighty said concerning Al-Khidry,

﴿ فَوَجَدَا عَبْدًا مِّنْ عِبَادِنَآ ءَاتَيْنَٰهُ رَحْمَةً مِّنْ عِندِنَا وَعَلَّمْنَٰهُ مِن لَّدُنَّا عِلْمًا ﴾

which means, "Then they found one of Our slaves, unto whom We had bestowed mercy from Us, and whom We had taught knowledge from Us." (Al-Kahf, 18:65)

And He, the Almighty said to His Messenger (peace be upon him),

﴿ إِنَّا فَتَحْنَا لَكَ فَتْحًا مُّبِينًا ۝ لِّيَغْفِرَ لَكَ ٱللَّهُ مَا تَقَدَّمَ مِن ذَنۢبِكَ وَمَا تَأَخَّرَ وَيُتِمَّ نِعْمَتَهُۥ عَلَيْكَ وَيَهْدِيَكَ صِرَٰطًا مُّسْتَقِيمًا ۝ وَيَنصُرَكَ ٱللَّهُ نَصْرًا عَزِيزًا ۝ ﴾

which means, "Verily, We have given you (O Muhammad) a manifest victory That Allah may forgive you your sins of the past and the future, and complete His Favour on you, and guide you on the Straight Path. And that Allah may help you with strong help." (Al-Fath, 48:1-3)

And He, the Almighty said,

﴿ ...وَأَنزَلَ ٱللَّهُ عَلَيْكَ ٱلْكِتَٰبَ وَٱلْحِكْمَةَ وَعَلَّمَكَ مَا لَمْ تَكُن تَعْلَمُ ۚ وَكَانَ فَضْلُ ٱللَّهِ عَلَيْكَ عَظِيمًا ﴾

which means, "Allah has sent down to you the Book (The Qur'ân), and Al-Hikmah (Islamic laws, knowledge of legal and illegal things i.e. the Prophet's Sunnah - legal ways), and taught you that which you knew not. And Ever Great is the Grace of Allah unto you (O Muhammad)." (An-Nisâ', 4:113)

And He, the Almighty said,

﴿ ...وَلَوْلَا فَضْلُ ٱللَّهِ عَلَيْكُمْ وَرَحْمَتُهُۥ مَا زَكَىٰ مِنكُم مِّنْ أَحَدٍ أَبَدًا... ﴾

which means, "And had it not been for the Grace of Allah and His Mercy on you, not one of you would ever have been pure from sins." (An-Nûr, 24:21)

Therefore, His Bounty is His Guidance, and His Mercy is His Grace and Kindness to them.

And He, the Almighty said,

$$ \text{﴿...فَإِمَّا يَأْتِيَنَّكُم مِّنِّي هُدًى فَمَنِ اتَّبَعَ هُدَايَ فَلَا يَضِلُّ وَلَا يَشْقَىٰ ﴾} $$

which means, "Then if there comes to you guidance from Me, then whoever follows My Guidance shall neither go astray, nor fall into distress and misery." (Tâhâ, 20:123)

Therefore, guidance is the means of preventing evil and disobedience, and mercy is the means of preventing distress, and this is what He mentioned at the beginning of Tâ-Hâ, by saying,

$$ \text{﴿ طه ۝ مَا أَنزَلْنَا عَلَيْكَ ٱلْقُرْءَانَ لِتَشْقَىٰ ﴾} $$

which means, "Tâhâ [These letters are one of the miracles of the Qur'ân, and none but Allah (Alone) knows their meanings.] We have not sent down the Qur'ân unto you (O Muhammad) to cause you distress." (Tâhâ, 20:1-2)

He combined the revelation of the Qur'ân and the means of overcoming distress regarding him, as He said concerning His followers,

$$ \text{﴿...فَلَا يَضِلُّ وَلَا يَشْقَىٰ ﴾} $$

which means, "shall neither go astray, nor fall into distress and misery." (Tâhâ, 20:123)

Therefore, guidance, favor, grace and mercy are all correlated; just as aberration and distress are inseparable. Allah, the Almighty said,

$$\text{﴿ إِنَّ ٱلْمُجْرِمِينَ فِي ضَلَٰلٍ وَسُعُرٍ ۝ ﴾}$$

which means, "Verily, the *Mujrimûn* (polytheists, disbelievers, sinners, criminals, etc.) are in error (in this world) and will burn (in the Hell-fire in the Hereafter)." (Al-Qamar, 54:47)

The word "*Sa'ar*" is the plural of "*Sa'îr*" which means the last degree of torture and distress. Allah, the Almighty also said,

$$\text{﴿ وَلَقَدْ ذَرَأْنَا لِجَهَنَّمَ كَثِيرًا مِّنَ ٱلْجِنِّ وَٱلْإِنسِ ۖ لَهُمْ قُلُوبٌ لَّا يَفْقَهُونَ بِهَا وَلَهُمْ أَعْيُنٌ لَّا يُبْصِرُونَ بِهَا وَلَهُمْ ءَاذَانٌ لَّا يَسْمَعُونَ بِهَا ۚ أُوْلَٰٓئِكَ كَٱلْأَنْعَٰمِ بَلْ هُمْ أَضَلُّ ۚ أُوْلَٰٓئِكَ هُمُ ٱلْغَٰفِلُونَ ۝ ﴾}$$

which means, "And surely, We have created many of the jinns and mankind for Hell. They have hearts wherewith they understand not, they have eyes wherewith they see not, and they have ears wherewith they hear not (the truth). They are like cattle, nay even more astray; those! They are the heedless ones." (Al-A'râf, 7:179)

Allah, the Almighty said again,

$$\text{﴿ وَقَالُواْ لَوْ كُنَّا نَسْمَعُ أَوْ نَعْقِلُ مَا كُنَّا فِي أَصْحَٰبِ ٱلسَّعِيرِ ۝ ﴾}$$

which means, "And they will say: "Had we but listened or used our intelligence, we would not have been among the dwellers of the blazing Fire!" (Al-Mulk, 67:10) Allah, the Almighty connects guidance and relief of the heart and a good life, as He connects aberration and constriction of the heart and a hard life. Allah, the Almighty says,

﴿ فَمَن يُرِدِ ٱللَّهُ أَن يَهۡدِيَهُۥ يَشۡرَحۡ صَدۡرَهُۥ لِلۡإِسۡلَٰمِۖ وَمَن يُرِدۡ أَن يُضِلَّهُۥ يَجۡعَلۡ صَدۡرَهُۥ ضَيِّقًا حَرَجًا ... ﴾

which means, "And whomsoever Allah wills to guide, He opens his breast to Islâm, and whomsoever He wills to send astray, He makes his breast closed and constricted." (Al-An'âm, 6:125)

And He, the Almighty says,

﴿ أَفَمَن شَرَحَ ٱللَّهُ صَدۡرَهُۥ لِلۡإِسۡلَٰمِ فَهُوَ عَلَىٰ نُورٖ مِّن رَّبِّهِۦ ... ﴾

which means, "Is he whose breast Allah has opened to Islâm, so that he is in light from His Lord (as he who is non-Muslim)?" (Az-Zumar, 39:22)

In the same way, Allah, the Almighty connects guidance and returning to Allah in repentance, as He connects aberration and harshness of heart. Allah, the Almighty said,

﴿ ...ٱللَّهُ يَجۡتَبِىٓ إِلَيۡهِ مَن يَشَآءُ وَيَهۡدِىٓ إِلَيۡهِ مَن يُنِيبُ ﴾

which means, "Allah chooses for Himself whom He wills, and guides unto Himself who turns to Him in repentance and in obedience." (Ash-Shûrâ, 42:13)

And He, the Almighty also said,

﴿ ...فَوَيۡلٞ لِّلۡقَٰسِيَةِ قُلُوبُهُم مِّن ذِكۡرِ ٱللَّهِۚ أُوْلَٰٓئِكَ فِى ضَلَٰلٖ مُّبِينٍ ﴾

which means, "So, woe to those whose hearts are hardened against remembrance of Allah! They are in plain error!" (Az-Zumar, 39:22)

Chapter: Bestowing and Preventing

Guidance, mercy and what follows them like favors and gifts are all elements of the attribute of bestowing. Aberration, punishment, and what follows them are all elements of the attribute of preventing. He, the Exalted, manages His creation between His Bestowing and Preventing, and all these are based on perfect wisdom, perfect authority, and perfect praise and therefore, there is no god but Allah.

The Intelligent Person does not Cling to this Material World

People cling to this worldly life because of the corruption in their hearts. The hearts of such people are completely centered round this life and they have no real desire for the Hereafter. It is not possible in such hearts to implant the deeds that will lead to the Hereafter. They remain firm in this material world, while they are cut off from the Hereafter. This is a kind of torment for them according to the degree to which they cling to this material world. Therefore, their desires remain stuck to it, and a barrier is set between them and that which they desire, to the extent that they lose hope to enjoy their pleasure.

Therefore, the intelligent person will remove the means of this pain and regret, and will cease to hold onto this worldly life, just as he takes the initiative to put an end to the causes of corruption. In spite of this, he will still receive his share of the world, while his heart is attached to the highest aim. (the Hereafter). It is only Allah whose Help should be sought.

Chapter: The Evil of Falsehood

Beware of falsehood because it spoils your natural ability to gain information, and it spoils your formation and your ability to teach people. The liar describes that which does not exist, and that which exists he says it does not exist, just as he describes truth as falsehood and falsehood as truth, and good as evil and evil as good. It spoils his conception and his knowledge, which become a punishment. Then he describes what is not true to the person who trusts him. The heart of a liar is far removed from the truth, and is inclined to that which does not exist and he prefers falsehood. When his ability to perceive has been spoiled as well as his knowledge, which is the basis of every voluntarily deed, these deeds would also be spoiled and the principle of falsehood would come into force. Therefore, it would proceed from him just like falsehood proceeds from the tongue, and so, he would not benefit from either his tongue or his deeds.

This is the reason why falsehood is the foundation of evil, just as the Prophet (peace be upon him) said, "Truthfulness leads to righteousness, and righteousness leads to Paradise. And a man keeps on telling the truth until he becomes a truthful person. **Falsehood leads to Al-Fajur (i.e. wickedness, evil-doing), and Al-Fajur (wickedness) leads to the (Hell) Fire**, and a man may keep on telling lies until he is written before Allah, as a liar." [54]

When falsehood proceeds from the heart to the tongue, it spoils it, and then it goes to the body, and spoils the good deeds, just like it spoiled the words of the tongue. Then falsehood prevails in his words, deeds and state. Therefore, corruption would become firmly embedded in him and its disease would extend to a state of destruction if Allah, the Almighty does not cure him with the remedy of truthfulness, which cuts off evil at its source.

That is why the origin of all the good deeds of the hearts is truthfulness, and their opposites such as ostentation, conceit, arrogance, pride, haughtiness, ingratitude, merrymaking, weakness, laziness, cowardice, disgrace and so on, have falsehood as their origin. Therefore, the origin of every good

---

[54] Recorded by Al-Bukhary, Kitâb Al-Adab, section of the word of Allah, the Exalted, ""..... يا أيها الذين آمنوا اتقوا الله, no. (6094), and Muslim (2606).

deed, done secretly or openly, is truthfulness. And the origin of every evil deed, done secretly or openly, is falsehood.

Allah, the Almighty, in return, rewards the liar by frustrating his interests, and rewards the truthful by helping him achieve his interests concerning this world and the Hereafter. Therefore, nothing can make us benefit more in this world and the Hereafter like truthfulness, and in the same way, nothing can make us earn more evil in this world and the Hereafter like falsehood. Allah says,

﴿ يَٰٓأَيُّهَا ٱلَّذِينَ ءَامَنُوا۟ ٱتَّقُوا۟ ٱللَّهَ وَكُونُوا۟ مَعَ ٱلصَّٰدِقِينَ ۝ ﴾

which means, "O you who believe! Be afraid of Allah, and be with those who are true (in words and deeds)." (At-Tawbah, 9:119)

Allah, the Almighty said again,

﴿ ...هَٰذَا يَوْمُ يَنفَعُ ٱلصَّٰدِقِينَ صِدْقُهُمْ... ۝ ﴾

which means, "This is a Day on which the truthful will profit from their truth." (Al-Mâ'idah, 5:119)

He, the Exalted, said again,

﴿ ...فَإِذَا عَزَمَ ٱلْأَمْرُ فَلَوْ صَدَقُوا۟ ٱللَّهَ لَكَانَ خَيْرًا لَّهُمْ ۝ ﴾

which means, "And when the matter (preparation for Jihâd) is resolved on, then if they had been true to Allah, it would have been better for them." (Muhammad, 47:21)

The Exalted also said,

﴿ وَجَآءَ ٱلْمُعَذِّرُونَ مِنَ ٱلْأَعْرَابِ لِيُؤْذَنَ لَهُمْ وَقَعَدَ ٱلَّذِينَ كَذَبُوا۟ ٱللَّهَ وَرَسُولَهُۥ سَيُصِيبُ ٱلَّذِينَ كَفَرُوا۟ مِنْهُمْ عَذَابٌ أَلِيمٌ ۝ ﴾

which means, "And those who made excuses from the Bedouins came (to you, O Prophet) asking your permission to exempt them (from the battle), and those who had lied to Allah and His Messenger sat at home (without asking the permission for it); a painful torment will seize those of them who disbelieve." (At-Tawbah, 9:90)

Chapter: "And it may be that you dislike a thing which is good for you"

Allah, the Almighty says,

﴿... وَعَسَىٰ أَن تَكْرَهُوا۟ شَيْـًٔا وَهُوَ خَيْرٌ لَّكُمْ ۖ وَعَسَىٰ أَن تُحِبُّوا۟ شَيْـًٔا وَهُوَ شَرٌّ لَّكُمْ ۗ وَٱللَّهُ يَعْلَمُ وَأَنتُمْ لَا تَعْلَمُونَ ۝﴾

which means, "And it may be that you dislike a thing which is good for you and that you like a thing which is bad for you. Allah knows but you do not know." (Al-Baqarah, 2:216)

In this Qur'ânic Verse, there are several judgments, meanings and benefits for the servant. If the servant knows that misfortune can produce a desirable thing, and that the desirable thing can produce a misfortune, he would not feel secure against the harm that can come from delight, and he would not lose hope of delight to come from harm, for he does not know the outcomes of things. Verily, it is Allah Who knows about that which the servant does not know, and in this context the following issues must be noted:

Nothing is more beneficial for him than abiding by the judgments of Allah, even if it is difficult for him at the beginning, because all its outcomes are good, delightful, and pleasurable. In the same way, nothing is more harmful for him than committing what is forbidden, even if he loves it. All its outcomes are pain, grief, evil and misfortune.

Furthermore, the mind bears little pain in comparison to the great pleasure and abundant good that it will experience, and likewise man is expected to avoid little in exchange for great rewards and preventing great pain and long term evil.

In this way, we can see that the perception of the ignorant does not go beyond the basics of life; his perception does not reach the goals, but the intelligent person always keeps his eye on the goals behind his actions in life.

The intelligent person perceives forbidden things like delicious food, which contain fatal poison. Whenever its pleasure arouses his interest, the reality of the poison would push him away from it. Also, he perceives the orders of Allah as bitter medicine that leads to good health and recovery.

Whenever its bitterness urges him not to take it, the reality of its usefulness leads him to comply. This requires knowledge that is more than the rudiments of the religion in order to understand the essential goals. It also requires strong patience to adjust oneself to it, in order to bear the difficulties that will be encountered for the sake of the goal. So if he loses certainty and patience, it would be difficult to achieve the goal, and on the other hand if his certainty and patience is strong, every difficulty would be rendered easy for him for the sake of permanent good and eternal pleasure.

There are other meanings of this verse. It also requires the servant to leave all his affairs in the Hands of the One Who knows the outcomes of all things, and to be pleased with whatever He chooses for him.

Also, the meanings of the verse include the fact that he should not propose or choose for his Lord, and should not ask Him for that which he has no knowledge of, for his harm and ruin may be in it and yet he does not know. He should simply ask his Lord to choose good for him and make him pleased with His choice, for that indeed would be the best ending. Also when he leaves all his affairs to his Lord, and is satisfied with His choice for him, Allah will support him by providing him with ability, determination and patience. He, the Almighty would also keep him away from the evil that the servant would have encountered if he had chosen for himself. He would show him some of the positive outcomes of His Choice, which he would not have attained if he had chosen for himself.

Such thinking relieves him of the burdens of trying to choose for himself as Allah frees his heart from estimations and arrangements, which fluctuate in difficulty. And in spite of this, the servant would always be surrounded by what was initially preordained for him. If he is pleased with the Choice of Allah, the preordainment would grant him what is praiseworthy, worthy of thanks and worthy of Allah's Mercy. Otherwise, the preordainment would incur on him all that is dispraised and unworthy of Allah's Mercy, because it was his own choice. When he truly leaves his affairs to Allah and truly becomes pleased with that, he would be surrounded by kindness and care in the preordainment, and he would be under the care and kindness of Allah. His Kindness protects him from that which he fears and His Care makes it easy for him to bear that which He preordained.

When the preordainment is implemented upon the servant, the greatest cause of its implementation would be his trying to avoid it. Therefore, there is nothing more beneficial for him than submission.

Chapter: The Conditions of Being Satisfied with Knowledge

No one benefits from the Grace of Allah, faith and knowledge except the person who knows himself, and does not go beyond his due estimation, and does not say that this is from me, but is certain that everything is from Allah. Such a person knows that He is the Real Granter of all things without a cause from the servant and without the servant actually deserving it. Therefore, the Grace of Allah makes the person deeply humble and he does not see any good at all in or from himself and he knows that all, which is good comes to him from Allah. So the Grace of Allah makes him humble and affects him deeply, even though he may not express it openly.

Therefore, whenever Allah repeatedly bestows grace upon him, he would become more and more humble, more deeply affected, more submissive, more loving, more fearing of Allah, and hopeful of Him. And this is the result of two kinds of noble knowledge:

His knowledge of his Lord, His Perfection, His Kindness, His Richness, His Generosity, His Benevolence, His Mercy and that all good is in His Hands. It is His Kingdom, and He gives to anyone He wills, and prevents it from anyone He wills. All praise and thanks are due to Him, and this is the most perfect praise. After that, comes the servant's own knowledge of himself, and perceiving his due limits, his just estimation, his defects, his injustice, his ignorance and that there is no good at all concerning himself, not in him or from him, and that if he is left to himself, he will surely destroy himself and be in a state of ruin. In the same way, his attributes will lead him to complete ruin, and his essential self is more insignificant and deficient than it. And any good that he has is related to his existence, and not to his own inclinations or actions.

When these two kinds of knowledge become an essential part of his characteristics and not just mere words, then he would know that all praise and thanks are due to Allah, and that all the Commandments and Good belong to Him, and that He is the Only One Who deserves praise and thanks, and that the servant of Allah is the one who deserves dispraise and blame.

Whoever failed to gain this knowledge would be inconsistent in his words, deeds and condition. He would be lost and would not be guided to the Straight Way that leads to Allah. So in order to follow the Straight Way the servant of Allah must know both kinds of knowledge theoretically and practically. The following statement illustrates this fact: Anyone who knows himself, knows his Lord, for the person who knows himself to be ignorant, unjust, defective, poor and humble, would know his Lord to be the complete opposite of these attributes. Therefore, he would acknowledge his due worth, and would not go beyond his limits. He would praise his Lord as He deserves. His deep love, fear, hope, repentance and trust would be turned to his Lord. Allah would be the dearest, the most Feared and the Most Hopeful to him, and this indeed is the true nature of worship.

It has been reported that a wise man wrote the following statement on the door of his house: no one would benefit from our wisdom except the person who knows himself and does not go beyond his limits. . Whoever is like this can enter or else it would be better for him to return until he is qualified.

Chapter: The Danger of Submitting to One's Desires

To restrain oneself from fulfilling unlawful desires is easier than to endure that which is the result of doing so, because giving in to one's desires will either cause pain and punishment or it will prevent a more perfect pleasure than could ever be experienced in this worldly life. Either it kills time to the extent that it causes regret, or it defiles honor, whose preservation is more beneficial and worthy to the servant. Either it takes away some wealth that would be better to be saved than to be wasted, or derogate a reputation that would be better to be praised.

Also it will either remove some grace that would be better to be preserved, or it debases you and makes you subservient to lowly people. Also it causes worry, grief, sadness and fear that is far more than the pleasure of fulfilling the desire, or it causes you to forget some knowledge that would be better to be remembered than satisfying one's desire. Either it makes an enemy rejoice and makes a friend sad, or prevents an expected grace from reaching you, or it causes a flaw or characteristic that will remain permanently. Indeed deeds are the means of developing qualities and character.

Chapter: The Limits of One's Characteristics

Human characteristics have limitations, which if surpassed, would be a transgression, and if one falls short of it, it would be a defect and a disgrace.

Therefore, **there is a limitation for anger**, which is courage and disdain for vice and deficiency. This is its perfection but if it surpasses that limitation, its owner would be guilty of transgressing and wrong doing. And if it falls short of him, he would be a coward and would not have disdain for vice.

Desire has a limitation, which is taking what is sufficient for this worldly life and the attainment of competency. However, when it falls short of that, it would be a disgrace and a waste, and when it surpasses that, it would be greed and a desire for that which is not praiseworthy.

Envy has a limitation, which is to compete in seeking perfection and to be unwilling to let someone do better than oneself. Whoever surpasses that in injustice and transgression, would wish for other people's grace to come to an end, and would seek to harm them. And when it becomes less than the required limit, it would be lowness and lack of ambition. The Prophet (peace be upon him) said, "Do not wish to be like anyone except in two cases: (the first is) a person, whom Allah has given wealth and he spends it righteously; (the second is) the one whom Allah has given wisdom (the Holy Qur'ân) and he acts according to it and teaches it to others." [55]

This is a kind of emulation that the envier imposes on himself in order to be like the one he envies, and it is not the disgraceful kind of envy, in which the envier wishes that the grace of the envied is removed.

Lust has a limitation, which is relief of the heart and mind from the toil of obedience, earning good qualities and making use of them. When it increases to more than its normal state, it would become a burning desire, and its owner would be on the level of animals. And when it becomes less than that, and is not a kind of devotion to seek perfection and favor, it would be a weakness and a disgrace.

Rest has a limitation, which is the revitalization of the self and one's perceptive faculties, in order to be ready for religious duties, earning good qualities and devoting oneself to all that is good., In this way they do not become weak because of toil and weariness and their effect does not become weak. When it goes beyond its normal limit, it would be apathy, laziness, wastefulness and many interests would be lost in this way. And when it becomes less than required, it would be harmful to one's faculties and a means of weakening them, and may even come to a stop with him.

Generosity has a limitation, and it lies between two extremes. When it surpasses its limit, it becomes extravagance, and when it becomes less than the required limit, it is stinginess and miserliness.

Courage has a limitation, and when it surpasses it, it would be rashness, and when it becomes less than the required limit, it

---

[55] Recorded by Al-Bukhary. Kitab Al-'Ilm, bab Al-Ightibat fil 'Ilm wal-Hikmah, no (73), and Muslim (816), At Tirmidhy (1936), and Ibn Majah, no, (4208), (4209).

would be cowardice and weakness. Its limit is to boldly engage on occasions that require courage, and to refrain on the occasions that require refraining. This is like what Mu'âwiyah said to 'Umar, "I have failed to understand whether you are courageous or a coward; you expose yourself to danger and risk to the extent that I say that you are one of the bravest people, and you become so frightened to the extent that I say that you are one of the most cowardly people". Thereupon, he answered,

Courage when there is an occasion

And a coward when there is no occasion

Jealousy has a limitation, which when surpassed is a blameworthy and evil thought about the innocent, and when it becomes less than the required limit, it would be carelessness and indifference concerning one's honor.

Humility has a limitation, which when surpassed would be lowness and disgrace. And when it is less than the required limit, it would turn to arrogance and pride.

Glory has a limitation, which when surpassed would be arrogance and a dispraised character. And when it is less than the required limit, it would turn to lowness and disgrace.

Moderation is the Best Way to Deal with all Matters

Controlling all these emotions with moderation is to adopt the middle way between the two extremes. The interests of this worldly life and the Hereafter are based on this, and not only that, but it is the standard to which the body can work effectively.

If any of its elements are diverted from moderation, and are caused to exceed beyond its due limits or became less than it, its good health would decrease accordingly. Besides, it includes all natural acts, such as sleeping, staying up at night, eating, drinking, copulation, movement, sport, privacy, social intercourse and so on. If moderation is not achieved it would become a defect. Among the noblest and the most beneficial kinds of knowledge, is the knowledge of limitations, especially legal limits; what is commanded and what is forbidden. The most knowledgeable person is the most knowledgeable of these ordained limits, for he is not confused about that which belongs to them and that which does not. Allah, the Almighty said in the Noble Qur'ân,

﴿ ٱلْأَعْرَابُ أَشَدُّ كُفْرًا وَنِفَاقًا وَأَجْدَرُ أَلَّا يَعْلَمُوا۟ حُدُودَ مَآ أَنزَلَ ٱللَّهُ عَلَىٰ رَسُولِهِۦ ﴾

which means, "The Bedouins are the worst in disbelief and hypocrisy, and more likely to be in ignorance of the limits (Allah's Commandments and His Legal Laws, etc.) which Allah has revealed to His Messenger." (At-Tawbah, 9:97)

Therefore, the most moderate person is the one who takes care of the limits of manners, deeds and legalities, in terms of learning and practicing them.

Chapter: Piety within the heart

Abu Ad-Dardâ[56] (may Allah be pleased with him) said, "Pious people are good both in cases of sleep or breaking fast. How can they envy the evil ones for their fasting and night prayers. The smallest amount of piety from a righteous person is better than worship the size of mountains from proud people." These great words show the perfection of the jurisprudence of the

---

[56] He is 'Uwaimir bin Mâlik, a pious companion, known for his courage and piety. He memorized the whole Qur'ân at the time of the Prophet (peace be upon him). He passed away in Syria in 32 A.H. See *Usd Al-Ghâbah*, vol.4, p.218, *Tajrîd Asmâ' As-Sahâbah*, vol.1, p.430, *Al-Istî'âb*, vol.3, p.1227.

Companions and their superiority over whoever came after them, (may Allah be pleased with them all).

You should know that the servant stops seeking Allah through his heart and intention and not through his body. In reality piety is in the heart and not in the body. Allah says,

$$\{ ذَٰلِكَ وَمَن يُعَظِّمْ شَعَٰئِرَ ٱللَّهِ فَإِنَّهَا مِن تَقْوَى ٱلْقُلُوبِ \}$$

which means, "Thus it is an obligation that mankind owes to Allah]. And whosoever honors the Symbols of Allah, then it is truly from the piety of the heart." (Al-Hajj, 22:32)

And He, the Almighty says,

$$\{ لَن يَنَالَ ٱللَّهَ لُحُومُهَا وَلَا دِمَاؤُهَا وَلَٰكِن يَنَالُهُ ٱلتَّقْوَىٰ مِنكُمْ... \}$$

which means, "It is neither their meat nor their blood that reaches Allah, but it is piety from you that reaches Him." (Al-Hajj, 22:37)

And the Prophet (peace be upon him) said, "The piety is here, (and while saying so) he pointed towards his chest."[57]

The intelligent servant of Allah is the one who walks on the straight path with his intention, great desire, and faithful determination with little effort and this is many times more than he who has none of these qualities ; such a person will experience much tiredness and hard travel, whereas the pious servant's intention and love remove all tiredness and beautify the journey he is on. Walking and proceeding to Allah, the Exalted is done through intention, sincere desire, and determination. Whoever has the intention even without the

---

[57] Recorded by Muslim, book of virtue, good manners, and joining of the ties of relationship, chapter on it is forbidden to perpetrate atrocity upon a Muslim, to humiliate him, to insult him, and inviolable is his blood, honor and wealth, no.2564.

deeds will precede whoever has lots of deeds but no intention. This matter requires a lot of explanation.

The Most perfect guidance:

The most perfect guidance is that of the Messenger of Allah (peace be upon him). This guidance gives Allah and the Prophet their rights. The Prophet besides being perfect, has a strong will and he used to perform the optional nightly prayer until his feet swelled, and he would fast until they would say, "He did not break his fast," and he would fight in the cause of Allah, mix with his companions and never avoid them, and he never neglected any optional acts of worship or supplications which are things that people cannot bear. Allah, the Exalted ordered His servants to fulfill both the laws of Islam and the realities of faith; one of them cannot exist without the other.

It was recorded in Musnad, "Islam is open and faith is in the heart."[58] So Islam is open and its owner does not reach the real hidden faith through it, and every real hidden faith that its owner does not perform (the open law of Islam), is useless regardless of its reality. If the heart is torn out of love and fear while the servant is not worshiping Allah and performing the open acts of worship, this will not save him from the Hellfire. Also if he only performs open deeds of Islam and does not have any real hidden faith within him, he will never be saved from the Hellfire.

If this becomes clear, then truthful people who seek Allah and the Hereafter are of two types:

One party spent what remains of their time after performing obligatory acts of worship in physical optional acts of worship and make that their habit without observing the deeds of the heart, its level, and judgments. They have the origin of real

---

[58] Weak hadith, recorded by Ahmad in his musnad, n.3/134, Al-Albâny approved its weakness in Al-Jâmi', no.2280.

hidden deeds but their intentions are all wasted. The other party spent what remains of their time after performing obligatory acts of worship in caring for the goodness of their hearts and seeking Allah alone. They make the power of their worship in the deeds of the heart by correcting their love, fear, hope, trust, and regret and find that the fewest supplications that they recite are preferred to them than a lot of physical optional deeds, which are not based in the heart. Whoever is granted this blessing from Allah and his heart seeks Allah alone either by love, fear, humiliation, or longing for Allah, he must not replace this feeling with anything else except by performing obligatory acts of worship even if this feeling is no longer present. But there is a hesitation concerning optional acts of worship; if he can he may perform them while having this feeling but if he is going to loose it, he should think about what is more preferable to Allah: is it by performing this optional act of worship even if his feeling is gone like helping a needy one, guiding a sinner, etc? Here he should prefer the optional act of worship and if he presents it to Allah seeking Him alone and seeking His closeness, Allah will grant him the feelings he had lost and even better than they were. But if this feeling is better than the optional deed, he should stick to it until it goes and then perform the optional act of worship, as feelings go away but optional acts do not have a special time.

This subject requires knowledge of jurisprudence, and the levels of deeds, and their importance. May Allah grant success, there is no god but Him.

Chapter: The Origin of Praised and Dispraised Morals

The origin of all dispraised morals is pride, disgrace, and lowness and the origin of all praised morals is piety and having high and lofty intentions. Arrogance, ingratitude, slander, vanity, envy, injustice, cruelty, tyranny, disobedience, refusing advice, obsession, seeking and loving authority and power, and to be praised for what he did not do are all caused by pride.

Lying, meanness, treason, hypocrisy, cunning, deception, greediness, fright, cowardice, miserliness, weakness, laziness, humility to other than Allah, and replacing what is better with what is worse, are qualities from disgrace and lowness,

while virtuous morals like patience, courage, justice, chivalry, abstinence, generosity, tolerance, forgiveness, bearing, unselfishness, raising oneself above lowness, humility, satisfaction, truth, sincerity, rewarding others for their good deeds with the same or better and neglecting their slips, abandoning what is useless, and purifying the heart from all dispraised morals are things that arise from piety and having high and lofty intentions. Allah, the Exalted informed us about the barren earth, when He sends down water (rain) to it, it is stirred to life and growth (of vegetation). The same occurs with creatures, which are created from the earth, when they get their share of Allah's blessings. Dispraised morals are like the fire that is high when it is well but when it goes out, it is low and mean. Good morals are like the earth and its creatures. Whoever has a high intention and is pious, will have every good moral and whoever is low and mean, will acquire every bad vice.

Chapter: The Requirements of Achieving Great Targets

Achieving high aims depends upon having a firm intention and a strong will. Whoever looses them will never attain his goals, because when one's intention is firm, it adheres to the plan and if one's will is strong, the servant will walk along the right way that leads to that aim. Having a strong will opens the way and a resolute intention focuses one on the aim. If his aim coincides with the way that reaches to it, he will be successful. If his intention is weak he will not have a high aim. If his will is not strong, it will not lead him to his aim. The whole matter depends upon the will and intention of the servant and they will never be achieved without neglecting three matters:

First: innovations, which people make.

Second: abandoning worldly benefits and vain pleasures, which hinder him from his way and aim.

Third: purify one's heart from any vain desires that will distract his intention.

Chapter: The Wisdom of Ibn Mas'ûd

One of the sayings of Ibn Mas'ûd (may Allah be pleased with him) was that a man said in his presence, "I do not like to be from among the companions of the right hand, but I would like to be from among those who are nearest to Allah." 'Abdullâh said, "But there is a servant here, who wishes that when he dies he will not be resurrected again (meaning himself)."

He went out one day, and some people followed him, so he asked them, "Do you need anything?" They said, "No, but we want to walk with you (as your followers)." He said, "Go back; you are humiliating yourselves and may do so to me."

And he said, "If you knew about me what I knew about myself, you would pour dust upon my head." And he said, "I preferred the two unpleasant matters: death and poverty; by Allah they are in reality wealth and life, and I do not care which of them I may be afflicted with, as I will seek Allah in each of them; if it is wealth, it means I am going to meet Allah, and if it is poverty, I will be patient."

And he said, "As you walk in the night and day your age decreases and your deeds are recorded, and death will come suddenly. Whoever sows good deeds, he will harvest goodness, and whoever sows evil deeds, he will harvest regret. Everyone will reap what he sows; he will neither precede a slow man according to his fortune nor catch up with an eager man unless it is destined for him.

- Whoever does good, must know that it is Allah, who allowed him to do so, and whoever is protected from evil, must know that it is Allah, who protected him.

- Pious people are masters, jurists are leaders, and accompanying them will increase your good.

- They are two: guidance and speech. The best speech is the words of Allah and the best guidance is that of Muhammad (peace be upon him). The worst matter of all is innovations and every innovation is a novelty, so do not be disturbed by hopes and do not waste time. Whatever is coming is near at hand and whatever is far will not come. Whoever is unhappy was destined to be so, when he was in his mother's womb and the happy servant is the one who takes the examples of others. Killing a Muslim is disbelief, abusing him is an evil doing and the Muslim is not allowed to abandon his brother Muslim for more than three days; he must greet him when he meets him, answer him when he calls him, and visit him when he is ill. The most evil account is that of lying. Lying contains no good, neither in cases of seriousness nor joking nor when a man promises his son something and does not fulfill it. Falsehood leads to wickedness and evil doing, and wickedness leads to the Hellfire and Truthfulness leads to righteousness, and righteousness leads to Paradise. It would be said to the truthful person that he was truthful and pious, and it would be said to the lying person that he was lying and wicked. Muhammad (peace be upon him) said to us, "And a man keeps on telling the truth until he becomes a truthful person and a man may keep on telling lies until he is written before Allah as a liar."

- The most truthful speech is the Book of Allah, the most correct word is the word of piety, the best religion is that of Ibrâhîm (Abraham, peace be upon him), the best Sunnah is the sunnah of Muhammad (peace be upon him), the best guidance is the guidance of the Prophets, the most honorable talk is remembering Allah, the best account is the Qur'ân, the best matters are its consequences, and the worst matter is innovation. Whatever is little but sufficient is better than what is a lot but distracting. A soul that you save from evil is better than an emirate that you cannot control. The worst excuse is when it is the time of death and the worst regret is on the Day of Resurrection. The worst error is that which is done after guidance. The best wealth is the wealth of the soul. The best provision is piety. The best content of the heart is certainty, and doubt is disbelief. The worst blindness is blindness of the heart. Wine is a collection of evil, and unrighteous women are the traps of Satan. Adolescence is a kind of insanity, and wailing is a deed from the pre-Islamic era.

- Among people are those who attend Friday prayer and hardly pay attention to it and remember Allah with his tongue but not with his heart. The gravest sin is lying, and whoever pardons people Allah will pardon him. Whoever restrains his anger, Allah will reward him, and whoever forgives, Allah will forgive him. Whoever is patient during disasters, Allah will recompense him. The worst of profits is usury, and the worst kind of eating is devouring an orphan's property. Whatever satisfies the soul, is enough for you. The destiny of each of you is the grave. Matters depend upon their consequences. The most honorable way of dying is the death of a martyr. Whoever is proud, Allah will humiliate him, and whoever disobeys Allah, will obey Satan.

- People who have memorized the Qur'ân should be known by the night when people are sleeping and he is awake, and by the morning when people are not fasting but he is, by his sadness when they are happy, by his crying when they are laughing, by his silence when they are slandering, and by his piety and humility when they are arrogant. He who has memorized the Qur'ân should be tearful, sad, wise, patient, and calm, he should not be rude, inattentive, loud or cruel.

- Whoever assaults others because of his authority, Allah will degrade him. Whoever is humble because of his piety, Allah will elevate him. Allah has a gathering and Satan has a gathering. The gathering of Allah promises good and believes in right, while the gathering of Satan threatens evil and doubts right. If you see such a gathering seek refuge with Allah.

- People have many good sayings, and whoever's words agree with his deeds, he would have been granted goodness, and whoever's sayings contradict his deeds, he is simply scolding himself.

- I hate to find a lazy, empty man, who neither works for his worldly living nor for the Hereafter. He whose prayer did not command him to do right and did not forbid him from doing wrong. It will not be of any use to him; it will only increase the distance between him and Allah.

- Undoubtedly one should never please people by displeasing Allah, should not praise anyone for that which Allah had bestowed on you, and never blame anyone for that which Allah did not grant you. The blessings of Allah will not be gained according to someone's desires nor will they be removed because of someone's hatred. Allah in His justice and patience makes the soul happy by being content, and makes sadness and grief when one doubts and is discontent.

- As long as you are performing prayer, you are knocking at the door of Allah, and whoever is knocking at the door of Allah, Allah will open it for him.

- Man almost forgets the knowledge he has gained because of the sins he has committed.

- Do not neglect knowledge and guidance, or the light of night, renewed hearts, and wearing worn clothes. In this way you will be known in the heavens and hidden from the people of the earth.

- The hearts of man pass through two phases: activity and inactivity, so seek your hearts while they are in the state of activity and control them in the phase of inactivity.

- Knowledge is not being able to narrate several accounts but by being pious.

- The disbeliever may have a stronger and healthier body but he has the sickest heart among them, and the believer has the healthiest heart among people but perhaps the weakest body. By Allah, if your hearts are sick and your bodies are healthy, you would be lower than an insect in the sight of Allah.

- The servant of Allah will not reach the reality of faith until he reaches its top, and he will not reach its top until poverty becomes preferable to him more than wealth, humility more preferable than honor, and until the one who praises or dispraises him are equal in his sight. Man comes out of his house with his religion and returns with nothing. A person comes to you while he cannot do anything for you nor your soul, either good or bad, and swore by Allah to others that he is good and he flatters you, and he returns and does nothing from what he wanted and Allah is not pleased with him.

- If I mocked at a dog, I would be afraid of being changed into one.

- Sin is whatever the heart is not comfortable with.

- In every look, Satan will seduce you.

- With happiness comes sadness. Every house that once was filled with joy will be faced with examples and each one of you is a guest and his money is a loan; the guest will travel and the loan will be repaid.

- Later in time there will be nations whose best deeds will be reciting among themselves and listening to evil reciters.

- If man wanted to be treated justly by his soul, he should visit those whom he would like to be visited by. The right is heavy but healthy, and evil is light but harmful.

- Perhaps one desire causes long term sadness.

- There is nothing on earth that badly needs to be imprisoned more than the tongue.

- If adultery and usury appeared in a town or village, it is a sign of its coming destruction.

- Whoever could put his treasure in heaven so that it would neither be eaten by worms nor stolen by thieves; he must do so, as the heart of man is his treasure.

- Do not imitate anyone concerning religion; if he believes you, you believe and if he disbelieves you, you will disbelieve. If you must imitate, you should imitate dead people as the living are not protected from seduction.

- None of you should be weak. They said, "What do you mean by weak?" He said, "He says, 'I am with the people; if they are on the right way I will be on the right way and if they go astray I will go astray. One should adjust himself to adhere to Islam even when people disbelieve."

  A man said to him, "Teach me words that are complete and useful." He said, "Worship Allah and do not worship any partners with Him, adhere to the Qur'ân whatever it says, and whoever calls you to the right accept it from him even if he is far from you and odious, and whoever calls you to what is wrong reject him even if he is a lover and close to you."

- The servant of Allah will be brought on the Day of Resurrection and he would be ordered to render back his trust, and he would say, "O My Lord! From where? The worldly life has gone." Then this trust would be shaped as it had been during this worldly life but it will be in the bottom of Hellfire, and he would fall down after it, put it on his shoulder, and begin to come up until he thought that he is about to come out, but it would fall again and he would fall after it forever."

- Submit your heart in three situations: when listening to the Qur'ân, during gatherings of remembering Allah, and during times of solitude. If you do not find your heart in these three situations, ask Allah to grant you with a heart, as you do not have one.

  Al-Junaid said, "I visited a youth, who asked me about repentance and its reality. I answered him and said, 'To put your sin between your eyes (never to forget it) until death comes to you', and he said to me, 'No this is not the reality of repentance', so I said to him, 'What is the reality of repentance according to you?' He said, 'To forget your sin.' And he left me and went away.' So I asked the Prophet (peace be upon him) "O Abu Al-Qâsim! What is it according to you?' He said, 'It is like what the youth said.' He said, 'How is that?' He said, 'If I was in a state of alienation then Allah moved me from this to a state of devotion, then remembering alienation when one is devoted, is alienation."

Chapter: Sincerity and Love that are Praised cannot Coexist

Sincerity and love that are praised cannot coexist in one heart just like water and fire cannot coexist. If you urge yourself to seek sincerity, you should kill greed first by using a knife made of despair, and you should neglect praise and thanks and be ascetic like asceticism in this worldly life. If you killed greed and abandoned praise and thanks, sincerity would be easy for you.

If you said, "What will help me to kill greed and abandon praise and thanks?" You can say, "What will help you to kill greed is by surely knowing that every matter that the servant could be greedy about is in the hands of Allah, and surely no one else has the keys to this lock. Allah alone can bestow it upon His servant. The servant should know that there is neither praise nor thanks nor dispraise or blame that can harm you or be useful to you except that of Allah. Once a Bedouin said to the Prophet (peace be upon him), "My praise beautifies and my dispraise disgraces.' He said, 'The one who can do that is Allah, the Exalted and ever Majestic.'"[59] Do not praise the one whose

---

[59] This hadith was mentioned by Al-Ḥâfizh bin Ḥajar in *Al-Fatḥ*, vol.8, p.591, he said, "Qatâdah (may Allah be pleased with him) narrated that a man came to the Prophet (peace be upon him) and said from without the inner apartments, "O Muhammad! My praise beautifies and my dispraise disgraces.' The Prophet (peace be upon him) said, 'The one who can do that is Allah, the Exalted and ever Majestic.'" Al-'Iz bin 'Abdus-Salâm mentioned it in his book,

praises of you will not beautify you, and do not dispraise the one whose dispraise will not disgrace you. Only praise the One whose beauty is in His praise and disgrace is in His dispraise. This cannot be done except through being patient and having firm belief. Whenever you lose patience and belief, you will be like the one who wanted to travel by sea without a boat. Allah, the Exalted says,

$$\text{﴿ فَاصْبِرْ إِنَّ وَعْدَ اللَّهِ حَقٌّ وَلَا يَسْتَخِفَّنَّكَ الَّذِينَ لَا يُوقِنُونَ ﴾}$$

which means, "So be patient (O Muhammad). Verily, the Promise of Allah is true, and let not those who have no certainty of faith, discourage you from conveying Allah's Message (which you are obliged to convey)." (Ar-Rûm, 30:60)

And He, the Almighty says,

$$\text{﴿ وَجَعَلْنَا مِنْهُمْ أَئِمَّةً يَهْدُونَ بِأَمْرِنَا لَمَّا صَبَرُوا وَكَانُوا بِآيَاتِنَا يُوقِنُونَ ﴾}$$

which means, "And We made from among them (Children of Israel), leaders, giving guidance under Our Command, when they were patient and used to believe with certainty in Our *Ayât* (proofs, evidences, verses, lessons, signs, revelations, etc.)." (As-Sajdah, 32:24)

Chapter: Pleasure Depends upon Determination

The pleasure of each one of us depends upon his value, determination, and honor. The one who has the most honorable soul, the firmest determination, and is the most valuable among people is the one who finds his pleasure in knowing Allah, loving Him, longing to meet Him, and pleasing

---

Qawâ'id Al-Ahkâm, vol.1, p.162, that some people said to the Prophet (peace be upon him), "O Muhammad! Give me, as my praise beautifies and my dispraise disgraces.' He said, 'The one who can do that is the Lord of all the worlds.'"

Him by doing what He likes; his pleasure is in seeking Allah and dedicating his determination to Him. Below that there are several ranks that only Allah knows their numbers, until the ranks end with he whose pleasure is in seeking the most mean and low matters from among all kinds of indecency: in speech, deeds, and works. If the pleasure of the first rank was offered to him, his soul would neither accept it nor pay any attention to it and maybe his soul would suffer from it, as whoever is in the first rank will neither accept the pleasure of that in the last rank nor pay attention to it.

Whoever experiences the most complete pleasure among people is the one who gathers the pleasures of the body, heart and soul. He is enjoying his lawful pleasures in a way that is neither decreasing his reward in the Hereafter nor depriving him from the pleasure of knowledge and being close to Allah. Such a person is from among those about whom Allah says,

﴿ قُلْ مَنْ حَرَّمَ زِينَةَ ٱللَّهِ ٱلَّتِىٓ أَخْرَجَ لِعِبَادِهِۦ وَٱلطَّيِّبَٰتِ مِنَ ٱلرِّزْقِ قُلْ هِىَ لِلَّذِينَ ءَامَنُوا۟ فِى ٱلْحَيَوٰةِ ٱلدُّنْيَا خَالِصَةً يَوْمَ ٱلْقِيَٰمَةِ ... ﴾

which means, "Say (O Muhammad): "Who has forbidden the adoration with clothes given by Allah, which He has produced for his slaves, and *At-Taiyibât* [all kinds of <u>Halâl</u> (lawful) things] of food?" Say: "They are, in the life of this world, for those who believe, (and) exclusively for them (believers) on the Day of Resurrection (the disbelievers will not share them)." (Al-A'râf, 7:32)

Whoever has the lowest share of pleasure is the one, who enjoys it in a way that deprives him of the pleasures of the Hereafter and is like those about whom Allah says on the Day of Resurrection,

﴿ ... أَذْهَبْتُمْ طَيِّبَٰتِكُمْ فِى حَيَاتِكُمُ ٱلدُّنْيَا وَٱسْتَمْتَعْتُم بِهَا ... ﴾

which means, "You received your good things in the life of the world, and you took your pleasure therein." (Al-Ahqâf, 46:20)

Both parties enjoyed their pleasures but in different ways. Some enjoyed them in a way that is permissible, so they gathered the pleasures of this worldly life and the Hereafter. Others enjoyed them according to their desires and either they were permissible or not, so they were deprived of the pleasures of this worldly life and missed the pleasures of the Hereafter. Neither the pleasures of this worldly life lasted nor the pleasures of the Hereafter. Whoever wants pleasure, its continuance, and a good life, should use the pleasure of this worldly life to take him to the pleasure of the Hereafter. That means to use it to dedicate his heart to Allah, His orders, and to worship Him; to use this pleasure as an aid and power to help him fulfill his aim not just some desires. If he was among those who were deprived of the pleasures of this worldly life, he should seek what he missed in the pleasures of the Hereafter and control himself during this life by abandoning in order to gain them all in the Hereafter. The pleasures of this worldly life are the best supporters and helpers for whoever truly seeks Allah and the Hereafter and dedicates his determination to what is in the Hereafter. Missing the pleasures of this life is the best helper for he who seeks Allah and the Hereafter, and whoever enjoys the benefits of life in a way that will not decrease his share of pleasures in the Hereafter, he will enjoy both pleasures but if he does not he will lose everything.

The Results of Abandoning Sins

Glorified be Allah, the Lord of all the worlds. If we consider the results of abandoning sins, we would cease to commit sins. Abandoning sins will result in raising one's magnanimity, protecting honor, keeping glory, and preserving wealth, which Allah makes for our benefit during this worldly life and the Hereafter, having the love of creatures, judging between them, a good way of living, granting relief to the body, strength to the heart, relief to the soul, joy to the heart, delight to the chest, being safe from the dangers of dissoluteness and wantonness, having only a little sadness, grief, and distress, honoring the soul by not accepting humiliation, protecting the light of the heart by being turned away from the darkness of sin, showing the way to the heart which cannot be seen by the disbelievers, providing subsistence from sources that we could never imagine, making easy whatever is hard for the disbelievers, helping him to obey, aiding he who is learning, and increasing other's supplications for him. This is all regardless of what he gains like beauty, glory in the hearts of people, support and protection from others if he was hurt, protection of his honor if he was slandered, answering his supplication and being close to Allah, and close to the Angels and being far from the Satans among the humans and the jinn. People will compete to serve him and fulfill his needs and to gain his love and company. He will not fear death but he will be happy to meet Allah and receive his reward. The world will be low in his eyes while the Hereafter will be great. He will seek the greatest property, supreme achievement in the Hereafter, tasting the sweetness of obedience, the sweetness of faith, the supplications of the angels that carry the Throne and the other angels around him, the happiness of the two angels that are recording his deeds and their supplications, an increase of knowledge, understanding, and faith, loving Allah, longing to meet Him and happiness at his repentance. Allah will reward him with happiness and joy that are not even close to the happiness experienced when committing sins.

These are some of the results that are gained in this worldly life when the servant abandons sins. If he dies, the Angels will meet him announcing the good news from his Lord that he will enter Paradise and that there is neither fear nor grief for him. He will leave the prison of this life to go to the garden of Paradise; enjoying its pleasures until the Day of Resurrection.

And on the Day of Resurrection, while the people will be sweating and hot he will be in the shade of the Throne, and when they are gone, he will be taken by the right hand with his pious companions and the successful party. Allah says,

$$﴿ ذَٰلِكَ فَضْلُ ٱللَّهِ يُؤْتِيهِ مَن يَشَآءُ ۚ وَٱللَّهُ ذُو ٱلْفَضْلِ ٱلْعَظِيمِ ۝ ﴾$$

which means, "That is the Grace of Allah, which He bestows on whom He wills. And Allah is the Owner of Mighty Grace." (Al-Jumu'ah, 62:4)

Chapter: The Piety of 'Umar bin 'Abdul 'Azîz

Ibn Sa'ad [60] said in *At-Tabaqât* about 'Umar bin 'Abdul 'Azîz [61] that when he delivered a speech on the pulpit and feared to be touched with conceit, he would stop the speech. And when he wrote a note and feared conceit, he would tear it up and say, "O Allah, I seek refuge with you from the evil of myself."

You should know that when a servant begins a speech or deed, with which Allah's Pleasure is sought, seeking Allah's Favor upon him and His Good Fortune for him, and that it is from Allah and not from him or his knowledge, thought, might

---

[60] He is Muhammad bin Sa'ad bin Munî' Al-Basry Az-Zuhry, a trustworthy historian. He was one of the memorizers of hadith. He (may Allah have mercy upon him) died in 230 A. H. Adopted from Tahdhîb At-Tahdhîb (9\182), Aj-Jarh wat-Ta'dîl (7\1433), Mîzânul-I'tidâl (3\560) and Lisânul-Mîzân (7\359) and Siyar A'lâmu-Nubalâ' (4\348).

[61] He is 'Umar bin 'Abdul 'Azîz bin Marwân bin Al-Hakam Al-Umawy, from Quraish tribe, his nickname is Abu Hafs. Historians considered him as the fifth of the Rightly Guided Caliphs. The period of his reign was two and a half years. He (may Allah have mercy upon him) died in 101 A. H. Adopted from Tahdhîb At-Tahdhîb (7\475), Târikh Al-Bukhâry Alkabîr (6\174), Aj-Jarh wat-Ta'dîl (1\663) and Siyar A'lâmu-Nubalâ' (5\114).

and strength, and moreover, it is He who created the tongue, then the heart, the eye and the ear are for him.

Therefore, He who favored him with that is the One Who favored him with the ability to speak and act. If he keeps this in his mind and heart, he would not be caught in the trap of conceit, whose origin is overt consideration of oneself, and taking no consideration of his Lord's Favor, Good Fortune and Support.

If these remarks are far away from his heart and mind, his self would assert itself, and there would be conceit, and his speech and deeds would be corrupted. At times, he would be hindered from completing his task, and this would be mercy upon him, so that he does not forget to consider the Favor and Good Fortune provided by Allah. And at other times, he would be able to complete it, but he would have no fruit, and if he has fruit, it would be weak, and not as he had desired. At other times, its harm would be more than its benefit, and there would be a lot of evil according to his negligence of good fortune and favor, and his conceit. According to this situation, Allah, the Almighty directs His servant to righteous speech and deeds, so as to enlarge their fruit for him or frustrate them for him and prevent him from the fruit. Therefore, nothing is more harmful to deeds than conceit and seeing oneself as actually the originator of one's deeds.

Therefore, when Allah wills good for His servant, He makes him witness His Favor, Good Fortune and Support for him in everything he says or does, and then he would not be conceited. And then He would make him witness his carelessness, and he would repent to Him and seek His Forgiveness and become shy to ask for a reward.

On the contrary, if He concealed it from him, and the servant found himself to be indispensable for the performance of his deeds, and found himself to be perfect and became self satisfied, his deeds would not be accepted, or gain the satisfaction of Allah.

Therefore, the person who he profoundly knowledgeable about Allah performs deeds for the sake of Allah, while observing in them His Favor, Grace and Good Fortune, repenting for any defect and being shy in front of Allah for failing to give Him His due right. The ignorant people perform deeds for the sake of their own vain desires and interests, observing themselves in them, and regarding them as a favor to his Lord and being satisfied with his deeds. Therefore, this is one category and that is another category, and they are far from each other.

Chapter: The Benefits of Deserting Evil Habits

In order to attain the pleasure of Allah, one should desert all bad habits and abandon anything that hinders one from achieving this goal. And "*'Awâ'id*" means: to enjoy the pleasure of living in gentleness, relaxation, and that which people are used to as forms and situations that people have adopted and placed them in the position of Islamic law. They disapprove of the person who violates them, but do not disapprove of the one who violates clear Islamic law. They might accuse the person of unbelief, heresy or perversity. They might as well abandon him and punish him for violating these forms.

For the sake of these forms, they have abandoned the Prophet's Sunnah (peace be upon him), and they made them equal to the Messenger (peace be upon him) by supporting them. Therefore, the good for them is that which is in conformity with these forms and the bad is that which differs from them.

These situations and forms have prevailed among different groups of people like kings, leaders, Islamic jurists, the poor, those who command good and forbid bad and the common people. Children have grown up in this environment, and adults have been educated according to them, and they have adopted them as ways of life, and moreover, they are dearer to them than the Prophet's Sunnah. Those who support these forms are shut off from the right path, and those who have abided by them have separated themselves from the Prophet's Sunnah. Whoever adopts them will be disappointed with Allah, the Almighty, and whoever follows them without the Book of Allah and the Sunnah of His Messenger (peace be upon him), will not be accepted by Allah. These are the greatest barriers and obstacles between the servant and being close to Allah and His Prophet (peace be upon him).

Chapter: Hindrances

There are open and secret hindrances. They hinder the heart from its advancement to Allah and prevent it from its course. There are three kinds: polytheism, innovation in religion and wrongdoing. The hindrance of polytheism disappears with pure monotheism, the hindrance of innovation in religion disappears with the adoption of the Sunnah, and the hindrance of wrongdoing disappears with repentance.

These hindrances do not become clear to the servant until he is ready and constant in obeying Allah. By then, these hindrances would appear to him, and he would feel them according to the degree of determination and sincerity in his commitment to Allah. Otherwise, as long as he has not taken any step towards Allah, he would not see or feel any hindrance at all.

Chapter: Attachments

Attachments are everything that the heart gets deeply attached to, besides Allah and His Messenger, like worldly pleasures, desires, leadership, being in the company of people and loving them. There is no way at all to cut off or reject these three matters except by strong attachment to the highest issue. Man does not abandon his beloved or that which he is used to, except for the sake of another beloved one who is dearer to him than the former. And whenever his attachment to his desires becomes stronger, his attachment to others would be weaker, and vice versa. To be attached to desires is to have a strong desire for them, and that is according to one's knowledge about it, its honor and its excellence.

Chapter: The Status of the Messenger (peace be upon him)

When the Messenger (peace be upon him) perfected the feeling of great need for Allah, the Almighty, He made him necessary to all the creatures in this world and in the Hereafter. Their need for him in this world is stronger than their need for food, drink and air with which they live. Their need for him in the Hereafter means they would seek his intercession with Allah in order to free them from the suffering of that critical day. All of them would be unable to intercede, but he would intercede for them, and he is the one who would ask for the door of Paradise to be opened for them.

Chapter: Signs of Happiness and Misfortune

Some of the signs of happiness and success are that whenever the servant's knowledge has been increased, he would be more humble and more merciful. Whenever he becomes more knowledgeable, he would fear Allah more and be more cautious. Whenever he gets older, he would be less greedy. Whenever he becomes wealthier, he would be more generous. Whenever he becomes more important, he would be closer to the people, and be more and more at their service.

The signs of misfortune are that whenever he becomes more knowledgeable, he would be more arrogant. Whenever he performs more deeds, he would be more boastful, disdain people and have a very good opinion of himself. When he gets older, he would be greedier. Whenever he becomes wealthier, he would be stingier and whenever he becomes more important, he would be more conceited. These are trials from Allah, the Almighty to try His servants, and according to these trials, some people become happy and others become miserable.

In the same way, wonders are trials and tests from Allah, like sovereignty, authority and wealth. Allah, the Almighty said about His Prophet Sulaimân (Solomon) (peace be upon him), when he saw the throne of Balqîs,

﴿ ...هَذَا مِن فَضْلِ رَبِّي لِيَبْلُوَنِي ءَأَشْكُرُ أَمْ أَكْفُرُ... ﴾

which means, "This is by the Grace of my Lord to test me whether I am grateful or ungrateful!" (An-Naml, 27:40)

That is to say grace is a trial and test from Allah, in order to bring to light the gratitude of the grateful and the ingratitude of the ungrateful.

In the same way, ordeals are a severe trial from Him, Exalted be He. He afflicts with grace as well as with misfortune. The following Qur'ânic verses will illustrate this fact,

﴿ فَأَمَّا ٱلْإِنسَٰنُ إِذَا مَا ٱبْتَلَىٰهُ رَبُّهُۥ فَأَكْرَمَهُۥ وَنَعَّمَهُۥ فَيَقُولُ رَبِّيٓ أَكْرَمَنِ ۝ وَأَمَّآ إِذَا مَا ٱبْتَلَىٰهُ فَقَدَرَ عَلَيْهِ رِزْقَهُۥ فَيَقُولُ رَبِّيٓ أَهَٰنَنِ ۝ كَلَّا ۖ بَل لَّا تُكْرِمُونَ ٱلْيَتِيمَ ۝ ﴾

which means, "As for man, when his Lord tries him by giving him honour and gifts, then he says (puffed up): "My Lord has honoured me." But when He tries him, by straitening his means of life, he says: "My Lord has humiliated me!" Nay! But you treat not the orphans with kindness and generosity (i.e. you neither treat them well, nor give them their exact right of inheritance)!" (Al-Fajr, 89:15-17)

That is to say that honor and gifts from Allah do not always mean that He is pleased with the servant, and at the same time, straightening the means of life for the servant does not always mean he is being degraded.

Chapter: Deeds are an Establishment whose Foundation is Faith

Whoever wants his establishment to be high, should consolidate its foundation and take great care of it, because it is according to the consolidation of the foundation that his establishment can reach the heights and stay firm. Therefore, deeds and grades are considered as an establishment and its foundation is faith. Whenever the foundation is firm, it would be able to hold the establishment and add more to it. And when any part of the establishment is destroyed, it would be easy to repair. However, when the foundation is not firm enough, the establishment would not be able to be constructed, and would not be stable. When any part of the foundation is destroyed, the establishment would collapse or would not stay long before it is destroyed.

The person who is profoundly knowledgeable of Allah would be interested in consolidating the foundation and strengthening it. And the ignorant person would be interested in constructing but without taking care of the foundation, and in no time, his establishment would collapse. Allah, the Almighty said in the Qur'ân,

﴿ أَفَمَنْ أَسَّسَ بُنْيَـٰنَهُۥ عَلَىٰ تَقْوَىٰ مِنَ ٱللَّهِ وَرِضْوَٰنٍ خَيْرٌ أَم مَّنْ أَسَّسَ بُنْيَـٰنَهُۥ عَلَىٰ شَفَا جُرُفٍ هَارٍ فَٱنْهَارَ بِهِۦ فِى نَارِ جَهَنَّمَ ... ﴾

which means, "Is it then he, who laid the foundation of his building on piety to Allah and His Good Pleasure, better, or he who laid the foundation of his building on an undetermined brink of a precipice ready to crumble down, so that it crumbled to pieces with him into the Fire of Hell?" (At-Tawbah, 9:109)

Therefore, the foundation regarding the establishment of deeds is like energy for the human body. If there is enough energy, it would be able to maintain the body and prevent many diseases. However, if there is not enough energy, it would fail to maintain the body, and diseases would find their way to it very easily.

For this reason, you should found your deeds on a basis of strong faith, and if anything happens to this strong faith after that, it would be easy to cope with it. And this basis is comprised of two matters:

One is: to have good knowledge of Allah, His Orders and His Beautiful Names and Attributes.

Two is: to have pure submission to Him and His Messenger (peace be upon him) and leave other than Him. This is the strongest foundation a servant can found his deeds on, and according to it, his faith would increase and increase.

Therefore, strengthen the foundation, preserve your faith, continue to be zealous for your faith, spare no effort when things are too much for you, be moderate when you achieve your goal, otherwise, you would always have weak faith and an evil intention and you would not be able to exert any effort.

Say goodbye to this worldly life because the final Farewell is close at hand. When the construction is complete, you should decorate it with good manners and kindness to people, then surround it with a fence of caution that is impossible to be broken through by an enemy, and let there be no defect to be seen through it. And then draw the curtains around its doors, and close the gate with silence from that which you fear. Then install a key to it, like remembering Allah, with which you can open and close it as you like. When you open the door, you open it with the key, and when you close it, you close it with the same key. In this way, you would have built a stronghold with which you have fortified yourself from your enemies. When the enemy went around it, he would not find any entrance, so, he would be disappointed with you.

You should continue to take care of the stronghold at all times, because if the enemy failed to enter from the door, he would initiate for you a way of committing sins from a far distance.

Therefore, if you neglect him, these sins would reach you, and you would soon see the enemy with you in the stronghold, and it would be very difficult for you to get rid of him, and one of the following will apply to you:

- Either he overcomes you in the stronghold and takes possession of it
- Or he lives with you in it.
- Or he keeps you busy by making you fight him without taking care of your more significant interests.

However, if he is able to get to you through committing sins, he would cause you three problems:

- He would ruin your stronghold.
- He would invade its contents and supplies.
- He would show the defect to thieves of his kind. You would continue to suffer from their invasions one after the other, until they weaken your strength and undermine your determination, and you would end up by abandoning the stronghold and leaving it to them.

This is the state of affairs of many people with the enemy. That is why you see them displeasing their Lord by pleasing themselves, and moreover, by pleasing a creature like themselves, which has no power either to harm them or to do them any good. They waste the gain of religion with the gain of wealth. They ruin themselves with that which is transient and will not remain with them.

They rush after the worldly pleasures, while it gives its back to them. They renounce the Hereafter, while it has charged them. They contradict their Lord by following their own vain desires. They rely on life and forget about death. They remember their desires and shares, and forget about that which Allah charged them with, and they care for that which He has guaranteed for them. They do not care for that which He has ordered them to do. They rejoice at worldly pleasures and feel sorry when they miss their share in it, but they do not feel sorry when they miss Paradise and what it contains.

They do not rejoice at faith the way they rejoice at the Dirham and the Dinar. They ruin their reward with their sins, their guidance with perversity and their good with evil. They mix their faith with uncertainty, and their lawful deeds with the unlawful. They hesitate in the confusion of their ideas and thoughts. They neglect Allah's guidance, which He guided them to. And what is more, the enemy uses the owner of the stronghold to ruin his own stronghold with his own hands.

Chapter: The Bases of Infidelity

There are four bases of infidelity: They are pride, envy, anger, and desire.

Pride can be prevented through submission to Allah, envy through advice and offering it, anger through justice, and desire through devoting oneself to worship. If the base of pride falls, submission would be easy for him, if the base of envy falls, accepting advice and offering it would be easy, if the base of anger falls, justice and humility would be easy, and if the base of desire falls, patience, virtue, and worship would be easy for him. Removing mountains from their places would be easier than removing these four from whoever was afflicted with them, especially if they have become solid bases, habits, and firm characteristics. No deed will be worthy and no soul will be pure as long as these four are found in the servant. The more hard he works, the more these four will spoil his deeds. All evil results from them. If they grow in the heart, they will change right to wrong and wrong to right and truth will be considered falsehood and falsehood will be considered truth. This worldly life will be close to him and the Hereafter will be far. If you think carefully about the disbelief of a nation, you will find that it resulted from these four, and their punishment will be according to their intensity. Whoever surrenders to these four would be opening the doors of all sooner and later evils, and whoever avoids them, would be closing the doors of all evils, as they prevent submission, devotion, repentance, accepting right and advice of Muslims, and being modest to Allah and His creatures.

The origin of these four is being ignorant of Allah and of himself. If he knew his Lord, the attributes of His perfection and the qualities of His majesty and knew himself, and his defects and faults, he would never be proud, or angry, and would never envy anyone about what Allah granted him. Envy in reality is a way of showing enmity toward Allah; he hates the blessings of Allah to be granted to another servant while Allah loves it, and such a person likes it to vanish while Allah hates that. He is against Allah in His judgments, destiny, love, and hate. That is why Satan is in reality his enemy; as his sin resulted from pride and envy. Removing these two is done through knowing Allah, acknowledging Him, being satisfied with Him, repenting to Him, removing all anger from his soul and knowing that it is not worthy to be angry and seek revenge. If you do so, you will prefer it more than its creator and the most important thing to remove such a disease is to make it accustomed to be angry and satisfied because of Allah and for Him. Whenever it feels something of anger or satisfaction when seeking Allah, in exchange it will lose something from anger and satisfaction.

The cure of desire is true knowledge and learning that giving the soul all it desires is the greatest cause behind depriving it from these desires, while protecting it from them is the best way to gain them. The more you close the door to desires, the more you would be reaching the desires in the most perfect way.

Anger is like a lion; if its owner sets it free, it will eat him. Desire is like a fire; if its owner starts it, it will burn him. Pride is like fighting against a king to take his Kingdom, if it does not destroy you it will expel you, and envy is like showing enmity to one who is more powerful than you. Whoever overcomes his desire and anger, Satan will depart from him and whoever's desire and anger beat him, Satan will stick to him.

A Most Precious Gem Characteristics of those who do not Know Allah

Those who do not know Allah, His names, or His attributes and those who deny their reality are making Allah hateful to His creatures and closing the way for them to love and get close to Him by obeying Him. We will mention some examples:

Such people persuade weak souls by saying that obedience will not bring them the pleasure of Allah, the Exalted even if it was sincerely done and the servant, who exaggerates in obeying Allah both in secret and public, there is no trust or guarantee that the servant is safe from harm, and that Allah used to take His pious servant from the concave to the brothel, from monotheism to polytheism and playing music, and turns the heart from faith to disbelief. They quote evidence to prove their claims but they do not understand these proofs. They claim that this is the reality of monotheism and they recite the verses of Allah in which He says,

﴿ لَا يُسْأَلُ عَمَّا يَفْعَلُ ... ﴾

which means, "He cannot be questioned as to what He does." (Al-Anbiyâ', 21:23)

And He, the Almighty says,

﴿ أَفَأَمِنُوا مَكْرَ ٱللَّهِ فَلَا يَأْمَنُ مَكْرَ ٱللَّهِ إِلَّا ٱلْقَوْمُ ٱلْخَاسِرُونَ ﴾

which means, "Did they then feel secure against the Plan of Allah. None feels secure from the Plan of Allah except the people who are the losers." (Al-A'râf, 7:99)

And He, the Almighty says,

﴿ ... وَٱعْلَمُوا أَنَّ ٱللَّهَ يَحُولُ بَيْنَ ٱلْمَرْءِ وَقَلْبِهِ ... ﴾

which means, "And know that Allah comes in between a person and his heart (i.e. He prevents an evil person to decide anything)." (Al-Anfâl, 8:24)

They claim that Satan is the source of their knowledge and that it used to be the head by Angels and that every place in both the heavens and the earth had the favor that Satan had bowed in it but destiny was unjust toward it and Allah turned its good eye into the most evil one. They reached the degree that some of their masters said, "You should be afraid of Allah exactly as you are afraid of a lion to jump on you without committing any sin." As proof they recite a hadith of the Prophet (peace be upon him). The Prophet (peace be upon him) said, "A man amongst you may do (good deeds until there is only a cubit between him and Paradise and then what has been written for him decides his behavior and he starts doing (evil) deeds characteristic of the people of the (Hell) Fire."[62] And they mentioned that some of the predecessors said, "The most grievous of the great sins is to feel secure against the plan of Allah and to despair of the mercy of Allah."

Imam Ahmad bin Hanbal recorded that 'Ûn bin 'Abdullâh[63] or another heard a man invoking Allah and saying, "O Allah! Do not let me feel secure of Your plan." So he blamed him and said, "Say, 'O Allah! Do not make me among those who feel secure of Your plan.'" And they based that on their incorrect beliefs, which deny wisdom, justification, and reason and that all the deeds of Allah are not according to any wisdom or cause; He does according to His wish, which is far away from wisdom, justification, and reason. He does not behave for a reason; it is simply lawful for Him to fiercely punish His pious people and generously reward His enemies and the people of sin, as both cases are equal to Him. The impossibility of this matter will become known only by reporting from Allah, the Truthful that He will never do that. Injustice will never come from Allah. It is like making one body into two places at the same time, gathering night and day in one hour, and making a thing visible and invisible at the same time. This is the reality of injustice according to them. If a scholar thinks about it himself, he would find that if we are not secure of His plan, how can we trust Him? How can we depend on obeying and following His orders while we just have this small period of time in front of us to live? If we abandon pleasures, neglect desires, and bear heavy acts of worship while we know that we can not trust Him; He can change our faith into disbelief, monotheism into

---

[62] Recorded by Al-Bukhâry, book of beginning of creation, chapter on mentioning Angels, no. 3208, and recorded by Muslim, no. 2643.
[63] 'Ûn bin 'Abdullâh bin 'Utbah bin Mas'ûd Al-Hadhly, Abu 'Abdullâh, from Kûfah. He was a poet, preacher, and narrator. He (may Allah be merciful to him) passed away in 115 A.H. See *Tahdhîb At-Tahdhîb*, vol.8, p.171, *Târîkh Al-Bukhâry Al-Kabîr*, vol.7, p.131, *Siyar A'lâm An-Nubalâ'*, vol.5, p.103, and *At-Tabqât*, Ibn Sa'd, vol.6, p.218.

polytheism, obedience into disobedience, and piety into impiety, and can punish us forever, and then we will be loosing both this worldly life and the Hereafter.

If such belief increases in their hearts and souls, after that whenever they are ordered to perform acts of worship and neglect desires, they will be like the one who says to his son: if you write, your teacher becomes better, behave yourself and do not disobey him, he may punish you, and if you become lazy, neglectful and disobedient, he may honor you and make you close to him. The father strengthened this belief in his son's heart saying that he cannot trust or believe in neither any threat of any teacher for his wrongdoing nor believe in the promise of good for his good deeds. And when the boy grew up and became more qualified to handle business and position, his father said to him: this is the sultan of our country, who takes a thief from prison and makes him the minister and the Emir and takes the pious man from his job and puts him in prison forever, or kills or crucifies him. When the father said so, he made him hate the sultan and never trust him for any threat or promise. He removed any love for this sultan from his son's heart and replaced it with fear. Fear from an unjust person, who punishes the innocent. This miserable son lost the belief that deeds are either useful or harmful. He neither feels happiness when doing good deeds nor feels bad when doing evil deeds. This is what such people are doing to other humble people who listen to them and believe their words. Whoever wants to make people hate religion and Allah, he can simply say the same thing.

Those who call to this method believe that he is propagating monotheism, destiny, refuting the people of innovations, and supporting religion. By Allah, a wise enemy is better than an ignorant friend. Allah wrote all reality and His Messengers are all witnesses, especially the Qur'ân. If those who call for justice follow the method that Allah and His Messenger used in calling people, the world would be a better place. Allah, the Exalted revealed His words and He is the Truthful and the Faithful that He is treating people according to their deeds and rewarding them according to their actions. The good servant never fears any injustice; his good deeds will never be wasted. The servant never loses even a whit of his good deeds. Allah says,

﴿ ...وَإِن تَكُ حَسَنَةً يُضَٰعِفْهَا وَيُؤْتِ مِن لَّدُنْهُ أَجْرًا عَظِيمًا ۝ ﴾

which means, "But if there is any good (done), He doubles it, and gives from Him a great reward." (An-Nisâ', 4:40)

Allah also punishes those who commit sin without doubling or erasing it through repentance, regret, and asking for forgiveness, while good deed are doubled ten times until seven hundred times.

He, the Almighty reforms evil servants, accepts the hearts of those who are disobedient, forgives sinners, guides people who are astray, rescues those who are spoiled, teaches the ignorant, leads those who are confused, reminds those who forget, and shelters fugitives. But He punishes those who increase in disobedience and violate His limits, after calling them several times to repent, ask forgiveness, and acknowledge His Divinity. After loosing all hope in their response, acknowledging His Divinity, and His oneness, Allah punishes them for some of their disbelief, tyranny, and rebellion. If the servant thinks about his condition, he would feel guilty, and admit that Allah was not unjust toward him and that he was simply unjust to himself. Allah says about the people of the Hellfire,

﴿ فَاعْتَرَفُوا بِذَنبِهِمْ فَسُحْقًا لِّأَصْحَٰبِ ٱلسَّعِيرِ ۝ ﴾

which means, "Then they will confess their sin. So, away with the dwellers of the blazing Fire." (Al-Mulk, 67:11)

And He, the Almighty says about those whom He ruined in this worldly life that they said when they saw His punishment,

$$\left\{ \text{قَالُوا۟ يَٰوَيْلَنَآ إِنَّا كُنَّا ظَٰلِمِينَ ۝ فَمَا زَالَت تِّلْكَ دَعْوَىٰهُمْ حَتَّىٰ جَعَلْنَٰهُمْ حَصِيدًا خَٰمِدِينَ ۝} \right\}$$

which means, "They cried: "Woe to us! Certainly! We have been *Zhâlimûn* (polytheists, wrong-doers and disbelievers in the Oneness of Allah, etc.). And that cry of theirs ceased not, till We made them as a field that is reaped, extinct (dead)." (Al-Anbiyâ', 21:14-15)

And He, the Almighty says that the owners of the garden, which He burnt when they saw it said,

$$\left\{ \text{قَالُوا۟ سُبْحَٰنَ رَبِّنَآ إِنَّا كُنَّا ظَٰلِمِينَ ۝} \right\}$$

which means, "They said: "Glory to Our Lord! Verily, we have been *Zhâlimûn* (wrong-doers, etc.)." (Al-Qalam, 68:29)

Al-Hasan said, "The people of the Hellfire entered Hell while praising Allah in their hearts and could not prevent that. That is why Allah says,

$$\left\{ \text{فَقُطِعَ دَابِرُ ٱلْقَوْمِ ٱلَّذِينَ ظَلَمُوا۟ ۚ وَٱلْحَمْدُ لِلَّهِ رَبِّ ٱلْعَٰلَمِينَ ۝} \right\}$$

which means, "So the roots of the people who did wrong were cut off. And all the praises and thanks be to Allah, the Lord of the *'Alamîn* (mankind, jinn, and all that exists)." (Al-An'âm, 6:45)

That is to say, Allah cut off their roots and He is to be praised for doing so according to His wisdom and justice and giving the suitable punishment in its due time. That is why He said in another verse when He sets His judgments of His servants; the people of good to Paradise and people of evil to Hellfire,

﴿ ...وَقُضِىَ بَيْنَهُم بِٱلْحَقِّ وَقِيلَ ٱلْحَمْدُ لِلَّهِ رَبِّ ٱلْعَالَمِينَ ﴿٧٥﴾ ﴾

which means, "And they (all the creatures) will be judged with truth, and it will be said. All the praises and thanks be to Allah, the Lord of the 'Alamîn (mankind, jinn and all that exists)." (Az-Zumar, 39:75)

He did not mention those who praise Allah, He left it general; as if the whole universe thanks Him when they see His wisdom, justice, and favor. That is why He says on behalf of the people of the Hellfire,

﴿ قِيلَ ٱدْخُلُوٓا۟ أَبْوَابَ جَهَنَّمَ... ﴿٧٢﴾ ﴾

which means, "It will be said (to them): "Enter you the gates of Hell." (Az-Zumar, 39:72)

It is as if the whole universe is saying so even their bodies, and souls, and the heavens and the earth. He, the Exalted tells us that as He is going to destroy His enemies, He is going to save His pious people, and He is not going to destroy them according to His mere wish.

When Nûh (Noah, peace be upon him) asked Him to save his son, Allah tells us that He will drown him because of his evil deeds and disbelief and did not say: I drowned him according to My wish and will without a reason or a sin. And Allah guarantees to increase those who fight in His cause in guidance and did not say that He will destroy their efforts and mislead them.

And He also guarantees to increase in guidance those who are pious and seek His pleasure. He tells them that He only misleads those who violate their oaths with Him and He only misleads those who prefer evil more than guidance. In that case, He will then seal up their hearts and ears. He changes the heart of whoever does not accept His guidance when it comes, does not believe in it, and neglects it, so He changes his heart and eyes as a punishment for him for what he did. And if Allah knew, in any of theses cases, that there is a chance of guidance, He would guide and lead them but they do not deserve His blessings and do not deserve His dignity. Allah, the Exalted removed causes, showed proofs, and enabled all the means of guidance. He only misleads dissolute and unjust servants, seals up the hearts of the aggressors, and throws into seduction after removing all the causes and showing all the proofs. He explains the means of guidance and that He only misleads the hypocrites because of their deeds. The covering that covers the hearts of the disbelievers is the result of their own deeds. Allah says,

$$﴿ كَلَّا ۖ بَلْ ۜ رَانَ عَلَىٰ قُلُوبِهِم مَّا كَانُوا۟ يَكْسِبُونَ ۝ ﴾$$

which means, "Nay! But on their hearts is the *Rân* (covering of sins and evil deeds) which they used to earn." (Al-Mutafifîn, 83: 14)

And He, the Almighty says about His enemies from among the Jews,

$$﴿ ...وَقَوْلِهِمْ قُلُوبُنَا غُلْفٌ ۚ بَل طَبَعَ ٱللَّهُ عَلَيْهَا بِكُفْرِهِمْ... ۝ ﴾$$

which means, "And of their saying: "Our hearts are wrapped (with coverings, i.e. we do not understand what the Messengers say)" - nay, Allah has set a seal upon their hearts because of their disbelief." (An-Nisâ', 4:155)

Allah tells us that He does not mislead whoever was guided until He shows him the paths and enables him to choose, and he chooses because of his unhappiness and bad nature, and he goes astray because he does not heed guidance, he is evil and he himself and his Satan are an enemy of Allah.

The Plan of Allah, the Exalted:

The plan, which Allah described is through punishing those who planned against His pious people and His Messengers. He faces their evil plan with His good plan. Thus their plots are the ugliest but the plan of Allah is the best as it is just. His plan is a punishment from Him for their deception against His Messengers and people, and there is nothing better than this deception and plan of Allah against the disbelievers.

Concerning the saying, "A man amongst you may do (good deeds) until there is only a cubit between him and Paradise and then what has been written for him decides his behavior and he starts doing the (evil) deeds characteristic of the people of the (Hell) Fire..." this is a good deed of the people of Paradise as it is shown to others; if it was a good and accepted deed that deserves Paradise that Allah loved and agreed with, He would never lose his good deed. " Until there is only a cubit between him and Paradise" can also suit this interpretation; deeds are calculated according to their results and their ends. This servant was not patient in order to complete his deed until its end and then obtain its reward. It contained a hidden vice that caused its ruin in its final stages. This vice and hidden evil betrayed him in the time of need. If there was no deception or vice, Allah would never turn his faith. The servant performs this deed with complete truth and sincerity without any reason that requires spoiling it, and Allah knows the secrets of His servants that are not known to each other.

Concerning Satan, Allah, the Exalted says to His Angels,

﴿ ...قَالَ إِنِّى أَعْلَمُ مَا لَا تَعْلَمُونَ ۝ ﴾

which means, "I know that which you do not know." (Al-Baqarah, 2:30)

Allah knew the disbelief, pride and envy that was in Satan's heart, which the Angels did not know. When they were ordered to bow, the contents of their hearts were revealed: obedience, love, piety, and yielding and they proceeded to obey. And the contents of the enemy's heart were revealed: pride, deception, and envy as it refused and was among the disbelievers.

The pious people fear His plan. They fear that Allah may let them down because of their sins and that their fate will be unhappy. They fear their sins, and hope for His mercy.

And when Allah, the Almighty says,

﴿ أَفَأَمِنُوا مَكْرَ اللَّهِ ... ﴾

which means, "Did they then feel secure against the Plan of Allah?" (Al-A'râf, 7:99)

It is referring to the disbelievers and the wicked. The verse means that those who disobey and feel secure against the plan of Allah when facing their evil plots are the losers and those who fear Him are those who know Him and fear His plan; He may delay His punishment until they get used to their sins and then the punishment would come suddenly.

Or they may forget Him and His remembrance, so He will abandon them as they abandon His remembrance and obedience and then they will be afflicted with distress and seduction. His plan here would be to abandon them. Also He knows about their sins and defects what they do not know about themselves, so the plan of Allah would come to them without their knowing.

Allah examines and afflicts them with what they cannot bear and they will be seduced and this is the plan of Allah.

Chapter: The Tree of Sincerity

A year is like a tree, the months are its boughs, the days are its branches, the hours are its leaves, and its breath is its fruit. Whoever's breath used to obey Allah, the fruit of his tree will be good and pure. Whoever's breath used to disobey Allah, his fruit will be evil. The time of harvest is on the Day of Resurrection and at that time the fruit will be shown, whether it is sweet or sour.

Sincerity and monotheism is a tree within the heart. Its branches are deeds and its fruit is the pleasures of life during this worldly life and permanent happiness in the Hereafter. The fruit of Paradise is neither limited nor forbidden, and the fruit of monotheism and sincerity in this worldly life are the same.

Polytheism, lying, and hypocrisy are also a tree within the heart. Its fruit is during life like fear, distress, sadness, and tightness of the chest and darkness of the heart, and in the Hereafter Az-Zaqqûm and a permanent punishment. Allah mentioned those two trees in verses of (chapter Ibrâhîm, 14)

Chapter: Degrees of Happiness

When the servant attains the age of puberty, he is to be given his oath, which Allah, His Creator and Owner entrusted to him. If he strongly handles his oath, accepts, and is determined to fulfill it, he deserves to be granted degrees and ranks, which are given to those who fulfill their oaths. If his soul has some doubts, and he supports it and sticks to his oath and says: I am qualified to fulfill the oath of my Lord, who is more qualified to accept, understand, or fulfill it than me? He first adheres to understanding his oath, thinking about it, and knowing the advice of his Lord to him, and then he adjusts his soul to obey this oath, work according to it, and fulfill it. He sees the reality of this oath and what it contains through his heart. He created an intention and a determination other than the one that was in his time of youth before he took this oath. He left behind the carelessness of youth and followed habits and nature, endured the honor of this intention, and tore the veil of darkness to the light of belief. Through his patience and sincere effort, he knew the favors that Allah has granted him.

The first among the degrees of his happiness is to have a keen ear and heart that understands what the ear would hear, if he hears, realizes, sees the good path, sees that the majority of people are going astray, keeps to it and does not go astray. The reason behind going astray is refusing the oath, accepting it unwillingly, accept it while lacking power and determination, or failing to urge themselves to understand it, think about it, work according to it, or fulfill it. The oath was offered to them while still in their youth and observing religion as a habit and according to what they used to see their parents doing. They received the oath while feeling satisfied with what they saw from their parents and ancestors. This is not enough for whoever aims his intention and heart at understanding the oath and working according to it as if this oath applied to him alone and it was said to him: think about what this oath contains and work according to it. If he did not receive his oath in this way, he would follow his ancestors, the habits of his family, friends, neighbors, and the people of his country. He would be satisfied to take religion as a habit. If Satan seduces him and reaches his intention and determination, it would accuse him of clanship and zealotry to his fathers and ancestors and convince him that this is right and whatever disagrees with it is false; guidance would be considered evil and evil would be considered guidance. This would indeed be fanaticism, which is not based on knowledge. As he is satisfied to follow his family and nation, he will have what they have and will also have to pay what they are paying. He is far removed from guidance and Allah abandons him to whoever he took as a friend. He will see any guidance that disagrees with his nation and family as evil and false. If he has a higher intention, a more honorable soul, and a higher worth, he would proceed to fulfill his oath and understand it and would know that the owner of this oath has a great stature that other people do not have. Through this oath he would know Allah. Allah will know that he knows Him, His attributes, names, doings, and judgments. The servant will know that Allah is self-existing, enables others to exist, is in no need of anyone while all others are in need of Him. That He established Himself on the Throne above all His creatures, that He sees, hears, accepts, becomes angry, loves, hates, manages the affairs of His kingdom, orders, and forbids, sends His Messengers to every place in His kingdom bearing His words, which are heard by whoever wishes from among His creatures. He stands firm on justice, awards according to both good and bad, is the Most Forbearing, the Most Merciful, the All-Thankful, the Most Generous, and the Well-doer. He is described with all perfection and is far above all defects, and He has no equal. The servant can see the wisdom of Allah in managing His kingdom and how He foreordains matters according to His will without opposing justice and wisdom. And when there is a confrontation between the mind, law, and nature, each one of them proved the truth in and of itself. The servant understands what Allah has described Himself with in His Book from the reality of His names that were revealed in His Book. The names with which Allah was introduced to His servants remain until the minds acknowledge Him and indeed nature testifies to Him.

If the servant knew and believed in his heart in the attributes of the owner of the oath, the light of these attributes would rise within his heart and would be as if he saw them with his own eyes. He would see their connection with creation and the commands of Allah, their effects in the sensual and spiritual world, and their effect on creatures; how they prevail, favor, come near, banish, give, and prevent. He would see with his heart the examples of His justice, favor, and mercy. Allah deserves to be worshiped according to irrefutable proof, valid judgments, perfect power, complete justice and wisdom, superiority above all His creatures as well as the fact that He is thorough, simultaneous, great, lofty, glorious, violent, and revengeful and with His mercy, He is charitable, kind, generous, forgiving, and patient. The servant would see the irrefutable proof with valid judgments that any creature could not rebel against, and how these attributes agree with and are in harmony and prove each other. He would discover that wisdom prevails, which is the aim and end of all judgments, which are the beginning of all things, and how their divisions come back to the origins and principles of aims as if he is watching the principles of wisdom in action. He would notice how cases are based according to wisdom, justice, benefit, mercy, and charity. There is no case that deviates from that until the end of the world and all that exists and people are judged on the Day of Resurrection, which will show His justice, and wisdom, and the truth of His Messengers and what they said about Allah to mankind; including humans and jinn both believers and disbelievers. And then it would be revealed to His creatures from His attributes that which they did not know before that. Even those who knew Him best during this life would praise Him because of the perfection of His attributes and honored descriptions, which he did not know during this life. This would be shown to His creatures and the reasons would be also shown to them according to which people deviated, went astray, and became negligent. The difference between knowing the reality of His names and attributes and knowing them during this worldly life will be like the difference between Paradise and Hellfire and seeing them, and even greater than that.

It would be also understood from the oath how His names and attributes require the existence of prophethood, decrees, and not to leave His creatures live in vain, as well as requiring what is included in the forms of commands and prohibitions, and what is required in the existence of reward, punishment, and resurrection. This is necessary because of His s names and attributes as to be deemed far above all that His enemies claim. The servant would see in the oath the generality of power and its effect on all creatures, which did not even miss one whit and that if Allah has any other gods alongside Him, the world would be destroyed, including the heavens, the earth, and all that is between them. He will see how Islam and the faith, which all creatures have comes from these Divine attributes, and how they require reward and punishment sooner or later. He will understand that it is impossible to combine acceptance of this oath and denying His attributes, His superiority above His creatures, communicating with man through His Books, and oaths. It also includes those who refuse to take this oath and fulfill it and even whoever accepted it but did not accept it as a whole.

Chapter: The Body and Soul

The body of the son of Adam was created from the earth and his soul from the government of Heaven and then they were joined. If he is hungry, stays awake, and keeps his body busy in serving Allah, his soul will find itself lighter and more peaceful so that it would long for the place from which it was created and miss its heavenly world. But if he secures food, blessings, sleep, and rest, the body will incline to remain at the place from which it was created and the soul would be pulled along with it and be in a prison. If it was not for the fact that it would get used to that prison, it would ask for help, as a tortured person does, to find relief from the pain resulting from the separation and departure from its own world from which it was created.

In general, the more the body is light, the more the soul will be light and seek its heavenly world, and the more the body is heavy and seeks desires and relief, the heavier the soul will be and it will come down from its heavenly world and become lower and more earthly. You may see the soul of a man in Heaven while his body is on the earth. Another person serves Allah with his body and his soul is low and wandering about in lowly matters. When the soul separates from the body, it would either catch up with its high or low place. With the high, it would find every blessing, happiness, beauty, pleasure, and good living while with the low it would find every distress, grief, suffering, sadness, and bad and difficult thing. Allah says,

﴿ ...وَمَنْ أَعْرَضَ عَن ذِكْرِى فَإِنَّ لَهُ مَعِيشَةً ضَنكًا ۝ ﴾

which means, "But whosoever turns away from My Reminder (i.e. neither believes in this Qur'ân nor acts on its orders, etc.) verily, for him is a life of hardship." (Tâhâ, 20:124)

"My Reminder" is His words, which He revealed to His Messenger, and "turns away" is by neglecting and abandoning working according to these words, and the majority of explanations saw that "life of hardship" is torture in the grave. Ibn Mas'ûd, Abu Hurairah, Abu Sa'îd Al-Khudry, and Ibn 'Abbâs agreed on that and it has a traceable hadith.

This life of hardship is in return for relieving the body and soul with pleasures, desires and relief. The more you enrich the soul, it will restrain the heart until you live a life of hardship, and the more you restrain the soul, it will enrich the heart until that heart will be delighted and relieved. Hardship in this worldly life, following piety will find its relief in partition and the Hereafter, and relief in this worldly life following desires will find its hardship in the partition and the Hereafter. You should choose one of the two: the better, more pleasant, and more lasting. You may distress the body in order to relieve the soul but do not distress the soul to relieve the body; relief and distress of the soul is greater and more lasting while relief and distress of the body is shorter and easier.

Leaving Sins First

A wise man will never order people to abandon life; as they cannot leave it, but he may order them to leave sins. Leaving life is a favor for them while leaving sins is an obligatory act of worship. How can they be ordered to do a favor while they do not fulfill the obligation? If it was hard for you to leave sins, exert your effort to make them love Allah through mentioning His blessings, favors, benefits, and attributes of perfection. The hearts are naturally disposed to love Allah, and if they were deeply attached to Him, leaving sins would be easy. Yahyâ bin Mu'âdh said: the wise person when seeking this worldly life is better than the ignorant one who leaves it.

The wise man calls people to Allah while they are still enjoying their worldly life and the answer would be easy but the pious person calls them to Allah through leaving this worldly life. Weaning human beings is hard when they are used to being fed from this breast (this worldly life), but we should choose the better and greater suckling mother; as milk influences the nature of man. The milk of a bad mother results in a bad child. The best kind of suckling is what is had after starvation. If you have the power to bear the pains of weaning, get a reasonable amount, as some kinds of indigestion cause death.

Chapter: Three Precious Gems

There is a great difference between observing duties while in difficulty, and observing them while in a good condition.

Verily, the real servant of Mine is the one who remembers Me at the time of distress (fighting).

﴿ يَٰٓأَيُّهَا ٱلَّذِينَ ءَامَنُوٓاْ إِذَا لَقِيتُمْ فِئَةً فَٱثْبُتُواْ وَٱذْكُرُواْ ٱللَّهَ كَثِيرًا لَّعَلَّكُمْ تُفْلِحُونَ ﴾

which means, "O you who believe! When you meet (an enemy) force, take a firm stand against them and remember the Name of Allah much (both with tongue and mind), so that you may be successful." (Al-Anfâl, 8:45)

It is not astonishing to see someone in good health, free and performing religious deeds, but the astonishing thing is to see someone who is weak, unhealthy, has many irons in the fire, does not have a stable condition and at the same time observes his religious duties, without failing to perform anything he is supposed to do.

Chapter: Knowing Allah

Knowing Allah, Exalted be He, is of two kinds:

One: awareness of confession, which includes all people: the righteous and the wicked, the obedient and the disobedient.

Two: awareness that necessitates being shy of Him, showing love to Him, being aware of Him in the heart, yearning to meet Him, fearing Him, turning to Him and repenting to Him, being at ease with everything concerning Him and fleeing from creation to Him.

This is the special awareness that is on the lips of all people. Their various levels can only be counted by the One Who informed them about Himself and made them aware of some of His knowledge that He concealed from others, and each one of them indicated this awareness according to his status and that which had been disclosed to him.

The most knowledgeable in creation about Him said, "I do not count any praise for You, You are as You have praised Yourself."[64] He also said that on the Day of Resurrection, Allah, the Almighty would reveal to him some words of praise that he is not able to pronounce now.

Concerning this awareness, there are two large sections:

Section one: thinking and meditation on all the Qur'ânic Verses, and the special understanding about Allah and His Messenger (peace be upon him).

---

[64] Recorded by Muslim, Kitâb As-Salâh, Bâb, that which is said while in the state of bowing down and prostration, no. (486).

Section two: thinking about His Visual Signs, and meditating on His Wisdom in them, His Strength, His Courtesy, His Kindness, His Justice, His Fairness and always maintaining His creation with justice. In a few words: to be knowledgeable of the meaning of His Beautiful Names, their Majesty, their Perfection, His Uniqueness, and their connection with the creation and the orders of Allah. He would then be an expert concerning His Commandments and Prohibitions, an expert concerning His Fate and Destiny, an expert concerning His Beautiful Names and Attributes, an expert concerning religious judgments and the judgment of this worldly life, and that is just as it is in the Qur'ânic verse,

﴿...ذَٰلِكَ فَضْلُ ٱللَّهِ يُؤْتِيهِ مَن يَشَآءُۚ وَٱللَّهُ ذُو ٱلْفَضْلِ ٱلْعَظِيمِ ۞﴾

which means, "That is the Grace of Allah which He bestows on whom He pleases. And Allah is the Owner of Great Bounty." (Al-Hadîd, 57:21)

Chapter: Licit and Illicit Gains

There are four ways of gaining wealth:

<u>Wealth</u> gained by obeying Allah and spent in the way of Allah, and that is the best wealth.

<u>Wealth</u> gained by disobeying Allah and spent in disobeying Allah, and that is the worst.

Wealth gained by doing harm to a Muslim, and spent in doing harm to a Muslim, that is also the worst.

<u>Wealth</u> gained licitly, and spent on lawful desires, and that is neither for him nor against him.

These are the principle ways of gaining wealth and spending them.

There are some other ways that branch out from them:

Wealth gained rightly, and spent illicitly.

Wealth gained illicitly, and spent rightly. Therefore, spending it is its expiation.

Wealth gained in a doubtful way, and its expiation is to spend it on dutifulness to Allah.

And just as reward, punishment, praise and dispraise are connected to spending wealth, in the same way, they are connected to gaining it. Moreover, a man will be asked about his expenditure, where he gained it, and on what he spent it.

Chapter: Consolation of the Believers

There are different ways of consoling the believers:

Consolation with wealth.

Consolation with high rank.

Consolation with body and service.

Consolation with advice and instruction.

Consolation with supplication and seeking forgiveness for them.

Consolation by sympathizing with them.

These forms of consolation are according to the faith of the servant. Whenever the faith is weak, the consolation would also be weak. But whenever the faith is firm, the consolation would also be so. The Messenger of Allah (peace be upon him) was the person who consoled his Companions (may Allah be pleased with them) the most, and his followers' consolation is according to the degree in which they follow him.

Some people once visited Bishr Al-Hâfî on a very cold day. He had no clothes on and was shaking. They said, "O Abu Nasr, what is this?, he said, "I remembered the poor people and the cold weather they are suffering from, and as I have nothing to console them, I decided to sympathize with them in their cold weather."

Chapter: Unawareness Causes Hardship

Being unaware of the way leading to Allah, its difficulty and purpose causes many problems and has little benefit, because the person may exert great effort in performing supererogatory duties, while neglecting a religious obligation. He may preoccupy himself with a deed connected with the body, while having something else in the heart, or a deed of the heart, without any action from the body. He may have great determination concerning a deed, without observing its purpose. He may perform a deed without being cautious of its evil consequences, while performing the deed and after performing it.

He may undertake a deed without acknowledging Allah's Kindness in it, by feeling that he participated in the fulfillment of the deed, and not by the Grace of Allah. It may be a deed where he failed to observe his heedlessness in it, and excuse for it. It may be a deed where he did not give its due in full like advice and kindness, while thinking that he gave it its due. All these decrease the fruit of the deed, in addition to a lot of trouble. It is Only Allah Who grants success.

Chapter: The Journey to Allah, Exalted be He, and its Obstacles

When the servant is determined to follow the way that leads to Allah, Exalted be He, he would be confronted with tricks and hindrances. Initially, he may be deceived by lusts, sovereignty, pleasures, spouses and clothes, and if he yields to them, he would give up, and if he rejects them and does not yield to them and was sincere in his cause, he would be tried with his children, by receiving more importance among people, by people supplicating for him, by people seeking blessing from him, and so on. If he yields to them, he would not be able to continue on the way to Allah, and that would be his share. And if he is able to reject them, and does not yield to them, he would be tried by miracles and discoveries.

If he yields to them, he would cease to continue on his journey to Allah, and that would be his share. If he does not yield, he would be tried by renunciation, the pleasure of being with Allah, the honor of solitude and giving up worldly pleasures. If he yields to that, he would be quitting the purpose.

And if he does not yield to that, he will continue, keeping an eye on his duty to Allah, and that which pleases Him, in order to be His true servant, no matter how or when. Whether this situation was the cause of his difficulty or rest; whether he enjoyed it or suffered from it, and whether it made him be with people or isolated him from them.

He does not choose for himself, except that which his Lord and Master chooses for him. He must approve of His Order and fulfill it according to his ability. His own self is less important to himself than placing its rest and pleasure over the pleasure of His Master and His Order. This would be the servant who would have reached the end of the journey, and was able to fulfill His orders and nothing was able to prevent him from his Master. And it is only through Allah that real success is achieved.

Chapter: Kinds of Grace

There are three kinds of grace:

Grace that is present, and the servant is aware of it.

Grace that is expected and hoped for.

Grace the servant is enjoying but does not feel it.

If it pleases Allah to perfect His Grace upon His Servant, He would make him aware of His Present Grace, and grant him the ability to be grateful as a preservation of this grace, for it disappears with disobedience; but with gratitude, it remains. He would also make it easy for him to perform deeds that would bring forth the expected grace, and make him see the causes that ruin this grace, and help him to stay away from them. In no time, it would come to him in abundance. And then, He would make him aware of the grace he is enjoying but not feeling.

It is reported that a Bedouin once visited Hârûn Ar-Rashîd and said, "O Commander of the believers, may Allah preserve for you the grace that you are enjoying, by making it easy for you to keep being grateful, and may He fulfill for you the grace you hope for, by making it easy for you to do the things He likes and continue to obey Him, and make you aware of the grace you are enjoying but you are not aware of, so that you become grateful to Him." He was pleased with these words and said, "How great are his words!"

A Great Principle: The Beginning of Knowledge and Action

The beginning of every theoretical capacity of awareness, and a practical capacity, is ideas and thoughts. They cause imagination, and imagination leads to will, and will necessitates action, and repeating that many times produces a habit, therefore, the correctness of these steps is according to the correctness of the ideas and thoughts, and their corruption is according to their corruption.

The correctness of ideas is when the person observes his Owner and Lord, yearns for Him and focuses on Him, for He is the cause of all that is correct. He is the One Who grants right guidance. His protection includes all kinds of protection for His servant and turning away from Him is the cause of all perversity and misfortune.

The servant gains all sorts of good and right guidance according to the degree of his awareness of His Grace, His Oneness, ways of Knowing Him, ways of submitting to Him, considering Him to be present with him, watching him, looking at him, observing him, and looking into his thoughts, will and intention. By then he would be shy of Him, and glorify Him so highly to the extent that he would not allow himself to be seen by Him doing things he does want people to see him doing.

When he considers his Lord as exaltedly as this, approaches Him, honors Him, selects and supports Him, according to that, Allah, the Almighty would keep baseness and bad thoughts away from him. And whenever he keeps away from Him and turns his back on Him, He would approach these base things and bad thoughts. By then He would prevent all perfection from him, and he would be exposed to all sorts of defects.

Therefore, man is the best of creatures when he approaches his Creator and abides by His Commands and abandons what He has forbidden, performs deeds according to His Pleasure and prefers Him to his vain desires. And he would be the worst of creatures when he moves away from Him, and refuses to come near Him to obey Him and seek His Pleasure.

Therefore, when he chooses to be near Him and prefers Him over his vain desires, then he would have applied his heart and mind and faith upon himself and his Satan; he would have applied his reason upon his temptation, and his guidance upon his vain desire. But when he chooses to be away from Him, then he would have applied his own self, his vain desire and Satan upon his mind, heart and senses.

Ideas and Scruples

You should know that ideas and scruples lead to thoughts, and thoughts lead to remembrance, and remembrance leads to will, and will leads to action, then it becomes firm and finally it becomes a habit. It would be easier to put a stop to it from the beginning than to terminate it when it has become strong and complete.

It is well known that man has not been given the ability to terminate ideas, for they fall upon him just like breath, except that the power of faith and mind help him adopt the best of them, be pleased with them and feel at ease with them. It also helps him push away the worst of them and hate them, as some of the Companions said, "O Messenger of Allah! Verily we perceive in our minds that which every one of us considers too grave to express.' He (peace be upon him) said, 'Do you really perceive it?' They said, 'Yes.' Upon this he remarked, 'That is pure faith.'" [65]

And in another wording the Messenger (peace be upon him) said, "All praise and thanks be to Allah, Who turned his cunning with scruple."

There are two points of views concerning this statement:

One: rejecting and hating it is pure faith.

Two: its existence and throwing it into the heart by Satan is pure faith, because he threw it into the heart in order to be in conflict with faith and eliminate it.

Certainly, Allah, the Almighty has created the mind just like a mill, which does not stop and has to have something to grind. If grain is put into it, it would grind it, and if soil is put into it or pebbles, it would also grind them. Therefore, thoughts and ideas that occur in the mind are like the grain that is put in the mill, and the mill can never remain without working.

Therefore, there are some people whose mill grinds grain to produce flour in order to benefit themselves and other people, but the bulk of them grind sand, pebbles, straw etc. When it is

---

[65] Recorded by Muslim, Kitâb Al-Îmân, section of Scruples in the faith and what should be said when perceived, no. (132), and Abu Dâwûd (5111).

time for kneading and baking, the reality becomes apparent to him.

Chapter: The Heart is Never Void of Thoughts

When you reject an idea that comes to you, that which is after it would be rejected. But when you accept it, it would be a wandering thought, then it would prey upon the will, and with the help of the thought, they would use the body. If it is difficult to be used, they would both turn to the heart with hope and lust, and you would direct it to what is desired.

It is a well known fact that reforming ideas is easier than reforming thoughts, and reforming thoughts is easier than reforming will, and reforming will is easier than amending the evil of a deed, and amending it is easier than putting an end to habits.

The best medicine therefore, is to preoccupy yourself with things that concern you, away from that which does not concern you, because thinking about things that do not concern you is the beginning of all evil things. Whoever thinks about that which does not concern him, would miss that which concerns him, and he would be preoccupied with something that contains no good, far away from the best thing for him.

Therefore, thoughts, ideas, will and intention are the best things you should reform in yourself, because they are your characteristics and your reality, with which you can be closer to or away from your Lord, without whose nearness and Pleasure, you would never find happiness. And all misfortunes are because of your being away from Him and His displeasure with you. Whoever is low and despicable in his ideas and the domain of his thoughts, would be the same in the rest of his concerns.

Be careful not to make it possible for Satan to control your thoughts and will, for he would ruin them for you to the extent that it would be very difficult for you to make them right. He would throw upon you all kinds of harmful scruples and thoughts. He would come in between you and your thoughts about that which benefits you. And what is more, it is you who would be helping him against yourself, by making it easy for him to possess your heart and your ideas; so he gains control of them over yourself.

Your likeness to him is as the likeness of the owner of a mill in which, good grain is ground. Then a man came to him with a load of soil, dung, coal and scum in order to grind them in his mill. If he rejects him and does not make it possible for him to throw that which is with him in the mill, he would be able to continue grinding that which is useful for him. But if he makes it possible for him to throw them into the mill, they would ruin the grain that is in it, and the mill itself would be ruined.

That which Satan throws into the heart is usually one of the following thoughts: thinking about things that exist, if they were other than the way they are now. About things that have not existed, if they were to exist, how they would be. About things that can be thought about such as immorality and prohibited things. Illusory imagination that has no reality at all or about null and void things. That which cannot be perceived like the kinds of things that have been kept secret from his knowledge. He would throw these ideas into him that would not come to an end, and make them the center of his concern and thought.

The remedy for this is to preoccupy your thoughts with knowledge and concepts that are useful for you, regarding the Oneness of Allah and His Rights, and about death and its aftermath like Paradise and Hellfire. Also it is important to preoccupy yourself with learning the problems of deeds and the ways to avoid them.

You should preoccupy yourself with will and intention and that which is useful for you and reject that which is harmful.

According to the most knowledgeable people of Allah, wishing for treason and preoccupying yourself with it, is more harmful to the heart than treason itself. You can find this in the example of a king. Among the King's retinues and servants is one who would like to betray him and his heart and thoughts are full of this, yet at the same time he serves him and performs his duties. If the king comes to know his secret and intention, he would hate him so profoundly that he would punish him with what he deserves.

He would be more hated to him than a man who is far away from him, and has committed some crime, but whose heart is with the king, and does not contain any wish for treason. The first one leaves it due to being weak and busy with that which he is doing, while his heart is full of it, but the second one commits these crimes, while his heart is void of any treason or desire to do it. Therefore, he is better than the first one.

In general, the heart is never void of thought. It is either concerned with a duty concerning the Hereafter, or worldly pleasures.

We have previously mentioned that the mind is like a mill that runs with that which is thrown into it. If some grain is thrown in, it would run with it. And if glass, pebbles or dung is thrown in, it would run with it too. It is Allah, the Almighty Who is the Lord, the Owner and Manager of that mill. He has appointed an angel to throw in it that, which is beneficial to run with it, and Satan throws that which harms it.

The angel visits it one time, and Satan visits it at another time. The grain that the angel throws is an indication of goodness and belief in the promise. And the grain that Satan throws is an indication of evil and disbelief in the promise.

The mill runs according to the grain. And the owner of the harmful grain would not be able to throw it except if he finds the mill void of useful grain, and the one who is running it has neglected it and turned away from it. By then, he would take the initiative to throw that, which he likes.

In general, if the one who runs the mill abandons it and gives up taking care of it by not throwing useful grain, the enemy would find the way to ruin it and run it with that which he has. And the way to reform this mill is by being preoccupied with that which concerns you. And as for its destruction, it is by being preoccupied with that which does not concern you.

How excellent the statement of a wise man is, as he put it: when I found that worldly pleasures are more likely to spoil the Hereafter, and saw that it is bound to be ruined, I turned away from it all to that which people of understanding do not differ in opinion.

Shafîq bin Ibrâhîm [66] said, "The door of success has been closed against the creation due to six matters":

their being preoccupied with grace without being grateful.

their interest in knowledge and neglecting action.

rushing to sin and delaying repentance.

being attracted by the company of the righteous but failing to follow their deeds.

This worldly life is turning away from them, while they strongly desire it.

The Hereafter is drawing near to them, while they are turning away in heedlessness.

I said, the source of that is lack of desire for (Paradise) and lack of fear of Hellfire, as well as weakness of certainty and insight,

---

[66] He is Shafîq bin Ibrâhîm bin 'Aly Al-Azdy Al-Balkhy. He was an ascetic, pious mulsim, one of the famous sheikhs of Kharasân. He was martyred (may Allah have mercy upon him) in the Battle of Kulân behind the River, in 194 A. H.

and disgrace and lowness of the self, and exchanging that, which is better for that which is lower. Otherwise, if the self was truly noble and great, it would not accept such lowness.

Therefore, the source of all good with success is from Allah and His Will. And this is also the source of nobility of the self and its greatness. And the source of evil is its lowness and pettiness. Allah, the Almighty said in the Glorious Qur'ân,

﴿ قَدْ أَفْلَحَ مَن زَكَّاهَا ۝ وَقَدْ خَابَ مَن دَسَّاهَا ۝ ﴾

which means, "Indeed he succeeds who purifies his ownself (i.e. obeys and performs all that Allah ordered, by following the true Faith of Islâmic Monotheism and by doing righteous good deeds). And indeed he fails who corrupts his ownself (i.e. disobeys what Allah has ordered by rejecting the true Faith of Islâmic Monotheism or by following polytheism, etc. or by doing every kind of evil wicked deeds)." (Ash-Shams, 91:9-10)

That is to say that the successful one is he, who honors it, invests it by obeying and performing all that Allah ordered. And the unsuccessful one is the one who belittles it and degrades it by disobeying what Allah has ordered.

Therefore, honored servants are only pleased with the highest, best and most praised matters. But the inferior servants hover about lowness and fall upon them just as a fly falls upon the dirt.

The honored and high self does not accept wrongdoing or immorality, theft or treason, for it is greater and higher than them. And the despised and low self is the opposite of that, for every self inclines to that which suits and resembles it. The following verse illustrates this fact,

﴿ قُلْ كُلٌّ يَعْمَلُ عَلَىٰ شَاكِلَتِهِ ... ۝ ﴾

which means, "Say (O Muhammad to mankind): "Each one does according to Shakilatihi (i.e. his way or his religion or his intentions, etc.)" (Al-Isrâ', 17:84)

That is to say that everyone performs deeds according to that which suits and corresponds to him. He performs deeds according to the way that coincides with his character and nature. Everyone follows his way, his faith and habits that he got used to and was created with.

Therefore, the immoral person performs deeds according to that which resembles his way of life, as repaying grace with sins, and turning away from the Benefactor. And the believer performs deeds according to his way of life, as being grateful to the Benefactor, showing his love and praise to Him, making himself loved by Him, being shy of Him, observing Him, glorifying Him and exalting Him.

Chapter: He who does not Know himself, does not Know his Creator

How can the one who does not know himself, know His creator? Know that Allah, the Exalted created a heart within your chest. Allah, the Almighty established Himself on the Throne by Himself and is clear to His creatures if their hearts are pure. On the bed of the heart there is a carpet of content and on its right and left sides there are utilities of its laws and commands. There is a door that is opened to it hoping for Paradise, His mercy, and longing to meet Him. It was rained on with truth, which planted all kinds of fruitful trees from among the forms of worship and remembering Allah. In the middle of this garden there is a tree of knowledge which brings forth its fruit at all times by the leave of its Lord, which are things like loving, repentance, piety, fearing, and happiness at being close to Him. He watered it with meditation, understanding, and working according to His words. Inside the house a lamp is hung that is lit with knowing and believing in Allah. After that he built a wall around it that prevents any disease and corruption from entering. Whoever seeks to harm the garden will not succeed. He appointed guards from the Angels to protect him in his wakefulness and repose. Then he let the owner of the house and the garden know about the dweller; as his aim is always to repair the house so as to gain the satisfaction of the dweller and if he felt any problem in the house, he would repair it at once fearing that the dweller may leave. How good the house is and how good the dweller is.

Glorified be Allah, the Lord of all the worlds. There is a great difference between this house and another house that is captured by destruction and has become a shelter for insects and bugs; a place for all that is dirty. Whoever wants relief, can find this ruined house without a dweller or a keeper. It is not prepared for relief, it is dark and has a foul odor, and is full of dirt and destruction. No one wants to be in it except insects and worms. Satan is on its bed, the bed has a carpet of ignorance accompanied with desires, its right and left sides have utilities of desires, a door is opened to it and it leads to betrayal, loneliness, seeking this worldly life, and neglecting the Hereafter, and it is rained upon by a heavy rain of ignorance, desire, polytheism, and innovations, which planted all kinds of thorns, colocynth, and fruitful trees from among sins and breaches that provoke committing what is forbidden and neglecting worship. In the middle of the garden there is a tree of ignorance and neglecting Allah which brings its fruit at all times in the form of sins, debauchery, amusements, impudence, and following every desire. From among its fruit is distress, sadness, and pain, but they are hidden because the soul is busy with amusements. But when it wakes up from its drunken state it suffers from all kinds of distress, sadness, hardship, and anxiety. He watered this tree by following desires, deceptive hope, and pride.

Then he abandons this house with its darkness and destruction in a way that did not prevent any corrupt, animal, harmful, or dirty thing from entering. Whoever knows his house, the value of he who dwells in it, the value of its treasures and the supplies he benefits from in his life and himself, and whoever is ignorant of these, would be ignorant about himself and would loose his happiness.

At-Tastary was asked once, "A man eats one meal during his day.' He said, 'The way of truthful people.' They said, 'What about two meals?' He said, 'The way of the believers.' They said, 'What about three?' He said, 'Tell his family to build a place of fodder for him.'"

Al-Aswad bin Sâlim said: to perform two rak'ahs is preferred to me than Paradise and all that it contains. It was said to him: this is wrong. He said: neglect your words and listen: Paradise will please me and the two rak'ahs will please My Lord; pleasing My Lord is more important that pleasing myself.

- A learned man on earth is like basil from Paradise, if one of his followers smells it, his soul will long for Paradise.

- The heart of the lover is placed between the loftiness and beauty of the one he loves. If he notices His loftiness, he would fear and glorify Him and if he notices His beauty, he would love and long for Him.

A Precious Gem: Levels of Knowing Allah

There are among people those who know Allah through His favors, blessings, and grace, others know Him through His forgiveness and mercy, others know Him through revenge and force, others know Him through knowledge and wisdom, pride and glory, mercy, piety, and kindness, overpowering and ownership, and through answering supplications, helping in grief, and fulfilling needs.

The highest among those in knowing Allah is the one who knows Him through His words; he knows the Lord has all the attributes of perfection and all the characteristics of glory, far above having a parallel, and free from any defects and faults. He has every good name and every perfect attribute, the doer of all that He intends, above all matters and accompanies every matter, capable of every matter and builds every matter, absolute master, speaks with His Divine words, greater than every matter and more beautiful than anything, the most merciful among those who show mercy, the most powerful among those who have power, and the most wise among those who have wisdom. The Qur'ân was revealed to inform His servants about Him, the Way that leads to Him, and the conditions of those who followed in His way after knowing Him.

A Precious Gem: Allah will not Change the Condition of a People until They Change Themselves

Quite often the servant of Allah is granted abundant blessings but he becomes bored and longs to change it for another which he claims is better. In fact, Allah, the Merciful does not deprive him of this blessing, and He excuses him for his ignorance and bad choice until the servant is unable to bear the blessing, feels discontent, and complains about it. Then Allah will take it away from him. When he gets what he wished for and sees the great difference between what he had before and what he has now, he is filled with worry and regret and he wishes to have what he had before. If Allah wishes good for His servant, He would make him see that whatever blessings he now has is from Allah and He will show him that Allah is pleased with him, and the servant would praise Him. If he is deceived by his soul to change this blessing, he would ask Allah for guidance.

There is nothing more harmful to the servant than becoming bored from the blessings of Allah; as he neither sees them as a blessing, praises Allah for them, nor is happy with them but he becomes bored, complains, and considers them as a means of distress. He does not think that these things are from the greatest blessings of Allah. The majority of people are opposed to the blessings of Allah. They do not feel the blessings of Allah, and moreover, they exert their effort to drive them away because of their ignorance and injustice. How often is a blessing bestowed on a person while he is exerting his effort to drive it away and how often does he actually receive it while he is pushing it away, simply because of his ignorance and injustice. Allah says,

﴿ ذَٰلِكَ بِأَنَّ ٱللَّهَ لَمْ يَكُ مُغَيِّرًا نِّعْمَةً أَنْعَمَهَا عَلَىٰ قَوْمٍ حَتَّىٰ يُغَيِّرُوا۟ مَا بِأَنفُسِهِمْ ﴾

which means, "That is so because Allah will never change a grace which He has bestowed on a people until they change what is in their ownselves." (Al-Anfâl, 8:53)

And He, the Almighty says,

﴿ ...إِنَّ ٱللَّهَ لَا يُغَيِّرُ مَا بِقَوْمٍ حَتَّىٰ يُغَيِّرُوا۟ مَا بِأَنفُسِهِمْ... ﴾

which means, "Allah will not change the good condition of a people as long as they do not change their state of goodness themselves (by committing sins and by being ungrateful and disobedient to Allah)." (Ar-Ra'd, 13:11)

What can be worse than the enmity of a servant toward the blessings he has received? In so doing, he supports his enemy against himself. His enemy arouses fire in his blessings and he increases the fire unawares. He enables his enemy to light the fire and then he helps his own enemy to blow on it until it becomes strong. Finally, he seeks help against the fire and blames fate.

Chapter: The Beauty of Allah, the Exalted

The most precious kind of knowledge e is to know Allah, the Exalted through His beauty. This is granted to the truly pious among His creatures, while others know Him through one of His attributes, while those who know Him the best know Him through His perfection, glory, and beauty. There is nothing like Him in His attributes. If we assume that all creatures are beautiful and we think of the most beautiful one we know, and compare their inner and outer beauty to that of Allah, the Exalted, it will be like we are comparing the light of a candle to the sun. Surely, if He withdraws the veil from His face, the splendor of His countenance would consume His creation. The beauty that is contained in the inner and outer elements of this worldly life and the Hereafter comes from the effect of His creation. What then, is the extent of beauty of the Creator?

He has all glory, power, charity, generosity, knowledge, and favor. With the light of His face, all darkness disappears. As the Prophet (peace be upon him) said in supplication of At-Tâ'if, "I seek refuge with Your Face that darkness will go and without which both the affairs of this life and the Hereafter will go astray."

'Abdullâh bin Mas'ûd (may Allah be pleased with him) said, "Allah does not have either night or day: the light of the Heavens and the earth is from the light of His face." Allah, the Exalted is the light of the heavens and the earth and on the Day of Resurrection when Allah will judge mankind, the earth will shine from His light. From among the names of Allah is "the most Graceful." It was recorded in the sahîh that the

Prophet (peace be upon him) said, "Verily, Allah is Graceful and He loves Grace."[67]

The beauty of Allah is on four levels: the beauty of self, the beauty of His attributes, the beauty of His deeds, and the beauty of His names. All His names are beautiful, His attributes are all attributes of perfection, and His deeds are all wise, just, and merciful, and He considers the benefit of man. Only Allah knows the beauty of self and what it is like, and His creatures only have some definitions that He bestowed upon some of His servants that He honored. This beauty is preserved away from others and is covered by a veil and a lower garment, as the Messenger (peace be upon him) said, "Pride is my cloak and majesty is my lower garment." And because pride is wider and greater, it deserves the name of cloak, as Allah is the Greatest and the Most High.

Ibn 'Abbâs said, "Allah covered His self with attributes and covered His attributes with deeds. What do you think about a beauty that is covered by the attributes of perfection and of glory and loftiness?"

From this some other meanings of beauty can be understood. The servant achieves progress from knowing the deeds and then the attributes, and from knowing the attributes to knowing the self. If he saw something among the beauty of deeds, he would reach the beauty of attributes and then he reaches the beauty of the self.

So all praise and thanks are due to Allah, the Exalted, and none of His creation can praise Him as He deserves, but only as He praises Himself and He deserves to be worshiped, loved, and praised. He loves His attributes and deeds as He loves His self. All of His deeds are beautiful and precious and there is nothing hateful among His deeds. There is nothing in

---

[67] Recorded by Muslim, book of faith, chapter forbiddance of pride, no.91.

the universe that is loved and praised except Allah, the Exalted. And whatever is loved other than Him, if love is for the sake of Allah, this love is lawful otherwise it is not. And this is the reality of Lordship. s The true Lord is the one that is loved and praised. What then if we add to that His charity, favor, mercy, forgiveness, and piety?

The servant should know that there is no god but Allah, so he would love and praise Him for His self and for His perfection and should know that there is no one that grants secret and public favors and blessings except Him, so he would love Him for His compassion and blessings. As there is nothing similar to Him, loving Him is not like any kind of love; loving with submission is the kind of worship that Allah created all things for. It is the utmost love with the utmost humility and it cannot be shown except to Allah. Indeed to show it to other than Him is polytheism that Allah does not forgive if the doer dies in that state.

Praising Him includes two matters: being informed about His praiseworthy acts and His attributes of perfection, and loving Him because of them. If someone informs another person about their praiseworthy acts without loving him, he is not praising him. And whoever loves him without informing others about his praiseworthy acts, he is not praising him until he combines the two matters. Allah, the Exalted praises Himself by Himself and praises Himself by the tongues of those who praise Him from among the angels, the Prophets, the Messengers, and the believers. They praise Him according to His wish and by His permission. He is the one, Who enables them to praise Him, and all things are done with His permission. All blessings begin and end with Him; they begin with His praise and end with His praise. He inspires His servant to repent and is happy with it while it is from His favor and generosity and He inspires His servant to obey, helps him to do that, and rewards him for it! He is in no need of anything but all things are in deep need of

Him at all times. The servant needs Him to help him to achieve his aims. Whatever is not permitted by Him will never be and whatever is not done for His sake is useless.

Chapter: Allah is Full of Grace and He loves Grace

When the Prophet (peace be upon him) said, "Verily, Allah is Graceful and He loves Grace,"[68] he meant an indirect kind of beauty included in all matters. As when he (peace be upon him) said in another hadith, "Verily, Allah is Clean and He loves cleanliness."[69] And, "O people, Allah is Good and He therefore, accepts only that which is good."[70] And it was recorded in As-Sunan, "Verily, Allah loves to see the effect of His blessings on His servant."[71] Abu Al-Akhwas (may Allah be pleased with him) narrated that the Prophet (peace be upon him) saw him while he was wearing rags, so he said, "Do you have any wealth?' He said, 'Yes.' Then the Prophet (peace be upon him) asked, 'What kind?' He said, 'Allah granted me camels and sheep.' He said, 'Let His blessings and dignity be seen on you.'"[72]

Allah, the Exalted loves to see the effect of His blessings on His servant; it is among the beauty that He loves. It is a way of praising Him for His blessings, which is an inner beauty and He also loves to see the outer beauty brought about by His blessings on His servant and the inner one by thanking Him. And as Allah loves grace, He provided man with clothing and decoration that beautifies their outer appearance, as well as piety that will beautify their inner selves. Allah, the Almighty says,

---

[68] Mentioned above.
[69] Recorded by At-Tirmidhy, book of good manners, chapter on what is mentioned about cleanliness, no.2799.
[70] Recorded by Muslim, book of charity, chapter on acceptance of charity by honest work and its growth, no.1015.
[71] Recorded by At-Tirmidhy, book of good manners, chapter on what is said about, " Verily, Allah loves to see effect of His blessings ....", no.2819.
[72] Recorded by Abu Dâwûd, no.4063, and At-Tirmidhy, no.2006.

﴿ يَٰبَنِىٓ ءَادَمَ قَدۡ أَنزَلۡنَا عَلَيۡكُمۡ لِبَاسٗا يُوَٰرِي سَوۡءَٰتِكُمۡ وَرِيشٗاۖ وَلِبَاسُ ٱلتَّقۡوَىٰ ذَٰلِكَ خَيۡرٞۚ ... ﴾

which means, "O Children of Adam! We have bestowed raiment upon you to cover yourselves (screen your private parts, etc.) and as an adornment, and the raiment of righteousness, that is better." (Al-A'râf, 7:26)

And He, the Almighty says about the people of Paradise,

﴿ ... وَلَقَّىٰهُمۡ نَضۡرَةٗ وَسُرُورٗا ۝ وَجَزَىٰهُم بِمَا صَبَرُواْ جَنَّةٗ وَحَرِيرٗا ۝ ﴾

which means, "And gave them *Nadratan* (a light of beauty) and joy. And their recompense shall be Paradise, and silken garments, because they were patient." (Al-Insân, 76:11-12)

Allah beautifies their outer face by that light, their inner one with joy and their bodies with silken garments. As He loves beauty in sayings, deeds, clothing, and appearance, and He hates ugliness in sayings, deeds, clothing, and appearance. He hates ugliness and its people and loves beauty and its people. But the two groups were misled concerning this subject: one group said that all that Allah has created is graceful, and He loves whatever He created, and we live with all that He created and do not hate any part of it. And whoever sees any of His creatures, will find that they are all graceful. Allah mentions this saying,

﴿ ٱلَّذِىٓ أَحۡسَنَ كُلَّ شَىۡءٍ خَلَقَهُۥۖ ... ﴾

which means, "Who made everything He has created good." (As-Sajdah, 32:7)

And He, the Almighty says,

$$\{\ ...صُنْعَ ٱللَّهِ ٱلَّذِى أَتْقَنَ كُلَّ شَىْءٍ...\ \}$$

which means, "The Work of Allah, Who perfected all things." (An-Naml, 27:88)

And He, the Almighty says,

$$\{\ ...مَّا تَرَى فِى خَلْقِ ٱلرَّحْمَـٰنِ مِن تَفَـٰوُتٍ...\ \}$$

which means, "You can see no fault in the creations of the Most Beneficent." (Al-Mulk, 67:3)

And the most pious among them is he who declares that beauty is absolute and that there is no ugliness in the universe. Their hearts lack all jealousy for the sake of Allah because of His love for beauty. While others worship Allah and perhaps some of them might exceed the limits and claim that his alleged lord is revealed in this shape and eminent in it. If he was a consolodationist,[73] he would say that it was an aspect from among aspects of right and would call it aesthetic aspects.

Chapter: Kinds of Beauty

The other group disagreed with them and said that Allah, the Exalted dispraised the beauty of outer figures and the perfection of the body and creation. He, the Almighty says about the hypocrites,

---

[73] Translator's Note:
Consolidation (ittihâd): A doctrine adopted by some deviant mystic groups and is based on some pagan beliefs. Consolodationists (ittihâdiyûn) believe that the entity of God is consolidated or unified with the entities of His Creatures, so that both entities become all in one. (Definitior translated with summary from *Al-Mawsû'ah Al-Muyassarah fy Al-Adyân wal-Madhâhib wal-Ahzâb Al-Mu'assirah (Concise Encyclopedia of Religions, Doctrines, and Contemporary Parties)* by the World Assembly of Muslim Youth, Third Edition).

﴿ وَإِذَا رَأَيْتَهُمْ تُعْجِبُكَ أَجْسَامُهُمْ ... ۞ ﴾

which means, "And when you look at them, their bodies please you." (Al-Munâfiqûn, 63:4)

And He, the Almighty says,

﴿ وَكَمْ أَهْلَكْنَا قَبْلَهُم مِّن قَرْنٍ هُمْ أَحْسَنُ أَثَاثًا وَرِءْيًا ۞ ﴾

which means, "And how many a generation (past nations) have We destroyed before them, who were better in wealth, goods and outward appearance?" (Maryam, 19:74)

Al-Hasan said: it is the outer shape. And Muslim recorded that the Prophet (peace be upon him) said, "Verily Allah does not look at your bodies nor at your faces but He looks at your hearts and deeds."[74] They said that it is known that He does not deny perception but that this perception is not what brings about love. They said that He forbade wearing silken clothes, and gold (for men), eating from gold and silver vessels, which are among the most beautiful things in the world. Allah says,

﴿ وَلَا تَمُدَّنَّ عَيْنَيْكَ إِلَىٰ مَا مَتَّعْنَا بِهِۦ أَزْوَٰجًا مِّنْهُمْ زَهْرَةَ ٱلْحَيَوٰةِ ٱلدُّنْيَا لِنَفْتِنَهُمْ فِيهِ ... ﴾

which means, "And strain not your eyes in longing for the things We have given for enjoyment to various groups of them (polytheists and disbelievers in the Oneness of Allah), the splendor of the life of this world that We may test them thereby." (Tâhâ, 20:131)

---

[74] Recorded by Muslim, book of virtue, good manners, and joining the ties of kinship, chapter on 'it is forbidden to perpetrate atrocity upon a Muslim, to humiliate him, to insult him, and inviolable is his blood, honor and wealth,' no.2564.

And the Prophet (peace be upon him) said, "Wearing old clothes is a part of faith."[75] Allah dispraises spendthrifts. Wasting food and drink is like wasting clothing.

To solve this dispute it must be said: beauty of shape, clothing, and appearance is of three kinds: some of it is praiseworthy, some is dispraised, and some would be neither praised nor dispraised. The kind that is praised is what is done for the sake of Allah and that which helps in obeying Him, fulfilling His orders, and answering His demands. The Prophet (peace be upon him) used to adorn himself to meet delegations, as he used to wear clothing of war preparing himself to fight, and when he wore silken clothes during wars, everything he did was praised as it was done for the sake of Allah, raising His word, supporting His religion, and irritating His enemy, while that which is dispraised is what is done seeking this worldly life, gaining authority, pride, and desires and if it was done for a human being. The majority of souls do not have any intention to do other than this. What is neither praised nor dispraised is that which is at variance with these two aims and the two descriptions.

What is meant here is that this honorable hadith includes two great bases: the first is knowledge and the second is behavior, which is to know Allah, the Exalted through His beauty, which has no similarity and to worship Allah through what He loves from among the beauty of sayings, deeds, and manners. Allah loves His servant to beautify his tongue through speaking the truth, his heart through sincerity, repentance, and trust, his body through obeying, and through showing the blessings of Allah in his clothing, purifying it from all dirt, impurities, ritual impurities, and undesired hair, and performing circumcision and cutting

---

[75] It has an authentic chain of transmission, recorded by Abu Dâwûd, book of combing the hair, no.4161, and Ibn Mâjah in book of asceticism, no.4118. Ibn Hajar said: it has an authentic chain of transmission, see *Fath Al-Bâry*, chapter on combing hair and beginning with the right side.

one's nails. The servant will know Him through His attributes of beauty and become acquainted with Him through the beauty of His deeds, sayings, and manners. He would know Him through the beauty, which He is described with and will worship Him through the beauty, which is His law and religion.

Chapter: Sincerity of Determination and Deeds

There is nothing more useful to the servant of Allah than being sincere with his Lord in all matters, especially sincerity in determination. The servant should be sincere in both his determination and in his deed. Allah, the Almighty says,

﴿ ...فَإِذَا عَزَمَ ٱلْأَمْرُ فَلَوْ صَدَقُوا۟ ٱللَّهَ لَكَانَ خَيْرًا لَّهُمْ ﴾

which means, "And when the matter (preparation for *Jihâd*) is resolved on, then if they had been true to Allah, it would have been better for them." (Muhammad, 47:21)

He will find happiness by being sincere in both determination and the truth of his deeds. Sincerity of determination is achieved through resolving and removing any hesitation. If he is sincere in his determination, the truth of his deeds still remains to be fulfilled, which is dedicating one's power and efforts without loosing anything from either the inner or the outer. Determination prevents weakness of will and intention, and the truthful deed prevents him from laziness and apathy. And whoever is true to Allah in all matters, Allah will grant him more than He does with others. This truth is a means that results from combining true sincerity and pure trust. The most truthful among people are those who are granted these characteristics.

A Precious Gem: The Will of the Servant

Allah has will and He orders His servant who also has a will to fulfill His commands, and if Allah wills to support and help him, he would fulfill His commands, but if He leaves him to his own will and soul, the servant will follow the desires of his soul as he is a mere human. That is why Allah dispraised him in His book from this point and only praised him for being a Muslim, a believer, patient, charitable, thankful, pious, etc. which is more than just being a human being, who has a will. It is not enough to just have a will unless it is combined with something extra, which is success. It is just like having good eyes is not enough to see unless you also have a good light.

Chapter: Glorifying Allah

It is the pinnacle of injustice and ignorance to ask to be glorified and honored by people while your heart does not glorify or honor Allah. You are honoring a creature and glorifying and protecting him from seeing you in the real state that Allah sees you in. Allah says,

$$\text{﴿ نَا لَكُمْ لَا تَرْجُونَ لِلَّهِ وَقَارًا ۝ ﴾}$$

which means, "What is the matter with you, [that you fear not Allah (His punishment), and] you hope not for reward (from Allah or you believe not in His Oneness)?" (Nûh, 71:13)

That is you do not glorify Him or honor Him. As Allah says,

$$\text{﴿ ...وَتُوَقِّرُوهُ... ۝ ﴾}$$

which means, "And honor Him." (Al-Fath, 48:9)

Al-Hasan said: why do you not know the worth of Allah and why do you not praise Him? Mujâhid said: you do not care to honor your Lord. Ibn Zaid said: you do not believe in obeying Allah. Ibn 'Abbâs said: you do not know the worth of His glory.

All these sayings bear one meaning, which is if they glorify Allah and know the worth of His glory, they would believe in His oneness, and obey, and praise Him. Obeying Him, avoiding sins, and feeling ashamed in front of Him are able to be done according to the amount one glorifies Him inside his heart. That is why some of our pious prececessors said: in order to increase the glorification of Allah inside the heart of anyone among you, mention Him when he is ashamed of mentioning Him and combine His name with other names. This is the way to glorifyAllah.

To glorify Allah is to never say He has an equal with any of His creation either in words as when one says, By Allah and by your life, I do not have anyone except Allah and you, and whatever Allah wishes and you wish, nor in loving, honoring, and obeying like obeying what a person orders or forbids, or even greater as the majority of unjust and dissolute people do. Also not to fear or hope for anything except Allah, or to care for Him less than you care for others. Man should never underestimate the worth of Allah and should never say that Allah used to forgive us. He should never give priority to creatures over Allah, nor put Allah and His Messenger on one side and people on the other, and join the side, which includes people and neglect the side, which has Allah and His Messenger. He should not dedicate his heart and soul to creatures while talking and give Allah the body and tongue without the heart and soul while worshiping Him, and he should never give priority to his desires over the orders of Allah.

All this is required to glorify Allah within the heart. And whoever fails to do that, Allah will never grant him honor and glory in the hearts of people but indeed, He would remove from their hearts any honor and glorification for him. Even if they honor him for fear of his evil acts, this is honor resulting from hate, not honor from love and glory. Also glorifying Allah is to feel ashamed to let Allah know his secret and conscience and know what He would hate. Also to feel ashamed in front of Him while in a place of privacy more than one feels ashamed in the presence of influential people.

What is meant here is how can the one who does not glorify Allah, His words, and the knowledge and wisdom that He granted him, ask people to glorify and honor him? The Qur'ân, knowledge, and speech of the Messenger (peace be upon him) are all warnings and restraints that have been sent to you in addition to white hair; it is a warning and a restraint for you, which exists within you. But neither what We have sent to you restrains you nor what is in your body advises you. Still you ask others for glorification and honor. You are like the one who was afflicted but did not profit from it and asks others to profit from his distress.

Whoever hears about the punishments and warnings that happened to others is not the same as he who sees them with his own eyes, so what about the one who tasted them in himself? Allah says,

﴿ سَنُرِيهِمْ ءَايَٰتِنَا فِى ٱلْءَافَاقِ وَفِىٓ أَنفُسِهِمْ ... ﴾

which means, "We will show them Our Signs in the universe, and in their ownselves." (Fussilat, 41:53)

His signs are known and heard throughout the universe and His signs in the souls are recognized by the pious. May Allah protect us from being disappointed. Allah says,

﴿ إِنَّ ٱلَّذِينَ حَقَّتْ عَلَيْهِمْ كَلِمَتُ رَبِّكَ لَا يُؤْمِنُونَ ۝ وَلَوْ جَآءَتْهُمْ كُلُّ ءَايَةٍ حَتَّىٰ يَرَوُا۟ ٱلْعَذَابَ ٱلْأَلِيمَ ۝ ﴾

which means, "Truly! Those, against whom the Word (Wrath) of your Lord has been justified, will not believe. Even if every sign should come to them, - until they see the painful torment." (Yûnus, 10:96-97)

And He, the Almighty says,

$$\left\{ \text{وَلَوْ أَنَّنَا نَزَّلْنَا إِلَيْهِمُ ٱلْمَلَٰٓئِكَةَ وَكَلَّمَهُمُ ٱلْمَوْتَىٰ وَحَشَرْنَا عَلَيْهِمْ كُلَّ شَىْءٍ قُبُلًا مَّا كَانُوا۟ لِيُؤْمِنُوٓا۟ إِلَّآ أَن يَشَآءَ ٱللَّهُ}... \right\}$$

which means, "And even if We had sent down unto them angels, and the dead had spoken unto them, and We had gathered together all things before their very eyes, they would not have believed, unless Allah willed." (Al-An'âm, 6:111)

The rational servant, who advocates success without having this, is completing the defects of his creation by virtue of his manners and deeds. Whenever his body loses the effect of worshiping Allah, he would increase his faith in another effect and whenever his body loses its power he would increase the power of his faith, belief, and seeking Allah and the Hereafter. If he was not like this, death would be better for him because he stops at a specific level of pain and corruption regardless of his defects and faults. It increases his pain, sadness, and regret, while if he lives for a long time it might be good and useful if it is used in remembering, catching what has past, seizing opportunities, and sincere repentance. Allah says,

$$\left\{ ...\text{أَوَلَمْ نُعَمِّرْكُم مَّا يَتَذَكَّرُ فِيهِ مَن تَذَكَّرَ}... \right\}$$

which means, "Did We not give you lives long enough, so that whosoever would receive admonition, - could receive it?" (Fâṭir, 35:37)

Whoever attains old age and life did not make him repair his defects and catch up with his past, and seize the rest of his life in order to seek the life of his heart and permanent pleasures, then his life would have been useless.

The servant is traveling either to Paradise or to Hellfire. If he had a long life and his deeds were good, his long journey would be the means of an increase in pleasure for him. The more the journey was long, the more the longing would be better and loftier. If he reached old age but his deeds were evil, his long journey would be a means of increase in his pain and punishment and a means to take him lower. The traveler is either being taken up or down. In a traceable hadith, the Prophet (peace be upon him) said, "The best amongst you is he whose life time extends during which he performs good deeds and the worst amongst you is he whose life time extends during which he performs evil deeds."[76]

Whoever is sincere in seeking Allah, whenever something from himself is damaged, he uses it to raise his heart and soul, and whenever something from his worldly life decreases, he would use it to increase his hereafter. Whenever he is prevented from some of the pleasures of this worldly life, he would use it to increase the pleasures of the hereafter, and whenever he is afflicted with distress, sadness, or grief, he would use it to increase the joys of the hereafter. The more there is a decrease in his body, life, pleasure, power, and authority, the more he gains in his resurrection and it would be a mercy and good for him, otherwise it would be a prevention and punishment for the sins he had committed either in public or secret or for neglecting an obligatory act of worship either in secret or in public, as the good of this worldly life and of the Hereafter depends upon these four. May Allah grant us success.

A Precious Gem: Life is a Journey

From the very moment of creation, mankind is on a journey. He is a traveler and is not allowed to halt except when he reaches either Paradise or Hellfire. The wise one among them is the one who knows that traveling is based on hardship and danger. It is usually hard to seek pleasures and relief during it,

---

[76] Recorded By At-Tirmidhy, book of asceticism, chapter on what is mentioned about long life time of believers, no.2329, Ad-Dârimy, book of softening of hearts, chapter on which among believers is the best, no.2742.

which are to be acquired after it is completed. Every footstep and every moan made during this journey will not stop him. It is proven that the traveler is preparing supplies, which will take him to his final end. And if he halts, sleeps, or rests, he is doing so while preparing himself to complete his journey.

A Precious Gem: Observing

Scholars agreed that keeping oneself busy with observing instead of walking seriously is in fact stopping, because if we use the time that is spent observing in performing any good deed either public or secret, increasing our knowledge, or strengthening our faith, it would have priority. Mankind will be resurrected according to the kinds of deeds he performed with knowledge, intention, and will. The body will be resurrected according to its deeds whether good or bad. When we are removed from this world, we will see the reality of that. As much as your heart is close to Allah, you will be removed from people and from mixing with them and as much as you keep your secret and your will, Allah will protect you. The core of all this is the truth of monotheism, then the truth of knowing the straight path, then the truth of will, and then the truth of deeds. And be very wary of people who seek you and know your aim, as it is a great disease.

A Precious Gem: The Satanic Ways of Tempting

Satan has three ways of tempting man:

One: increase and extravagance; to have more than one needs. This addition is the way, which Satan uses to enter the heart. To protect oneself from that is to be careful not to fulfill all the needs of the soul like food, sleep, pleasure, or rest. Whenever you close this door, you would be safe from any enemy.

Two: negligence; whoever remembers Allah is protected by the fortress of remembering Him. When he neglects that he will be opening the door of this fortress and the enemy will enter. It would then be difficult to drive him out.

Three: caring for what is not his business in all matters of life.

A Precious Gem: The Way to Success

Whoever wants to reach Allah and the Hereafter and attain all knowledge, craft, and authority in a way that he will be ahead of these matters and be followed in that, needs to be courageous, bold, in control of his desires, not to be governed by the authority of his imagination, renouncing all his needs, love what he is heading toward, knowing the way to it and the ways that interrupt it, and have a strong intention and a firm will that nothing would turn him away from its aim. Such a person would not be affected by blame or reproach, and would usually be quiet and think seriously. He would never be inclined to follow either the pleasure of praise or the pain of dispraise. He would be secure of what he needs from all the means of support, would not be provoked by disagreements, and would adopt the motto of patience and his relief would be found in working hard, love for high moral standards, being on time, being careful while mixing with people like a bird when it looks for its seeds, preserving himself through hope and fear, hoping for the results of being special above his kind, not to lose any of his senses in useless matters, and not to lose his mind in contemplating the levels of the universe. In order to achieve all that, he should abandon the habits and obstacles that lie between him and what he wants. The public used to say: to have hidden manners is better than losing one's manners in public.

A Precious Gem: The Best Kinds of Remembrance

Among those who remember Allah are those who begin remembering with the tongue even if he is negligent. He continues to do so until his heart is involved too. Others do not agree with that and do not start while in a state of negligence, but instead wait until the heart is ready. He begins with his heart and then involves his tongue in remembrance. The first supplication goes from his tongue to his heart and the second from his heart to his tongue without empting any of the contents of his heart. He just waits until he feels that the utterance is ready to be verbalized. When he feels that his heart will utter, then the heart's utterance would pass to verbal utterance. Then he would engross himself in that until he finds that every part of his being is supplicating Allah. The best and more useful kind of supplication is what the heart and tongue are involved in, to be from among the prophetic supplications, and whoever is reciting it feels its meaning and aims.

Chapter: The Most Useful and the Most Harmful of People

The most useful person is the one who allows a person to implant goodness inside him or to do him a favor, as this help is the means to attaining benefit and perfection. In fact, both the giver and the receiver benefit from this. The most harmful of people are those who overpower you until you disobey Allah. Such people only help you to harm yourself and decrease your morality.

A Precious Gem: Forbidden Pleasure

Forbidden pleasure is combined with ugliness and it will cause pain after the moment has passed. If you feel strongly inclined toward it, you should think about the pain it will leave behind. It is necessary to compare the two matters and discover the difference between them. Suffering pain while worshiping Allah is combined with a good soul that will bear the fruit of pleasure and relief. When the soul finds it heavy and thinks to stop the pain and then compares the end results of the two matters, he will surely prefer the way of hardship. If you feel pain because of deeds, you should think about the happiness, joy, and pleasure you will gain, then the pain will seem easy to bear. If you get hurt because of abandoning some kind of forbidden pleasure, you should think about the pain that follows it and compare the two kinds.

To make the correct choice, you must know the reasons and consequences of each act and then choose that which is more deserving and useful. Whoever succeeds at doing this, would choose the better and prefer it. Whoever thinks about this Worldly life and the Hereafter, would know that he will never gain either of them except by hardship. He should bear this hardship in order to gain the best and more lasting of them.

A Precious Gem: There is Right and Wrong in Everything

When Allah created man, He established an order and a system for each organ, and He ordained prohibitions for each organ, granted a blessing for fulfilling each of them, and specified a kind of pleasure and benefit that results from each one. If the servant acts while using each organ for the sake of Allah and avoids the prohibitions, he would be praising Allah for granting him the blessings of each organ and would complete the potential benefit and pleasure from each one. But if he neglects the orders of Allah and His prohibitions, Allah will not allow him to benefit from any of them and moreover, He will make it a cause of pain and harm.

Each organ of the body has the duty to worship Allah at all times, which will bring one closer to Him. If he keeps himself busy with worship, he will be close to Allah, but if he is busy with his desires, seeking relief, or being idle, he will fail. The servant is constantly fluctuating between being close to Allah and being far from Him. Allah, the Exalted says,

$$\{ \text{لِمَن شَاءَ مِنكُمْ أَن يَتَقَدَّمَ أَوْ يَتَأَخَّرَ} \}$$

which means, "To any of you that chooses to go forward (by working righteous deeds), or to remain behind (by committing sins)." (Al-Muddathir, 74:37)

Chapter: The People of Paradise and those of Hellfire

Allah, the Exalted created all things with a harmony between order and prohibition, and giving and preventing, so they became two parties: one party that neglected His order, ignored His prohibitions, failed to praise Him or be grateful to Him, and was dissatisfied when He prevented them from something they wanted. Such people are His enemies and their enmity increases or decreases according to the situations that confront them. Another party said: we are Your servants. If You give us an order we will hurry to fulfill it, if You prohibit us from something we will restrain ourselves, if You give something to us we will praise and thank You, and if You prevent us from something we wanted, we will ask You and supplicate to You. There is nothing between man and Paradise except the veil of this worldly life. When death tears down that veil, the pious people will remain forever in pleasure and happiness. When the evil ones face death, the final veil will also be torn down and there will be nothing between them and the hellfire. When death tears down this veil, they will remain forever in pain and regret.

The armies of this Worldly life and the Hereafter confront within your heart and want to know to which you belong. If you look sincerely within your heart, you will notice which one you prefer and you will fight against the other. No person can remain stagnant between them; you belong to one of them. The first group restrains desires, takes the advice of the mind, empties the heart so it can think about the aim behind their creation, the body performs what it was ordered to do, and it uses time to do what will benefit it in the Hereafter. It defeats their short life by rushing to perform good deeds. It lives in this worldly life while its heart is far removed from it. It lives for the Hereafter before going to it, it cares for Allah and obedience to Him, and seeks to perform that which will increase their rank in the hereafter, so Allah paid in advance by granting them the pleasures of Paradise; is close to them and fills their hearts with love and longing for Him and empties their hearts from whatever fills the hearts of others like loving this life and sadness and grief for losing it. So they feel a sense of ease with the same things that others feel are difficult. They love what others hate, and live this life with their bodies but their souls are with the Exalted.

Chapter: Some Qualities of Monotheism

Monotheism is fine, chaste, clean, and pure. An evil thought, word or action affects its standing in the heart of man, and just a moment, a word, or a hidden desire confuse it. And if its owner fails to hurry and remove this effect by doing its opposite, it will become stronger and turn into a habit that is hard to be removed.

These effects and impressions sometimes take place quickly and also vanish quickly, while others happen fast but are slow to vanish, and others are slow to happen and fast to vanish.

Some people have a strong sense of monotheism and are able to withstand the effects of evil like a great amount of water that catches only a little dirt. The person whose sense of monotheism is not so strong, will be easily deceived and his weakness will bear the harmful effects that strong monotheism does not.

A place that is marked by purity will show its owner the cause of its being soiled, so he has the chance to hurry and remove it but the place that does not reach this level of purity will not do that. Faith and monotheism go hand in hand and if they are very strong, they would defeat evil in a way that weakness cannot. The person who has good character will be forgiven for sins that the one with bad character will not be forgiven for. Having a sincere intention, a strong will and perfect obedience change evil effects just like lying, a bad intention, and weak obedience change good words and deeds according to their ways.

A Precious Gem: Only the Heart that is Founded on Monotheism Will Comprehend the Precious Qualities of Allah

Abandoning desires for the sake of Allah will rescue the servant from the punishment of Allah and will guarantee one to obtain His mercy. The precious qualities of Allah, the treasure of piety, pleasure, longing for Him, joy, and the happiness found in being close to Him will never happen to the heart that cares for anyone or anything besides Allah even if he was among the people of worship, piety, and knowledge. Allah, the Exalted refused to put His precious qualities into the heart that associates others with Him and whose intention is to follow other than Him. Instead He entrusts His precious qualities to the heart that considers poverty as wealth as long as it is close to Allah, and wealth as poverty if it is not close to Allah. It will consider honor as humiliation and humiliation as honor, as well as pleasure as punishment and punishment as pleasure. As a whole, the servant who possesses such a heart neither knows the meaning of life without Allah nor the meaning of death, pain, sadness, grief, and distress that is associated with being far from Him. The pious servant will gain two kinds of Paradise: the Paradise of this worldly life and the Paradise on the Day of Resurrection.

A Precious Gem: Al-Inâbah and Al-I'tikâf

Inâbah is devotion of the heart to Allah, the Exalted like devotion of the body inside the mosque without leaving it. That is to say, devotion of the heart is to love and glorify Allah and devote the actions of one's body to Allah by worshipping sincerely and following His Messenger. Whoever does not devote his heart to Allah alone, would devote it to different kinds of images. Allah says that Ibrâhîm (Abraham, peace be upon him) said to his people,

$$\{...\text{مَا هَـٰذِهِ ٱلتَّمَاثِيلُ ٱلَّتِىٓ أَنتُمْ لَهَا عَـٰكِفُونَ}\}$$

which means, "What are these images, to which you are devoted?" (Al-Anbiyâ', 21:52)

He and his people shared the reality of devotion but his nation chose devotion to graven images and he devoted himself to Allah, the Exalted. Images are actually the plural of an image, like pictures. When the heart is attached to, busy with and following anything other than Allah, this is devotion of the heart to images which appear to him in his heart similar to devotion to the images of idols. That is why the polytheism of pagans was by devoting their hearts, intentions, and wills to idols. For this reason the Prophet (peace be upon him) called whoever did so a servant of idols or images and invoked Allah against him. He (peace be upon him) said, "Miserable be the worshipper of the dinar and the dirham! Let him be miserable and a looser, and let him never be healed even from the prick of a thorn."

Mankind are all travelers in this worldy life and every traveler is heading toward his aim and will stop at the place that pleases him. Whoever seeks Allah and the Last Day is a traveler and his aim in his travel is seeking the pleasure of Allah, and this is his aim, intention and destiny. Allah says,

$$ \text{﴿ يَٰٓأَيَّتُهَا ٱلنَّفْسُ ٱلْمُطْمَئِنَّةُ ۝ ٱرْجِعِىٓ إِلَىٰ رَبِّكِ رَاضِيَةً مَّرْضِيَّةً ۝ فَٱدْخُلِى فِى عِبَٰدِى ۝ وَٱدْخُلِى جَنَّتِى ۝ ﴾} $$

which means, "(It will be said to the pious): "O (you) the one in (complete) rest and satisfaction! "Come back to your Lord, Well-pleased (yourself) and well-pleasing unto Him! "Enter you, then, among My honored slaves, "And enter you My Paradise!" (Al-Fajr, 89:27-30)

And Allah says that the wife of Fir'awn (Pharoah) said,

$$ \text{﴿ ...رَبِّ ٱبْنِ لِى عِندَكَ بَيْتًا فِى ٱلْجَنَّةِ... ۝ ﴾} $$

which means, "My Lord! Build for me a home with You in Paradise." (At-Tahrîm, 66:12)

She asked for His companionship and the home of the Hereafter before her earthly home.

Some Sayings of Sheikh 'Aly

In a state between wakefulness and sleep it occurred to me: do not show that you are in need of any other except Allah otherwise He will double your need for you as a consequence of violating your limits as His servant. He afflicted you with poverty so that you would be purified so do not rid yourself of the means of your reformation. Allah prescribed that poverty would be your destiny and your wealth would be with Him, and if you used your wealth to maintain a close relation with Him, He would use His to do the same, but if you used yours to seek your need from another, He would prevent His support to you as a means of exile from His door. Do not depend on anything that is lower and weaker than Him, as it will bring about evil results and destroy you. If you depend on your deeds, He will give you your due reward, if you depend on knowledge alone, He will take it away from you, if you depend on love, He will cause you to indulge in it, if you depend on learning alone, He will make it a means of your destruction, and if you depend on creatures, He will leave you to them. Be satisfied with Allah as Your Lord and He will be satisfied with you as His servant.

A Precious Gem: Sighing While Listening to the Qur'ân

Sighing while listening to the Qur'ân or other than it has a number of causes:

One: if while listening to the Qur'ân a person experiences a new degree that he never did before within himself and becomes scared, this happens to him. This is a sigh of longing to have this degree.

Two: if a sin is mentioned that he committed, he sighs out of fear and sadness. This is a sigh of fear.

Three: if a fault or weakness is mentioned which he cannot stop or control, it will cause him sadness. his is a sigh of sadness.

Four: when he perceives the perfection of his Lord and discovers that the way to Him is closed. This is a sigh of sadness and grief.

Five: if he forgets His Lord and is busy with other than Him and this recitation reminds him of his Lord and outlines the way to Him clearly and openly, this is a sigh of joy and happiness.

Anyway, the cause of sighing is the strength and significance of the event in comparison with the weakness of the person and his ability to bear it or overcome it, along with the power of the event when it happens inside him. If he shows it on his face, it would cause the effect to be weak and would bring about its end. This is the sigh, which comes from the true servant. The one who tastes that is either truthful, a thief, or a hypocrite.

A Useful Rule: Kinds of Thoughts

The origin of good and evil begins in one's thoughts. Thought is the bases of will and seeking piety, love, and hate. The most beneficial kinds of thoughts are those, which seek the benefits of the Resurrection and the ways to gain them and the evils of the Resurrection and the ways to avoid them. These are four of the loftiest thoughts, and there are four others that follow them: thought concerned with the benefits of this worldly life and the ways to gain them and evil thoughts concerning this worldly life and the ways to avoid them. These eight subjects comprise the thoughts that wise people think. The head of the first section is thinking about the blessings, favors, commands, and prohibitions of Allah, about the ways to know Him, His names and attributes from His Book and the Sunnah of His Messenger and whoever follows him sincerely. Thoughts of this kind will bring about love and knowledge. When he thinks about the Hereafter, its honor and immortality and about this worldly life and its meanness and ruin, he will wish for the Hereafter and will neglect the other. The more he thinks about the shortness of time and the absence of hope in front of him in this worldly life, he will become more serious and diligent and do his best to benefit from time and whatever avails him.

These thoughts will strengthen his intention and revive it after its death and will make him steer his course in one way while the others steer theirs in another way. Besides these thoughts, there are also evil thoughts which get established in the majority of hearts. These include thinking about what we are not supposed to think about it and being preoccupied with useless knowledge like the identity of Allah and His attributes and other things, which the mind cannot comprehend.

Also thinking about non beneficial pass times like playing chess, listening to music, and images and pictures of living things.

As well as this are some of the sciences which do not elevate the soul or bring about the development of man, like the details of logic, mathematics and physics and many schools of philosophy. Even if man understands the essence of such things, it does not bring about perfection or honor.

Thinking about desires, pleasures, and ways to fulfill them, is an aspect of evil thought. Even if man takes delight in them, their harm during this worldly life and the Hereafter are greater than the pleasure they provide.

Another example is thinking about what never happened. If it had really happened, what would it have been like? Like for example, thinking about what it would be like if one were a king, found a treasure, or owned a garden. What would be one's manners and how would one act, take, give, take revenge, etc? These are the thoughts of foolish people.

Thinking about such people and the aspects of their lives,etc are the kinds of thoughts of those who are far away from Allah, His Messenger, and the Hereafter.

Thinking about and planning traps and tricks by which one can achieve his desires and aims whether they are lawful or not.

Also thinking about the kinds of poetry that praise, criticize, express feelings of love, lamentation, and others, as they keep the servant busy and prevent him from thinking about his real happiness and eternal life in the Hereafter.

Also thinking about imaginary concepts that are not conceivable and moreover they are not necessary in human life. This is found in every science even in jurisprudence, the principles of Islam, and medicine. Such thoughts contain more harm than good and keep the servant of Allah busy instead of thinking about what is more useful.

An Important Rule: Making a Request and Patience Thereafter

Making a request is a seed of faith. If faith and requesting are combined they will have a good result. Trusting in Allah is the seed of relying on Him and if He, the Almighty is approached with sincerity, supplications will be answered. Fear is the seed of love, and when it is combined with patience, the result is obedience to Allah's commands and avoidance of what He has prohibited. Patience is the seed of belief, and it will make the servant a strong believer. Allah, the Almighty says,

﴿ وَجَعَلْنَا مِنْهُمْ أَئِمَّةً يَهْدُونَ بِأَمْرِنَا لَمَّا صَبَرُوا وَكَانُوا بِآيَاتِنَا يُوقِنُونَ ۝ ﴾

which means, "And We made from among them (Children of Israel), leaders, giving guidance under Our Command, when they were patient and used to believe with certainty in Our Âyât (proofs, evidences, verses, lessons, signs, revelations, etc.)." (As-Sajdah, 32:24)Following the Messenger (peace be upon him) truly is the seed of sincerity, and if they are all combined they will lead to acceptance of one's deeds. Hard work in useful purposes is the seed of knowledge, and when they are all combined, there will be success and happiness, but if they are not, they will be of no use. Tolerance is the seed of knowledge, and if they are combined they will bring about mastery of this worldly life and the Hereafter and the scholar will benefit from his knowledge. But if one of them separates from the other, he will benefit nothing. Determination is the seed of insight, and if they are united, the servant will gain all goodness in this Worldly life and the Hereafter and his intention will reach the highest levels of every place.

Lacking perfection is due to either lack of insight or lack of determination. Good intention is the seed of a healthy mind, if they are lacking all good is missed and if they are present, they will bring about all good. A true opinion is the seed of courage, and when they are combined there will be victory, but If they are lacking there will be disappointment and failure. Opinion found without courage, will result in cowardice and deficiency. If there is courage without opinion, there will be rashness and destruction. Patience is the seed of insight, and if they are combined, all good will be found in their unity.

Al-Hasan, said: if you wish, you will see a servant who has insight without having patience, and if you wish you will also see one, who has patience without insight but when you see who has both insight and patience, he is the successful one.

Advice is the seed of the mind. The stronger it is the more the mind will be strong and enlightened. Remembering and thinking are the seeds of each other, when they are combined, they will encourage one to forsake this life and seek the Hereafter. Piety is the seed of trust, if they are combined the heart will become straight. Preparing oneself is the seed to face weak hope, and all good is in their unity and all evil is in their separation. Sincere intention is the seed of strong determination, and if they are combined, the servant will attain his greatest aim.

An Important Rule: The Servant Exists between the Hands of Allah

The servant exists between hands of Allah at two times: while standing during performing prayer and standing on the Day of Resurrection. Whoever fulfills the rights of the first standing, will in fact be facilitating the second one, and whoever considers this easy and does not pay due attention to it, he will be making the other one difficult for himself. Allah, the Almighty says,

﴿ وَمِنَ ٱلَّيْلِ فَٱسْجُدْ لَهُۥ وَسَبِّحْهُ لَيْلًا طَوِيلًا ۝ إِنَّ هَٰٓؤُلَآءِ يُحِبُّونَ ٱلْعَاجِلَةَ وَيَذَرُونَ وَرَآءَهُمْ يَوْمًا ثَقِيلًا ۝ ﴾

which means, "And during night, prostrate yourself to Him (i.e. the offering of *Maghrib* and *'Ishâ'* prayers), and glorify Him a long night through (i.e. *Tahajjud* prayer). Verily! These (disbelievers) love the present life of this world, and put behind them a heavy Day (that will be hard)." (Al-Insân, 76:26-27)

An Important Rule: The Pleasure of the Hereafter is More Lasting

Pleasure from this point of view is that needed by man but it is better to be free of it if it will cause the loss of what is greater than it and, which is more perfect than it or if it will cause pain that is much greater than the pain that will be caused if we missed it. Here we find the difference between the wise and intelligent person and the foolish and ignorant one. Whenever the mind of man comprehends the difference between these two pleasures and the two kinds of pain associated with them and discovers that there is no comparison between the two, it will be easy for the mind to abandon the lower pleasure in order to gain the higher, and it will be easier to bear the easier pain and to avoid the harder one.

Since this is the case, the pleasure of the Hereafter is greater and more lasting, and the pleasure of this worldly life is lower and has a shorter duration. That is also the case concerning the pain of the Hereafter and that of this worldly life. The criterion here is according to one's faith and belief. If belief is strong and governs the heart, he will prefer the higher (eternal) pleasures more than the lower ones, and will bear the easier pain more than the hardest one in the Hereafter.

A Precious Gem: And Ayyûb (Job) when he cried to his Lord!

Allah, the Almighty says,

﴿ وَأَيُّوبَ إِذْ نَادَىٰ رَبَّهُ أَنِّي مَسَّنِيَ ٱلضُّرُّ وَأَنتَ أَرْحَمُ ٱلرَّٰحِمِينَ ﴾

which means, "And (remember) Aiyûb (Job), when he cried to his Lord: "Verily, distress has seized me, and You are the Most Merciful of all those who show mercy." (Al-Anbiyâ', 21:83)

Aiyûb (Job, peace be upon him) combined many elements in his supplication. He inferred the reality of monotheism, expressing his need to Allah, showing love for Him and longing for Him, acknowledging the attribute of His mercy and that He is the Most Merciful among those who show mercy, and being humble in front of Allah because of His attributes and by showing his need for Him. Whenever someone is in trouble and finds this feeling in himself, his distress will be removed.

A Precious Gem: You are my Protector in this Life and in the Hereafter

Allah says that Yûsuf (Joseph, peace be upon him) said,

﴿ ...أَنتَ وَلِيِّ۪ فِي ٱلدُّنْيَا وَٱلْءَاخِرَةِ تَوَفَّنِي مُسْلِمًا وَأَلْحِقْنِي بِٱلصَّٰلِحِينَ ﴾

which means, "You are my Walî (Protector, Helper, Supporter, Guardian, etc.) in this world and in the Hereafter, cause me to die as a Muslim (the one submitting to Your Will), and join me with the righteous." (Yûsuf, 12:101)

This supplication combined the acknowledgment of monotheism, submission to Allah, showing one's need for Him, being free of taking any supporters other than Him, expressing that dying while being a Muslim is the greatest aim of any servant. This entails acknowledging that we are in the hands of

Allah and not in the hands of any servant, confessing the truth of the Resurrection, and asking to join with the righteous.

An Important Rule: And there is not a thing but the stores thereof are with Us

Allah, the Exalted says,

$$ \text{وَإِن مِّن شَيْءٍ إِلَّا عِندَنَا خَزَائِنُهُ} ... $$

which means, "And there is not a thing, but with Us are the stores thereof." (Al-Hijr, 15:21)

This verse is a treasure from among treasures, which includesevery matter that is to be asked for, as the only One who has keys of this treasure is Allah and He is the One who owns the keys. If anyone or anything else is asked, they have no power or ability to fulfill the request. While the verse, in which Allah says,

$$ \text{وَأَنَّ إِلَىٰ رَبِّكَ ٱلْمُنتَهَىٰ} $$

which means, "And that to your Lord (Allah) is the End (Return of everything)" (An-Najm, 53:42) includes greater treasure which is that every aim if it was not for His sake, it is vain and useless. The end of all matters returns to whoever all matters end to Him. All matters returns to Allah, His creation, will, wisdom, and knowledge. He is aim of every need. Every lover that does not love for His sake, his love would be pain and suffer, every deed that is not for His sake, is vain and lost, and every heart that is not full of Him is miserable away from any happiness and success. Allah shows that all what servant may want is in His hands by saying what means, "And there is not a thing, but with Us are the stores thereof." (Al-Hijr, 15:21).

Allah revealed that all words and deeds should be performed for His sake by saying which means, "And that to your Lord

(Allah) is the End (Return of everything)" (An-Najm, 53:42). There is no need that we cannot ask from Allah, and the end of all matters is with Him.

Some Secrets of Monotheism

The heart never becomes straight or calm except by achieving closeness to Allah. All things should be loved or hated for the sake of Allah. It is impossible that any matter would end with two ends or that all creatures were created from two. Whoever loves, desires, wills, and obeys other than Allah, it would be in vain and whoever loves, desires, fears, and needs for the sake of Allah, he would gain His blessings, pleasure, and eternal happiness. Mankind is always confused between commands and prohibitions. Man is constantly in need and is obliged to receive help at times of commands and is in need of kindness during times of disasters. The kindness that would happen to him at times of disaster depends upon the way in which he fulfilled the commands. If he fulfills both the commands in secret and in public, he would be shown kindness both in secret and in public. But if he fulfills the commands in public without fulfilling them secretly within himself, he would be shown kindness in public, and his share of kindness within himself would be decreased.

The kindness that one is given within oneself, at times of disasters is calmness, relief, and not feeling worried, confused, or discontented. The servant should submit to Allah in humility seeking Him with all his heart, longing for Him with his soul, and remain busy by thinking about the kindness He has bestowed on him more than about his pain. He does not feel pain as he knows that Allah chooses the best for him and that he is a mere servant of Allah and under His judgments whether or not he is content. If he is content, he will feel contentment and if he is discontented, he will have the displeasure of Allah. This is kindness, which is the hidden fruit inside man and is a kind of hidden and secret treatment whose affect will be either increased or decreased.

A Precious Gem: Loving Allah

The servant can only be close to Allah when his will and love become attached to Him. This is the kind of love that seeks Him alone and is not covered with any falsehood or insincerity. It seeks to know His names, attributes, and deeds and its light would never hide the darkness of neglect, as the light of love does not cover the darkness of polytheism. The supplications of the sincere servant seek Allah, so there is no veil of forgetfulness or negligence to be found between the supplicant and Allah. The sincere supplication seeks Allah and his deeds would be seeking to fulfill His commands and avoid what He has forbidden. He would perform acts of worship because he was ordered to do so and loves to do them and avoids what is forbidden because he was forbidden to do so and so hates them.

This is how deeds are attached to His commands and prohibitions, which remove all the causes that induce one to do or avoid the vanities of life. Also trust and love are attached to Him by placing one's trust in Allah and being content with what He has chosen for him. Poverty and need are attached to Him alone and no other than Him, as well as fear, hope, happiness, and joy.

And if the servant experiences happiness from any creature, he knows that complete happiness and perfect joy and relief of the heart are in the hands of Allah. If any creature helps one to gain closeness to Allah, he will be happy and if that creature does not, he would be sad. There is no happiness except through what helps to reach Him and supports to obey Him. Allah told man that He does not like those who rejoice at this worldly life and its allurements and ordered man to be glad because of His favor and mercy, which is Islam, faith, and the Qur'ân, as the companions and followers explained.

A Valuable Rule: All Blessings are From Allah

The origin of this is to know that all blessings are from Allah alone: both the blessings of worship and pleasure. You should seek Him in order to help you in remembering and praising Him. Allah says,

﴿ وَمَا بِكُم مِّن نِّعْمَةٍ فَمِنَ ٱللَّهِ ۖ ثُمَّ إِذَا مَسَّكُمُ ٱلضُّرُّ فَإِلَيْهِ تَجْـَٔرُونَ ۝ ﴾

which means, "And whatever of blessings and good things you have, it is from Allah. Then, when harm touches you, unto Him you cry aloud for help." (An-Nahl, 16:53)

And He, the Almighty says,

﴿ ...فَٱذْكُرُوٓاْ ءَالَآءَ ٱللَّهِ لَعَلَّكُمْ تُفْلِحُونَ ۝ ﴾

which means, "So remember the graces (bestowed upon you) from Allah, so that you may be successful." (Al-A'râf, 7:69)

And He, the Almighty says,

﴿ ...وَٱشْكُرُواْ نِعْمَتَ ٱللَّهِ إِن كُنتُمْ إِيَّاهُ تَعْبُدُونَ ۝ ﴾

which means, "And be grateful for the Graces of Allah, if it is He Whom you worship." (An-Nahl, 16:114)

As these blessings are from Him and His favor and remembering and praising them are not gained except through His permission. Sin is the result of neglecting one's duty to Allah and the consequence of Allah leaving His servant to himself and if He, the Almighty does not remove this from His servant, he would never be able to remove it himself. The servant is obliged to ask Allah to remove its cause from him so that he will not commit it and if it happens he would be obliged to ask and supplicate Allah to remove its consequences and punishment. The servant is never satisfied with these three origins and will never gain success without them: praise, seeking health, and sincere repentance.

This essence of this subject is desire and fear and it is not in the hands of the servant but in the hands of Allah, who turns the hearts according to His will. If Allah granted His servant success, the servant will seek Him with his heart and fill it with desire and fear but if Allah leaves His servant, He will leave him to himself, and will not captivate his heart. Whatever Allah wishes, will be and whatever He does not wish, will never be.

Granting Success and Incurring Failure

I often wonder whether or not there is a reason for success and failure or whether they are just according to will. The truth is that their reason is based on the level of gratefulness in the servant. For a servant to be in a suitable situation to accept a blessing he must know its value, and its potential danger, praise He who bestowed it on him, glorify Him, and know that it is a blessing from Allah without having had anything to do with it nor deserve it. The servant should acknowledge the oneness of Allah, use this blessing to praise Him, admit that it is because of His favor, and then he would know his faults and defects as he knows he could never praise Allah properly. The servant should know that if Allah continues to grant him this blessing, it is a favor, charity, and blessing from Him and if He chooses to take it away from him, he deserves that.

The more Allah grants His servant blessings, the more humility, submission, praise, and fear of Allah the servant should have and if it is taken away from him it is because he did not praise Him as He deserves. The Almighty may take His blessings away from whoever does not acknowledge or care for them as they deserve. If the servant does not praise Allah as he should and misuses this blessing, undoubtedly Allah will take it away. Allah says,

$$﴿ وَكَذَٰلِكَ فَتَنَّا بَعْضَهُم بِبَعْضٍ لِّيَقُولُوٓا۟ أَهَٰٓؤُلَآءِ مَنَّ ٱللَّهُ عَلَيْهِم مِّنۢ بَيْنِنَآ ۗ أَلَيْسَ ٱللَّهُ بِأَعْلَمَ بِٱلشَّٰكِرِينَ ۝ ﴾$$

which means, "Thus We have tried some of them with others, that they might say: "Is it these (poor believers) that Allah has favored from amongst us?" Does not Allah know best those who are grateful?" (Al-An'âm, 6:53)

They are those who knew the value of those blessings, accepted, loved, and praised whoever granted them, and loved and thanked Him. Allah says,

$$﴿ وَإِذَا جَآءَتْهُمْ ءَايَةٌ قَالُوا۟ لَن نُّؤْمِنَ حَتَّىٰ نُؤْتَىٰ مِثْلَ مَآ أُوتِيَ رُسُلُ ٱللَّهِ ۘ ٱللَّهُ أَعْلَمُ حَيْثُ يَجْعَلُ رِسَالَتَهُۥ ... ۝ ﴾$$

which means, "And when there comes to them a sign (from Allah) they say: "We shall not believe until we receive the like of that which the Messengers of Allah had received." Allah knows best with whom to place His Message." (Al-An'âm, 6:124)

Chapter: The Causes of Failure

The cause behind failure is unsuitability of place, inconvenience, and lacking the ability to accept the blessing; if he was granted the blessing he would say: this is mine and I got it because I deserve it as Allah says,

$$﴿ قَالَ إِنَّمَآ أُوتِيتُهُۥ عَلَىٰ عِلْمٍ عِندِىٓ ... ۝ ﴾$$

which means, "He said: "This has been given to me only because of knowledge I possess." (Al-Qaṣaṣ, 28:78)

That is to say, because of the knowledge that Allah gave me and according to which I deserve this blessing and so it is my right. Al-Farrâ' said: I got it and I deserve it according to the favors I possess.

'Abdullâh bin Al-Hârith bin Nawfal[77] mentioned the blessings and ownership that Sulaimân bin Dâwûd (Solomon, the son of David, peace be upon him) possessed, then he recited that Allah says,

﴿ ...هَٰذَا مِن فَضْلِ رَبِّي لِيَبْلُوَنِي ءَأَشْكُرُ أَمْ أَكْفُرُ... ﴾

which means, "This is by the Grace of my Lord to test me whether I am grateful or ungrateful!" (An-Naml, 27:40)

He did not say: this is because of my honor. Then he mentioned Qârûn and recited,

﴿ قَالَ إِنَّمَآ أُوتِيتُهُۥ عَلَىٰ عِلْمٍ عِندِي... ﴾

which means, "He said: "This has been given to me only because of knowledge I possess." (Al-Qasas, 28:78)

He meant that Sulaimân (Solomon, peace be upon him) realized that whatever he gained is from his Lord and His favor and that he is afflicted with it and Qârûn thought that he deserved the blessings he received. Also Allah says,

﴿ وَلَئِنْ أَذَقْنَٰهُ رَحْمَةً مِّنَّا مِنۢ بَعْدِ ضَرَّآءَ مَسَّتْهُ لَيَقُولَنَّ هَٰذَا لِي... ﴾

---

[77] He is 'Abdullâh bin Al-Hârith bin Nawfal Al-Hâshimy Al-Qurashy. He was a pious imam. He, (may Allah be merciful to him) passed away at 84 A.H. See *Tahdhîb Al-Kamâl*, vol.2, p.673, *Tahdhîb At-Tahdhîb*, vol.5, p.180, *Taqrîb At-Tahdhîb*, vol.1, p.408, *Al-Jarh wat-Ta'dîl*, vol.5, p.30, and *At-Tafâwut*, vol.5, p.9.

which means, "And truly, if We give him a taste of mercy from us, after some adversity (severe poverty or disease, etc.) has touched him, he is sure to say: "This is for me (due to my merit)." (Fussilat, 41:50)

That is to say, I deserve it and it is mine; I own it.

The believer realizes that all blessings belong to Allah and His favor and that Allah grants him blessings without him deserving it. It is continual charity from Him to His servant and He has the right to deprive anyone from this as He wills. If Allah prevents people from receiving blessings, He never prevents them from what they deserve. If the servant fails to realize that, he might think that he deserves it and would become conceited thinking that he deserves this blessing and that he is better than others. As Allah says,

﴿ وَلَئِنْ أَذَقْنَا ٱلْإِنسَٰنَ مِنَّا رَحْمَةً ثُمَّ نَزَعْنَٰهَا مِنْهُ إِنَّهُ لَيَـُٔوسٌ كَفُورٌ ۝ وَلَئِنْ أَذَقْنَٰهُ نَعْمَآءَ بَعْدَ ضَرَّآءَ مَسَّتْهُ لَيَقُولَنَّ ذَهَبَ ٱلسَّيِّـَٔاتُ عَنِّىٓ إِنَّهُۥ لَفَرِحٌ فَخُورٌ ۝ ﴾

which means, "And if We give man a taste of Mercy from Us, and then withdraw it from him, verily! He is despairing, ungrateful. But if We let him taste good (favor) after evil (poverty and harm) has touched him, he is sure to say: "Ills have departed from me." Surely, he is exultant, and boastful (ungrateful to Allah)." (Hûd, 11:9-10)

Allah dispraises such a man because of his despair and being ungrateful during times of afflictions and because he is happy and proud when the affliction is removed. He failed to praise Allah, thank, and glorify Him when He removed the afflictions but Allah says that he said, "Ills have departed from me." If he had just said: Allah removes ills away from me by His mercy, Allah would never dispraise him but the servant forgets Who bestowed this blessing on him by ascribing it to himself and through feeling proud.

If Allah, the Exalted sees such a heart in His servant, this is one of the greatest causes of failure and letting him down. His place is not suitable to receive such perfect and complete blessings as Allah says,

﴿ إِنَّ شَرَّ ٱلدَّوَابِّ عِندَ ٱللَّهِ ٱلصُّمُّ ٱلْبُكْمُ ٱلَّذِينَ لَا يَعْقِلُونَ ۝ وَلَوْ عَلِمَ ٱللَّهُ فِيهِمْ خَيْرًا لَّأَسْمَعَهُمْ ۖ وَلَوْ أَسْمَعَهُمْ لَتَوَلَّوا۟ وَّهُم مُّعْرِضُونَ ۝ ﴾

which means, "Verily! The worst of (moving) living creatures with Allah are the deaf and the dumb, those who understand not (i.e. the disbelievers). Had Allah known of any good in them, He would indeed have made them listen, and even if He had made them listen, they would but have turned away, averse (to the truth)." (Al-Anfâl, 8:22-23)

Allah said that their place is not suitable to receive His blessings. Besides this there is another obstacle that prevents blessings from reaching them, which is their denial and neglect of what they know and perceive.

The causes of failure are based on the state of the soul and its adherence to its nature; the origin of creation. The causes of success are according to Allah, Who enables the servant to accept His blessings. The causes of success are from Him and from His favor and He created both this and that as He created all the parts of the earth; one part accepts plant life and the other does not. He created trees; one grows fruit and the other does not. He created the bee and enabled it to produce honey with different colors as well as the hornet, which cannot do that. He created good souls that are able to remember, praise, thank, glorify, and advise His servants and also created evil souls who are not able to do that. He is the All Wise and the All-Knowing. The scholar of Islam Abu Al-'Abbâs Ahmad bin

Taimiyah[78] (may Allah be merciful to him) talked about the interpretation of chapter of Al-'Ankabût saying the following.

Chapter: The Interpretation of the Beginning of Chapter Al-'Ankabût

Allah, the Almighty says,

﴿ الٓمٓ ۝ أَحَسِبَ ٱلنَّاسُ أَن يُتْرَكُوٓا۟ أَن يَقُولُوٓا۟ ءَامَنَّا وَهُمْ لَا يُفْتَنُونَ ۝ وَلَقَدْ فَتَنَّا ٱلَّذِينَ مِن قَبْلِهِمْ ۖ فَلَيَعْلَمَنَّ ٱللَّهُ ٱلَّذِينَ صَدَقُوا۟ وَلَيَعْلَمَنَّ ٱلْكَٰذِبِينَ ۝ أَمْ حَسِبَ ٱلَّذِينَ يَعْمَلُونَ ٱلسَّيِّـَٔاتِ أَن يَسْبِقُونَا ۚ سَآءَ مَا يَحْكُمُونَ ۝ مَن كَانَ يَرْجُوا۟ لِقَآءَ ٱللَّهِ فَإِنَّ أَجَلَ ٱللَّهِ لَـَٔاتٍ ۚ وَهُوَ ٱلسَّمِيعُ ٱلْعَلِيمُ ۝ وَمَن جَٰهَدَ فَإِنَّمَا يُجَٰهِدُ لِنَفْسِهِۦٓ ۚ إِنَّ ٱللَّهَ لَغَنِىٌّ عَنِ ٱلْعَٰلَمِينَ ۝ وَٱلَّذِينَ ءَامَنُوا۟ وَعَمِلُوا۟ ٱلصَّٰلِحَٰتِ لَنُكَفِّرَنَّ عَنْهُمْ سَيِّـَٔاتِهِمْ وَلَنَجْزِيَنَّهُمْ أَحْسَنَ ٱلَّذِى كَانُوا۟ يَعْمَلُونَ ۝ وَوَصَّيْنَا ٱلْإِنسَٰنَ بِوَٰلِدَيْهِ حُسْنًا ۖ وَإِن جَٰهَدَاكَ لِتُشْرِكَ بِى مَا لَيْسَ لَكَ بِهِۦ عِلْمٌ فَلَا تُطِعْهُمَآ ۚ إِلَىَّ مَرْجِعُكُمْ فَأُنَبِّئُكُم بِمَا كُنتُمْ تَعْمَلُونَ ۝ وَٱلَّذِينَ ءَامَنُوا۟ وَعَمِلُوا۟ ٱلصَّٰلِحَٰتِ لَنُدْخِلَنَّهُمْ فِى ٱلصَّٰلِحِينَ ۝ وَمِنَ ٱلنَّاسِ مَن يَقُولُ ءَامَنَّا بِٱللَّهِ فَإِذَآ أُوذِىَ فِى ٱللَّهِ جَعَلَ فِتْنَةَ ٱلنَّاسِ كَعَذَابِ ٱللَّهِ وَلَئِن جَآءَ نَصْرٌ مِّن رَّبِّكَ لَيَقُولُنَّ إِنَّا كُنَّا مَعَكُمْ ۚ أَوَلَيْسَ ٱللَّهُ بِأَعْلَمَ بِمَا فِى صُدُورِ ٱلْعَٰلَمِينَ ۝ وَلَيَعْلَمَنَّ ٱللَّهُ ٱلَّذِينَ ءَامَنُوا۟ وَلَيَعْلَمَنَّ ٱلْمُنَٰفِقِينَ ۝ ﴾

which means, "*AlifLâmMîm*. [These letters are one of the miracles of the Qur'ân, and none but Allah (Alone) knows their

---

[78] He is Imam Ahmad bin 'Abdul-Halîm bin 'Abdus-Salâm An-Numairy Al-Harrâny Ad-Dimishqy Al-Hanbaly. Abu Al-'Abbâs Taqiy Ad-Dîn. Passed away in 728 A.H.

meanings.] Do people think that they will be left alone because they say: "We believe," and will not be tested. And We indeed tested those who were before them. And Allah will certainly make (it) known (the truth of) those who are true, and will certainly make (it) known (the falsehood of) those who are liars, (although Allah knows all that before putting them to test). Or those who do evil deeds think that they can outstrip Us (i.e. escape Our Punishment)? Evil is that which they judge! Whoever hopes for the Meeting with Allah, then Allah's Term is surely coming. And He is the All-Hearer, the All-Knower. And whosoever strives, he strives only for himself. Verily, Allah is free of all wants from the *'Âlamîn* (mankind, jinns, and all that exists). Those who believe [in the Oneness of Allah (Monotheism) and in Messenger Muhammad, and do not apostate because of the harm they receive from the polytheists], and do righteous good deeds, surely, We shall remit from them their evil deeds and shall reward them according to the best of that which they used to do. And We have enjoined on man to be good and dutiful to his parents, but if they strive to make you join with Me (in worship) anything (as a partner) of which you have no knowledge, then obey them not. Unto Me is your return, and I shall tell you what you used to do. And for those who believe (in the Oneness of Allah and other items of Faith) and do righteous good deeds, surely, We shall make them enter in (the entrance of) the righteous (i.e. in Paradise). Of mankind are some who say: "We believe in Allah," but if they are made to suffer for the sake of Allah, they consider the trial of mankind as Allah's punishment, and if victory comes from your Lord, (the hypocrites) will say: "Verily! We were with you (helping you)." Is not Allah Best Aware of what is in the breast of the *'Âlamîn* (mankind and jinns). Verily, Allah knows those who believe, and verily, He knows the hypocrites [i.e. Allah will test the people with good and hard days to discriminate the good from the wicked (although Allah knows all that before putting them to test)]." (Al-'Ankabût, 29:1-11)

And He, the Almighty says,

﴿ أَمْ حَسِبْتُمْ أَن تَدْخُلُوا۟ ٱلْجَنَّةَ وَلَمَّا يَأْتِكُم مَّثَلُ ٱلَّذِينَ خَلَوْا۟ مِن قَبْلِكُم ۖ مَّسَّتْهُمُ ٱلْبَأْسَآءُ وَٱلضَّرَّآءُ وَزُلْزِلُوا۟ حَتَّىٰ يَقُولَ ٱلرَّسُولُ وَٱلَّذِينَ ءَامَنُوا۟ مَعَهُۥ مَتَىٰ نَصْرُ ٱللَّهِ ۗ أَلَآ إِنَّ نَصْرَ ٱللَّهِ قَرِيبٌ ﴾

which means, "Or think you that you will enter Paradise without such (trials) as came to those who passed away before you? They were afflicted with severe poverty and ailments and were so shaken that even the Messenger and those who believed along with him said, "When (will come) the Help of Allah?" Yes! Certainly, the Help of Allah is near!" (Al-Baqarah, 2:214)

And He, the Exalted says when He mentioned he who apostatizes and who is obliged,

﴿ مَن كَفَرَ بِٱللَّهِ مِنۢ بَعْدِ إِيمَٰنِهِۦ ... ﴾

which means, "Whoever disbelieved in Allah after his belief." (An-Nahl, 16:106)

And then He, the Almighty says,

﴿ ثُمَّ إِنَّ رَبَّكَ لِلَّذِينَ هَاجَرُوا۟ مِنۢ بَعْدِ مَا فُتِنُوا۟ ثُمَّ جَٰهَدُوا۟ وَصَبَرُوٓا۟ إِنَّ رَبَّكَ مِنۢ بَعْدِهَا لَغَفُورٌ رَّحِيمٌ ﴾

which means, "Then, verily! Your Lord for those who emigrated after they had been put to trials and thereafter strove hard and fought (for the Cause of Allah) and were patient, verily, your Lord afterward is, Oft-Forgiving, Most Merciful." (An-Nahl, 16:110)

People receive the Messengers of Allah in one of two ways: either to say: we believe, or refuse to say that and continue to do evil deeds. Whoever among them says: I believe, Allah will test him and make him choose in order to expose him as a liar from the one who is truthful. Whoever refuses to say: I believe, should not think that he can defeat Allah, for there is no one, who can do that. This is His way: He sends Messengers to His creatures and then people accuse them of lying and harm them. Allah, the Almighty says,

﴿ وَكَذَٰلِكَ جَعَلْنَا لِكُلِّ نَبِيٍّ عَدُوًّا شَيَٰطِينَ ٱلْإِنسِ وَٱلْجِنِّ ... ﴾

which means, "And so We have appointed for every Prophet enemies - *Shayâtin* (devils) among mankind and jinns." (Al-An'âm, 6:112)

And He, the Almighty says,

﴿ كَذَٰلِكَ مَآ أَتَى ٱلَّذِينَ مِن قَبْلِهِم مِّن رَّسُولٍ إِلَّا قَالُوا۟ سَاحِرٌ أَوْ مَجْنُونٌ ﴾

which means, "Likewise, no Messenger came to those before them, but they said: "A sorcerer or a madman!" (Adh-Dhâriyât, 51:52)

And He, the Almighty says,

﴿ مَّا يُقَالُ لَكَ إِلَّا مَا قَدْ قِيلَ لِلرُّسُلِ مِن قَبْلِكَ ... ﴾

which means, "Nothing is said to you (O Muhammad) except what was said to the Messengers before you." (Fussilat, 41:43)

Such evil people also harmed and showed enmity toward anyone who believeds in the Messengers and obeyed them. They would afflict the believers with pain and if he did not believe in them, he would be punished and this would be the cause or more and more pain. No doubt, every soul will suffer pain whether they are believers or disbelievers. However the believer suffers pain during this Worldly life, and then he will gain the reward in the Hereafter, and the disbeliever gets to enjoy this worldly life but then in the Hereafter he must endure lasting pain.

The Opinion of Ash-Shâfi'y Concerning Affliction and Being Given Power

A man asked Ash-Shâfi'y,[79] "O Abu 'Abdullâh! What is better for man: to be afflicted or to have power?' Ash-Shâfi'y said, 'He will not be given power until he has been afflicted; Allah afflicted Nûh (Noah), Ibrâhîm (Abraham), Mûsâ (Moses), 'Îsâ (Jesus), and Muhammad (peace be upon them all) and because they were patient, Allah bestowed power upon them. No one should think that he can avoid pain forever.'"

Whoever Pleases Allah and Displeases People

This is the great origin of power that the wise man should know. It is human nature that man tries to be civilized. He has to live with people and people have wills and imagination and demand him to agree with them in all matters and if he does not agree, they will harm and torture him and if he agrees with them, he will be tortured and harmed both by them and by others.

Whoever thinks about his situation and those of other people, would find several more situations like these. Every nation that wants to commit adultery, be unjust, and nullify religion, are guilty of committing some prohibited things that Allah has mentioned in the following verse,

---

[79] He is Muhammad bin Idrîs bin Al-'Abbâs bin 'Uthmân bin Shâfi' Abu 'Abdullâh. Imam, head of the famous school and one of the four Imams. The famous among his books are *Al-Umm, Ar-Risâlah*, and others. He (may Allah be merciful to him) passed away in 204 A.H. See *Tahdhîb At-Tahdhîb*, vol.9, p.25, *Târîkh Al-Bukhâry Al-Kabîr*, vol.1, p.42, *Al-Jarh wat-Ta'dîl*, vol.7, p.1130, and *Siyar A'lâm An-Nubalâ'*, vol.10, p.5.

﴿ قُلْ إِنَّمَا حَرَّمَ رَبِّيَ ٱلْفَوَٰحِشَ مَا ظَهَرَ مِنْهَا وَمَا بَطَنَ وَٱلْإِثْمَ وَٱلْبَغْىَ بِغَيْرِ ٱلْحَقِّ وَأَن تُشْرِكُوا۟ بِٱللَّهِ مَا لَمْ يُنَزِّلْ بِهِۦ سُلْطَٰنًا وَأَن تَقُولُوا۟ عَلَى ٱللَّهِ مَا لَا تَعْلَمُونَ ﴾

which means, "Say (O Muhammad): "(But) the things that my Lord has indeed forbidden are *Al-Fawâhish* (great evil sins, every kind of unlawful sexual intercourse, etc.) whether committed openly or secretly, sins (of all kinds), unrighteous oppression, joining partners (in worship) with Allah for which He has given no authority, and saying things about Allah of which you have no knowledge." (Al-A'râf, 7:33)

If such people are gathered in one place for example, in a university, an inn, a school, a village, or a city that has others with them, what can they do? What do they want except approval of the others, or for the others to remain silent and not to oppose them openly. If the others remained peaceful they may not be harmed by their evil but they might insult and punish them to keep them down and in their places. He might be asked to commit perjury or talk falsely about religion or to help in committing adultery and unjust deeds. If he refuses, they will harm him and show enmity to him and if he answered them they themselves will rule, harm, and insult him many times as much as they used to fear him before or he will be tortured. What should be done is what is mentioned in the hadith that was narrated by 'Â'ishah, which she sent to Mu'âwiyah. It was narrated as Mawqûf (discontinued) and Marfû' (traceable), "Whoever pleases Allah through displeasing people, Allah will save him from asking people."[80] And in another narration, "Allah will be pleased with him and will make people pleased with him and whoever pleases people by displeasing Allah, they will never save him from Allah." And in another narration, "Whoever praises him from among people will dispraise him."

---

[80] Recorded by At-Tirmidhy, book of asceticism, no.2414.

This applies to whoever supports kings and leaders with their evil aims and whoever supports the people of innovations in their novelties who are supposed to belong to the people of knowledge and religion. Whoever Allah guides and shows him the way, he will never commit prohibited acts and will bear their harm and enmity and then he will receive the reward for his efforts in the Hereafter. As it happened to the Messengers and their followers with those who harmed them and showed them enmity, like the emigrants of this nation and the scientists, worshipers, merchants, and supporters, who were afflicted.

Affliction is Inevitable

On certain occasions, it is lawful to show approval and hide one's denial like in the case of he who is forced to say words of disbelief. What is meant here is that it is inevitable that everyone will face affliction and harm. There is no way to be saved from affliction. That is why Allah, the Exalted mentioned this point in several places saying that people have to be afflicted and that affliction can be by means of happiness and misfortune. Man will be afflicted with what pleases and harms him, so he needs to be patient and praise Allah.

Allah, the Almighty says,

﴿ إِنَّا جَعَلْنَا مَا عَلَى ٱلْأَرْضِ زِينَةً لَّهَا لِنَبْلُوَهُمْ أَيُّهُمْ أَحْسَنُ عَمَلًا ۝ ﴾

which means, "Verily! We have made that which is on earth as an adornment for it, in order that We may test them (mankind) as to which of them are best in deeds. [I.e. those who do good deeds in the most perfect manner, that means to do them (deeds) totally for Allah's sake and in accordance to the legal ways of the Prophet]." (Al-Kahf, 18:7)

And He, the Almighty says,

www.ingramcontent.com/pod-product-compliance
Lightning Source LLC
Chambersburg PA
CBHW081104080526
44587CB00021B/3438